SHAKESPEARE'S DRAMA

UNA ELLIS-FERMOR

SHAKESPEARE'S DRAMA

edited by Kenneth Muir

METHUEN

LONDON AND NEW YORK

First published in 1980 by
Methuen & Co. Ltd
11 New Fetter Lane, London EC4P 4EE
Published in the USA by
Methuen & Co.
in association with Methuen, Inc.
733 Third Avenue, New York, NY 10017
This collection © 1980 Methuen & Co. Ltd
Chapters I-V and IX © 1961 Elaine Weston and Elsie Brown
Typeset by Red Lion Setters London WC1
Printed in Great Britain at the University Press Cambridge

British Library Cataloguing in Publication Data

Ellis-Fermor, Una
Shakespeare's drama.
1. Shakespeare, William – Criticism
and interpretation
I. Title   II. Muir, Kenneth
822.3'3   PR2976   80-40726

ISBN 0-416-74090-1
ISBN 0-416-74100-2 pbk
(University paperbacks; 724)

Printed in Great Britain by
Richard Clay (The Chaucer Press) Ltd,
Bungay, Suffolk

Contents

Acknowledgements

Chapters I-V and IX originally appeared in *Shakespeare the Dramatist* (1961, Methuen) ©Elaine Weston and Elsie Brown; Chapters VI-VIII and X originally appeared in *The Frontiers of Drama* (1945, Methuen).

Introduction

Una Ellis-Fermor, Hildred Carlisle Professor of English Literature at Bedford College, London, from 1947 until her death in 1958, although best known as a Shakespearian scholar, had wide interests in poetry and drama. She wrote a pioneer book on Marlowe, and standard works on Jacobean Drama and on the Irish Dramatic Movement. Towards the end of her life she translated six of Ibsen's plays and, as her writings reveal, she was acquainted with Greek drama, Racine and Corneille, and many modern European dramatists. One essay alone refers to twenty-five modern dramatists.

She was the first General Editor of the New Arden Shakespeare and the series owes much of its success to her foresight and planning, and also to her willingness to change her mind when occasion arose. It was originally intended to print the New Arden from the Old, with only the most necessary corrections to the text and notes, but she soon became convinced that such a course was impossible.

In 1948, just as the New Arden Shakespeare was started, Una Ellis-Fermor delivered the Annual Shakespeare Lecture of the British Academy, and this was intended to be the first chapter of a projected book on Shakespeare the Dramatist. When I edited under that title the chapters which had been drafted, I suggested that some of the gaps could be filled by chapters from *The Frontiers of Drama*. The present volume, therefore, combines the Shakespearian parts of the two books.[1]

1 I am grateful to Harold Brooks and Terence Hawkes for valuable suggestions, most of which I have been able to follow.

There are a number of omissions. The essays on *Timon of Athens* and *The Two Noble Kinsmen* were never intended to be part of *Shakespeare the Dramatist* and it is apparent from pencilled annotations that Una Ellis-Fermor had modified her position on both plays. The chapter entitled 'Shakespeare and Ibsen', admirable as it is, contains very little about Shakespeare. 'Some Functions of Verbal Music in Drama' was left unfinished, but from this I have salvaged a section on *Coriolanus* and added it to the chapter on that play. 'The Limitations of Drama', the first chapter of *The Frontiers of Drama*, is an introduction to that volume, and could not be detached from it. Another chapter in *The Frontiers of Drama* – 'A Technical Problem: The Revelation of Unspoken Thought in Drama' – was on a subject which was discussed later in the chapter on *Coriolanus*. Another reason for omitting that chapter is that it contains only a passing reference to Shakespeare.

Apart from the contents of these two books, Una Ellis-Fermor wrote two pamphlets on Shakespeare. One of them, 'Some Recent Research in Shakespeare's Imagery' (1937), is largely concerned with the work of others and she devotes much of her space to the first holder of the Bedford College Chair, Caroline Spurgeon, and to Wolfgang Clemen's *Shakespeares Bilder*. Naturally enough, Una Ellis-Fermor is enthusiastic about Professor Spurgeon's 'objective' and 'scientific' method, its limitations not then being apparent. The other pamphlet, 'The Study of Shakespeare' (1948), her inaugural lecture, contains nothing that is not implied in her other criticism. Nevertheless it is a useful and eloquent statement of her aims as a teacher of Shakespeare, and hence her aims as a critic. Her main argument is that bibliographical and textual studies, researches into the nature of the Elizabethan stage or into the background of the life of Shakespeare's contemporaries, even studies of the thought of his age, should all be regarded as means to an end. 'But we shall not confuse knowing them with knowing Shakespeare . . . it is as poet and dramatic artist that we must know him, not as a problem in texts or an illustration of prevailing habits of the Elizabethan mind.' In the same lecture Una Ellis-Fermor paid another tribute to Caroline Spurgeon: she stressed the importance of Shakespeare's imagery as 'one of the most potent sources of suggestion and illumination. Without admitting it to our imagination, we cannot enter the world of the poet'. In a broadcast talk, delivered in the following year, Una Ellis-Fermor again stressed the value of the investigation of imagery:

It has given us a knowledge of Shakespeare's habits and processes as a writer. This may act as a corrective to rash assumptions and perhaps play its part in the determining of doubtful cases of authorship, offering evidence complementary to the findings of that bibliographical and textual criticism which revolutionized Shakespeare scholarship at the beginning of this century. But I think its real value will always be rather that of the discipline to which I have just referred. It has taught modern criticism as a new awareness of one branch of Shakespeare's technique, and has taught it, by its occasional excesses no less than by its genuine achievement, that no branch of his technique can be studied in isolation or considered without reference to all other aspects of his dramatic art. Its value, that is to say, is aesthetic: it has brought us a step nearer to the understanding of Shakespeare the artist. But as a branch of aesthetics, it will, I think, prove fruitful only in so far as the dramatic function of the images is kept unwaveringly before the critic's mind. The dramatic functions of imagery are many and it would be foolish to suppose that those of us who have discovered some five or six have come to the end of the story.

In this stress on the dramatic function of imagery, Una Ellis-Fermor seems to have moved away from Caroline Spurgeon towards Wolfgang Clemen.

In her inaugural lecture she also made the point – one that Bradley stressed, although he is not always given the credit for it – that we must 'identify ourselves with the characters like actors studying parts; and because we are in the hands of a genuine dramatist – perhaps the only man of purely dramatic genius the world has ever known – we identify with *all* the characters, first in turn and then simultaneously'. Here is the germ of the British Academy Lecture and of the book that was to be called *Shakespeare the Dramatist*.

The parts she had written of that book do not include a consideration of one other aspect of Shakespeare, which she had stressed in her inaugural – the fact that the plays 'are the records of a poet's experience', as Keats and other poets have believed. The 'passionate perception of the significance and value of all things, from the minute to the sublime, of all experience . . . informs the long succession of the plays as individual works of art and as a sequence.' Although some parts of *Shakespeare the Dramatist* lacked the author's final revisions, those chapters included in the present book and the chapters from *The Frontiers of Drama* represent her criticism at its best. For, if one reads her work in chronological order, it becomes apparent how much she developed and matured between 1927, when her book on Marlowe was published, and the time of her inaugural twenty years later.

Christopher Marlowe was a pioneer work, the first full-length study of
the dramatist, and one which can still be enjoyed and admired, but it
suffers from a tendency to assume too close a link between the poet and his
creations and to treat some of his work as veiled autobiography. In writing
of *Doctor Faustus*, for example, Una Ellis-Fermor accuses the poet of
apostasy: 'He accepts, with a half-cowed and sometimes almost frantic
submission, the conventional idea that it is rejection of the superstitions of
his contemporaries that has ruined him.' She claims that Marlowe, in
numbering the vision of Helen 'among the wiles of Mephistophiles', is
'denying the two truest elements in his own nature, an instinct for beauty
so fine that it trembles upon the very borders between the sensuous and
the spiritual, and a ruthless, scientific honesty of thought and devotion to
truth that mark his nature as profoundly religious'. Marlowe is a more
uncomfortable figure than these words would suggest, and they ignore the
fact that Faustus, in taking 'Helen' as his paramour, is having intercourse
with a devil. The poet, moreover, is not half-cowed but merely
dramatizing the story of a man who had sold his soul to the devil.

The Jacobean Drama (1936) shows a considerable advance. It was
probably the best book on its subject when it was published, and after more
than forty years it has not been superseded. Yet, it must be admitted,
changes in the world have made some of its judgements seem to belong too
obviously to their period. Una Ellis-Fermor seems to avert her eyes from
the harsh satire of *The Widow's Tears*; she says nothing about *More
Dissemblers Besides Women*, with its multiple portraits of hypocrisy; and,
although she appreciates Middleton's citizen comedies, 'a world in which
roguery, Rabelaisianism, broad gusto, poetry and tenderness meet', she
regards *A Chaste Maid in Cheapside*, the masterpiece in that genre, as
looking forward to *Women Beware Women* and *The Changeling*.

The penultimate chapter, 'The Shakespearian Transmutation', is an
attempt to show Shakespeare's links with his contemporaries, and his
transformation of material he shares with them. This is partly due to the
'inward nature' of his characters, types which are transmuted into individuals. This point is illustrated by his treatment of the Machiavel figure
and of madness, and most tellingly by a comparison of Beaumont and
Fletcher's tragi-comedies with the plays of Shakespeare's last period:

by one of those paradoxes which this drama continually offers us,
Shakespeare used for the culminating expression of his faith in reality
that form which its inventors had devised as a means of escape. The
fairy-tale with him becomes charged with those implications which the

more immediate types of story could not present, becomes the vehicle of imaginative experience, and interprets the real world more truly than do the records of actuality.

Although her brief account of Shakespeare's development contains many perceptive comments, Una Ellis-Fermor was out of sympathy with the problem comedies, largely because she assumed, along with many critics from Keats to Murry, that Shakespeare's plays are in some sense a reflection of his personal life. She argued that in *Measure for Measure*,

> the lowest depths of Jacobean negation are touched. Cynicism has taken on a kind of diabolic vigilance; with the exception of the kindly, timid Provost, there is no character who is not suspect, and those whose claims to goodness or decency seem most vigorous are precisely those in whom meanness, self-regard and hypocrisy root deepest.

The characters of the underplot lack even 'the redeeming virtue of humour'; Claudio is another Bertram; and Isabella is 'hard as an icicle'. With Shakespeare, at this period of his career, the mingling of good and evil 'constitutes the denial, not only of the nobility of man, but of the very laws which pretend to guide him'.

> Before the comprehensiveness of this exposure, the imagination staggers, all the cynicism of individual speeches is as nothing beside the cynicism implicit in this orientation of the material; it is a world in whose fetid air no wholesome thing can grow. It is, in Shakespeare's thought, the very nadir of disgust and cynicism, a world where 'nothing is but what is not', where such order as there is in evil, where all passion and all enterprise is only 'the expense of spirit in a waste of shame'.

Few readers today would accept this as a true assessment of the play; indeed it was questioned by R.W. Chambers in his British Academy Shakespeare Lecture soon after it was written. There is sin in the play, but no cynicism, repentance and forgiveness rather than disgust. It is, perhaps, the most Christian of all Shakespeare's plays. But it should be remembered that modern appreciation of the play is the result of numerous critical appreciations – by Knight, Leavis, Bradbrook, Empson, Lascelles and many others – of some effective productions, notably that of Peter Brook, and the result above all of the 'permissive' society which is parallel in some ways to the Vienna of the play. By the time Una Ellis-Fermor began her work on *Shakespeare the Dramatist*, her attitude to the problem plays had been modified; but even in her brilliant essay on *Troilus* and Cressida in *The Frontiers of Drama* she argues that the content of Shakespeare's 'thought is an implacable assertion of chaos as the ultimate fact of being', despite the danger of attributing to the poet a belief that the chaos of the Greek camp and Troy is universal.

It is worth noting that in none of the finished chapters of *Shakespeare the Dramatist* – nor, indeed, in the plan of work connected with the book – is there any discussion of Shakespeare's comedies; and in the chapter devoted to Shakespeare in *The Jacobean Drama* the great comedies fell outside the period with which she was concerned.

All the essays included in this selection belong to the last years of Una Ellis-Fermor's life, at a time when she was directing a department, planning and editing the New Arden Shakespeare, and translating Ibsen. But these activities were not distractions from her critical work but contributors to it. It will be apparent that her consideration of the teaching of Shakespeare led her to lay down critical priorities; that editing the Arden edition involved a similar concern with fundamentals; and that translating Ibsen led her to fruitful comparisons with Shakespeare.

Her contribution to the criticism of Shakespeare depends on a number of qualities. Her wide knowledge of drama in six different languages and her specialized knowledge of Elizabethan and Jacobean drama enabled her to set Shakespeare in the context of his contemporaries, and also to compare him with other great dramatists. She was one of the first to recognize that Ibsen, even in his middle period, was essentially a poetic dramatist. If she sometimes seems to have imperfect-sympathies with the French classical dramatists – as when she complains that 'the processes of Racine's soliloquies still seem inhumanly coherent' – this followed from her central conception of the essence of drama.

Although she was not the first to single out Shakespeare's unique powers of characterization, she made fruitful use of Maurice Morgann's essay on Falstaff, and of the way in which, by setting up conflicting impressions, Shakespeare made his characters live. She went further: she avoided Morgann's eccentricities and paradoxes which covered up his profound insights; she stressed that the creation of character was the essential dramatic gift; and she analysed the *poetic* means of creating character; not merely, that is to say, by the introduction of apparent inconsistencies in words and actions, but also by the use of imagery and verbal music to differentiate one character from another. She brilliantly demonstrated this method in her analysis of the contrast between the outer and inner life of Coriolanus.

In her inaugural lecture, Una Ellis-Fermor suggested briefly the lines on which she would have discussed Shakespeare's development as a dramatist; but unfortunately she did not live to write what would have been the climax of *Shakespeare the Dramatist*, the chapter dealing with the development of his art.

Another quality which is not fully displayed in her published work, although apparent to her team of New Arden editors, was her ability to visualize a scene, and her instinctive knowledge of how the lines ought to be spoken to obtain their full effect. This is the more remarkable as she wrote only two pieces of dramatic criticism and had little experience of acting or directing.

I

Shakespeare the dramatist [1]

In speaking today of Shakespeare the dramatist I propose, with your
permission, to consider one question: To what degree and in virtue of what
quality in his genius is Shakespeare a dramatist? What, in other words,
constitutes the specifically dramatic quality in his writing and how nearly
is that the native habit of his mind? For it is evident that, in the Elizabethan period, when conditions fostered the art of drama, many writers
became practising dramatists who in another age would have sought
another medium; Ben Jonson was almost certainly one of these and so in
some degree was Marlowe on one hand and Webster on the other. Just so,
during the nineteenth century, many poets as evidently diverted their
imaginations from the drama, which offered them only an incomplete and
inhibited form of artistic communication. Was dramatic expression, then,
partly induced in Shakespeare, as it was in Marlowe, Jonson, and Webster,
by the favourable conditions, the prevailing mood of the age? Or was it
essential to his genius, innate in him, profiting no doubt by the
coincidence of man and moment, but not prompted, as in some of his
contemporaries, by the demands of that moment? May we, as a first step
towards answering this (and so my initial question), look for a moment at
the nature of drama, or, more precisely, at the nature of dramatic genius?

Clearly we are not concerned here with the obvious characteristics of
the literary form that we call drama; these, though derivative from, are not
the essential manifestation of, dramatic genius. If we remind ourselves of
them briefly it is rather that, having so recalled them, we may set them
aside before beginning to look for the generic and then the differentiating

qualities of the art and of the artist. We are not likely to meet with disagree-
ment, to need to justify ourselves, when we say that in a play which shows
competent craftsmanship as a play, we expect to find at least three things:
action, or a reasonably clear and coherent plot; characters, themselves the
sources of this action, who convince us that they are human beings, such
as we meet or might expect to meet; speech, the dialogue through which
plot and character are revealed, which satisfies us that it is such speech as
these men, meeting these events, might use. If one or other of these three
is notably defective, we find a piece of work which fails as a play, whether
or not it has in it fine poetry, subtle thought, or firm design. There is some
noble poetry in W.B. Yeats's *Shadowy Waters*, but there is not enough
action, in outward event or inner experience, to give it the vigour and
immediacy of drama. There is subtle and sometimes searching thought in
much modern drama, but such a play as Denis Johnston's *The Old Lady
Says No* fails to move the audience – as a play – because the central figures
are not imagined primarily as human beings. There is firm design and
some understanding of character in Browning's *Strafford*, but the words
do not strike upon our imaginations as they would if they were instinct
with the life of speech at any level of experience. If, however, all these ends
are duly served, the play will be at least a workman-like piece of
craftsmanship (it may, of course, be much more), even though the
emphasis be laid on the action, as in *The Spanish Tragedy*, on the
revelation of character, as in Maeterlinck's *Aglavaine et Sélysette*, or on
verbal wit, as in Etherege's *Man Of Mode*.

To determine, then, what dramatic genius is in its essence, we must
look below these formal characteristics, these outward signs of dramatic
thought, and ask what are the innate powers of mind which lead a poet to
apprehend life in terms of dramatic experience which, if they are not
thwarted by circumstance or conditions, will certainly direct his artistic
expression to dramatic, rather than to any other, literary form. We are not
concerned, that is, with the nature of the average play (which, like the
average novel, need not be a work of art at all) but, first, with the nature of
dramatic art, and then with that of dramatic genius; the first of these may
best be learned from the study of the major drama; the second can only be
so learned.

And so, setting aside technical and formal considerations, we examine
first the generic qualities which the great dramatist shares with certain
other major artists and then those qualities or powers which differentiate
the dramatist and drama. We call in evidence such dramas as, while
fulfilling the technical demand, so inform it with the universal and the

enduring that, when what is temporal and perishable has lost its meaning, an imperishable and eternal significance shines through, and Aeschylus speaks to men of today, not as an Athenian of two thousand years ago, but as a man whose essential experience is still ours. Passion, thought, and poetic imagination, unchanging even in the wreckage of the civilizations they worked upon, survive event and circumstance and reveal man's kinship with the indestructible spirit of which great art is an image. And it is somewhere here that we shall find our starting-point. Passion, thought and poetic imagination are, I think, the generic characteristics of dramatic genius and we can trace their manifestation in the substance of drama, and, if we wish, in the form, through the work of all the greatest dramatists. How, then, do these manifest themselves in drama, and what is Shakespeare's portion here?

It is perhaps upon the passion and intensity with which the dramatist apprehends the world of experience that great drama depends, in the first instance, for its power and its immediacy; though passion is, in the last analysis, inseparable from thought and poetic imagination, and these from each other. It is the intensity, first of his imaginative experience of the world about him, then of his artistic experience – the act of transmuting this into a work of art – that gives to the great dramatist his power to move men, to touch the depths of their imaginations, to free them, and to set at work the powers of life. Nor are there any narrow limits to the shape this mighty force may take when it informs the characters in a great drama. It may be released, or may appear to be released, almost without guidance, as in the terrifying whirlwinds of madness in a Lear or a Timon. It may be stifled, or appear to be stifled, in the marmoreal calm of the Chorus Leader in the *Oedipus at Colonus*: 'Not to be born at all Is best'[2] or in the deceptively prosaic utterance of Middleton's or Ford's tragedies, of Ibsen's late plays. A Macbeth, an Agamemnon, a Jocasta may, as men do in actual life, hold it with difficulty in some kind of restraint; a Clytemnestra, a Lady Macbeth, seemingly with less difficulty, may hide it altogether. A Medea, an Othello, a Borkman may, without crossing the border-line of madness, release a part of what is shattering the mind. It is the presence of the passion, not the mode or the extent of its expression, that matters, and it is our awareness of forces beyond our own imagination that strikes us into awe and receptivity in the presence of the *Agamemnon*, the *Oedipus, Othello, Lear*, or *Timon*. Whether it appears to be revealed or seems to be hidden is really of less moment than we think, for our subconscious minds, wiser in this than 'meddling intellect', recognize and respond to the hidden as swiftly as to the manifest.

This power is not the prerogative of the dramatist; it will be found in varying kinds and degrees in all great artists. But though diffused or mitigated passion, though moments only of concentration are compatible with the highest reaches of art in other kinds, the dramatist depends upon it as the very matter of his. We recognize its working in the debates in the second book and in other isolated passages in *Paradise Lost*; but *Samson Agonistes* is instinct with it throughout. In Dante and in Goethe it is again intermittent, giving place to description, to meditation, to reasoned reflection, even to satire; in Wordsworth there is still less direct expression, it is diffused in the underlying groundwork of the thought; the solemn exultation of the music, in his major poems, its only outward sign. But in the great dramatists it is sustained and seemingly inexhaustible; Marlowe, Webster, Racine (in this among the greatest) suffer no dilution and little or no intermission. The power and comprehensiveness of their passion would alone distinguish the great masters of drama from all but the occasional companionship of their fellows. And here Shakespeare, as our instinctive choice of plays suggests, is with Aeschylus and Sophocles.

But the great forces set at work by passion are not undirected. 'God spoke to Job out of the whirlwind', and over the passion evoked by the intensity of his apprehension presides, in the major dramatist, the directing thought which gives us what has been called the logic of poetry.[3] The operation of thought, the effect of the continual discipline of contemplation or reflection, is harder to discern in drama than in many forms of art. And this we should expect, for it is inseparable from the differentiating quality of drama (of which we shall have to speak later), that preoccupation with the life of man, doing and suffering, which affords – except in rare instances – but little opportunity for the direct expression of reflection. Such revelation as there is is therefore implicit and can often be consciously abstracted only by a deliberate consideration of the total effect of action, character, and sentiment interrelated within a given play held whole in the mind of the critic.

This is, in effect, to say that in some plays it cannot be abstracted at all, for nothing but the total play will give us its 'meaning'. What, after all, is the meaning of *Much Ado*? Or, for that matter, of *Antony and Cleopatra*? A governing idea, a sequence of thought, can, it is true, be traced in *Troilus and Cressida* or the group *Richard II, Henry IV, Henry V*, but even here thought and content are more nearly coterminous than it is always convenient to admit. The 'logic of poetry' remains, in fact, the logic of *poetry*, and thought is revealed, in each aspect of the play, precisely by the presence of the excellence proper to that aspect; if we consider the characters, we find in it the depth of Shakespeare's understanding of motive and human experience; if the structure, it is in the flawless relation of the form to its subject. If we look for a theme in Shakespeare's plays, we find none, other than the bottomless and endlessly extending wisdom that asks of his readers a lifetime's consecration to explore. The operation of thought, then, is easier to discern than the resultant thoughts; a man must be blind to whom Shakespeare's architecture spells nothing, but he would fall into as great a folly if he assumed that the operation of this governing and presiding intelligence must necessarily give indications which can be abstracted and restated as the conclusions of a philosopher, an historian, a moralist, or a psychologist. The dramatist's is an impersonal art; its ways are secret and his thoughts are often hidden in those ways. But the sign of thought, in profound and powerful, sometimes in prophetic, form, is in the strength and majesty of the work of art itself and each fresh exploration teaches us to recognize here the conscious and unconscious intellectual control of passion.

So it is (with reservations which will be noted later) with the thought of Aeschylus and with that of Sophocles, Euripides, Ibsen. it is true that in these a part (a progressively diminishing part) is explicitly stated in the commentary of the chorus or an equivalent modern agent; but the total thought remains coterminous with the content of the play, of which this is itself a part. And it is too easily forgotten that in the first and second and in some degree in the third of these dramatists there are formal and aesthetic relations between the choric odes and the rest of the play which reveal in terms of another mode some part of the theme and are indispensable to full conscious or unconscious apprehension of it.[4]

In all of these poets, then, the major dramatists of literature, the forces evoked by passion are directed by thought, serving to express it, as it in turn expresses them.

And so we 'enter that state of grace which is called poetry',[5] a mode of experience, a condition of mind which is inherent in and yet partially distinguishable from passion and from thought as they are from each other. By 'poetry' in this sense I would be understood to mean that apprehension of beauty which irradiates the mind of the poet, presenting order or form as an aspect of truth, and distinguishing it at that point from the mind of the philosopher or of the saint. This radiance, this sense of glory in things seen or felt or imagined and of the ultimate and underlying truth of which they in turn are images, is communicated to us in ways which again differ widely in each of the greatest dramatists. It is at work in the major lines of design which give form to structure and to character and in details of expression – imagery and verbal music. It is the ever-present sense of significance in all things, of some hidden reality in them ever about to become manifest. Its clarity is at its height in the work of Aeschylus, of Sophocles, of Shakespeare, where design and detail are alike instinct with it; it is intermittent in certain dramatists second only to the greatest; though always there, it burns low and sometimes almost invisibly in Ibsen. Like passion, the poetic apprehension of the universe may reveal itself in drama clearly or more obscurely. From the time of his full maturity it never fails in Shakespeare's authentic work; in Ibsen, at the opposite extreme, it is sometimes so deep buried as to leave us blind to its working. Yet the imagery of *Antony and Cleopatra* springs, though with fuller potency, from the same faculty as the occasional overtones of beauty in *Rosmersholm*, and the secret kinship of the two is revealed by the solemn yet continuous presence of such overtones, side by side with clear and distinctive imagery, in such a play as the *Oedipus at Colonus*.

Such, then, are the generic forces that we discover if we look below the outward characteristics of drama presented to us by a normally constituted play and inquire what is the essential attribute of dramatic genius. But these, being generic qualities, are shared in varying degrees and relations by all great literature. What, then, differentiates drama from other forms of literature and the dramatist from other writers?

The nature of this differentiation has already been indicated in some of the suggestions we have made. Put briefly, it consists in this, that the dramatist (with whom up to this point we must be prepared to admit a certain kind of novelist) is concerned with the life of man acting and suffering. Here and here only can he rightly find his material. However far he may make universal his implicit theme, his subject remains man's experience, and all that he says or implies must be said in terms of this medium. From this there follow, almost as corollaries, two inferences. First, that the dramatist's mood, his attitude, will itself show a characteristic differentiation, which we may think of as sympathy. He enters into the minds of his characters (ideally into the minds of all of them) and speaks, as it were, from within them, giving thus a kind of impartiality to his picture of life, sorrowing with him that sorrows, rejoicing with him that rejoices. In certain rare cases this may take the form of an equidistant detachment from, rather than active participation with, all his characters,[6] but this, for our purpose, is a distinction without essential difference. It is the equality of his relations with them all that is the essential feature. And in close conjunction with this inference we may draw a second. The dramatist's primary concern being man's life, acting and suffering, and his relation to this basic material being one of sympathy, the mode which offers him the fullest expression is direct revelation by the agents themselves. No other means will allow him so to concentrate upon the essentials of his subject, no other will present so economically the passions and thoughts of men as to leave men themselves, under due safeguards, to present them. And from what has been said of the nature of that sympathy which is a differentiating characteristic of dramatic genius, it follows that the genuine dramatist meets no obstruction in expressing his passion thus mediately instead of immediately, as the passion of his characters, not as his own; nor in the fact that his reading of life can only be expressed indirectly and by implication (in such ways as we have already indicated), and that even his sense of the poetry that irradiates his universe is at the mercy of the people of his drama.

Now, just as the different dramatists, though fundamentally akin, differ somewhat in the balance and relation of these generic qualities we began by considering, so, it will be found, do they differ in respect of this differentiating characteristic of dramatic sympathy and the technical mode that follows from it. Dramatists differ in their power, or their desire, of maintaining equidistant relations with their characters; at one extreme we find Marlowe, who in *Tamburlaine* and in *Faustus*, identifies himself with one or at most two characters and enters only intermittently into the others; at the other extreme we find Shakespeare, who speaks from within each of his creatures as it speaks. So also do they vary in the extent to which they express directly their own passion, their own perception of poetic truth, and make explicit or keep implicit their reading of life. Marlowe again is at one extreme in the first of these and Shakespeare at the other; in the second the extremes may be illustrated by Aeschylus on the one hand and Shakespeare again on the other. So far as his characters allow him, a dramatist may express with a measure of directness his emotion and his poetic delight. But those larger inferences from his experience which we call his reading of life can only, as we have said, be expressed implicitly, in terms of character and event and the relation between the two. In so far as he does in fact depart from this law, itself an inference from the differentiating characteristics of drama, in so far does he depart from the strict dramatic mode. This divergence, here possible to dramatists, may be briefly illustrated by the different methods of revealing thought through or independently of character and action. (Since, as has been indicated, the problems in the dramatic revelation of passion and of poetic experience are less crucial, the divergence in practice is less wide there and calls the less for illustration.)

Aeschylus, as is obvious, gives us in twofold form his comment on the world of his play; in one form it is implicit and dramatic, lying wholly within the dialogue; in the other, in the choric odes, it is explicit and to that extent non-dramatic, sometimes almost a direct statement of a theme. The two are complementary and in complete harmony, but each is dependent upon the other and neither alone would render fully his interpretation. This is true to a less degree of Sophocles. Euripides, perhaps simply because he came later in the tradition which had bequeathed the choric ode, but more probably because he instinctively laid more emphasis upon action and suffering, revealed his reading rather by the indirect, implicit method. More than any modern of comparable stature, Ibsen renders parts of his interpretation in terms of direct commentary, though he is dramatist enough to put suitable characters in charge of the operation.[7] Of the greatest dramatists of the world's literature, one alone, so far, has used the dramatic mode, and only the dramatic, for the revelation of his underlying thought. It is Shakespeare who baffles impertinent conjecture and unimaginative exegesis alike by affording us no re-expression of his implicit, dramatic utterance in terms of explicit commentary. The reading of life revealed by his plays cannot, as we have already noticed, be abstracted, for it is co-extensive with the plays themselves and can only be learnt by a lifetime spent in their world.

If, now, we look again at the properties of the resulting 'kind', those outward characteristics which, taken together, constitute the conventional forms of drama, can we discover anything more? I think we can, by this means, add something to what we have already said of the operation both of those generic forces and of those differentiating qualities which are at work in the mind of a dramatic genius. We may observe that they can transmute, not only traditional and conventional forms but even the limitations imposed not by convention but by the nature of the kind itself, and make both subservient to significant form.

When a traditional or conventional form comes into the hands of a dramatist of genius, when passion, thought, and poetic imagination have there expressed themselves in terms of sympathy and by means of direct presentation, we find the elements of a play (action, character, dialogue) transformed, so that each fulfils more than the bare functions necessary to make of the work drama rather than some other literary kind. Through the operation of those powers the relation between these elements becomes more fruitful; action or plot becomes significant form, itself an aspect of the play's meaning or thought; the revelation and grouping of character becomes the spatial aspect of the play's structure;[8] and dialogue or speech the vehicle for our necessary knowledge not merely of action and character, but of much upon which depends our understanding of the relations between the world of the play and the wider universe of which that world is a part. Contrast between scene and scene becomes in *Troilus and Cressida* an image of disjunction, in *Antony and Cleopatra* of synthesis; in the first play the theme is the discord of the universe, in the second it is the conflict in Antony's mind between an empire and a mistress, and the vastness of that empire images the magnitude of the conflict. The grouping of characters in each play serves the same end, somewhat as does the relation of colour and shape in pictorial composition; and imagery directly and verbal music indirectly relate the significance thus revealed within the play to that of the wider, surrounding universe.

When we consider such drama as this, which has passed beyond mere adequate craftsmanship to take its place among the great art-forms, we find that it, like all other arts, meets and conflicts with the limitations imposed by its form and seeks out means of transcending them. And it is the major dramatists, with whom we have been all along concerned, who discover and reveal to their fellows the possibilities inherent in the form, which can, paradoxically, enable them to transcend its limitations. Their discoveries may be defined by their followers or imitators, by those who are consciously or unconsciously taught by them, sometimes as branches of technique, sometimes almost as technical devices; but in the hands of the original masters they are the findings of far-reaching imaginative exploration. It is Aeschylus, so far as our knowledge allows us to judge, who perceives a further function of the choric ode, using it to refer outward, beyond the boundaries of the play's actual content, to a moral and spiritual universe of which his chosen portion of life is a significant part. But this is the least innately dramatic of all the modes of transcending limitation in scope, and what we have already said would lead us, even if we had not studied his work, to expect that Shakespeare would not use it. In fact, he does not. But since to remain in subjection to the limitations of a form is to write a work of art which may be the poorer for its submission, he finds his own ways to enlarge the content of his play, to deepen its significance, and to reach out beyond a given pattern of character and event to a universe of thought and experience of which they are but a representative fragment. Certain of the means by which he does this we can in part discern, though our description of their working must necessarily be imperfect. The soliloquy (very differently used by most of his predecessors and contemporaries and by many of his successors down to the present day) allows him to let down a shaft of light into the hidden workings of the

mind, to enable us to overhear its unspoken thought without in effect
suspending the outward movement of the action or breaking the impression of the immediacy and reality of the dramatic world. The imagery in
his dialogue, for which, again, the Elizabethan habit gave him precedent,
allows him, without extending the body of the speech, to let those same
words which convey to us our necessary knowledge of feeling, thought, or
event convey simultaneously many other things which our subconscious
minds apprehend even if our conscious thought does not, deepening and
extending our perception, now of the significance of the action, now of the
relation of the whole to that wider universe which surrounds it. The verbal
music, all that we include in the effects of rhythm and pitch inherent in the
words and disengaged from our language by Shakespeare's blank verse,
have a similar function and work simultaneously with imagery to similar
ends. He, moreover, can evoke, by rare and exquisite use of what may be
called the overtones of speech and action,[9] something other than, yet
simultaneous with, the words, images, and music which yet continue in
their appointed functions. Each of these powers latent in the medium of
dramatic dialogue was known to one or other of Shakespeare's contemporaries; Shakespeare alone uses them all, and, at the height of his power,
simultaneously, and he alone to all the ends I have suggested. Of the great
moderns, Ibsen is a master of the first and the last; of the soliloquy which
reveals the hidden thought of his characters and of the art which evokes
from speech the overtones that reveal something related to, yet other than,
that speech. But imagery tends with him, as never with Shakespeare, to
pass over into the less dramatic mode of symbol, and verbal music is
limited (though never destroyed) by his later dedication to the prose
medium.

It is perhaps at this point that we realize how often and how nearly we
have approached to begging the question in saying: 'This writer (or his
method) is more nearly dramatic than that.' Can we now attempt some
such statement without falling into that fallacy? Can we say that if, from
our chain of hypothesis and deduction, we can abstract for ourselves an
idea of what constitutes the innately dramatic mind, the mind that finds its
expression in a mode which is fully and strictly dramatic, then such and
such dramatists approach most nearly to this ideal? I think we can.

Clearly enough it has been to Shakespeare that we have been so often
tempted to point. Even in a brief and cursory survey of the obscure movements of the great generic powers, we find, and I think we find justly, that
Shakespeare, in the possession of the primal forces from which drama
derives, is with the greatest. Yet already there, and still more when we

pass to the differentiating characteristics of the art, he sometimes seemed to stand a little apart. We suspected, again somewhat in anticipation of the argument, that it is he alone who uses no modes but the dramatic; he alone who never steps out of his play to speak, disguised or undisguised, in his own person. Can we, with that in mind, point to any distinctive character- istic and say that this carries an artist to the heart of the dramatic experience and gives to his work full dramatic quality? Is there, in fact, in his approach to his material anything which sets apart the genuine dramatist, the man whose art is wholly dramatic from the first moment of its conception to the last detail of communication? Is there a faculty which makes possible for him a special mode of artistic experience,[10] and that mode the dramatic?

If we look again at the distinction we drew between the dramatic and the other forms of great poetic art, we shall find at the same time both the explanation of our conviction that Shakespeare's art is the most consist- ently dramatic and the answer to this last question. The method of a given artist, while derived primarily from his instinctive choice of material, is immediately determined by his approach to it, and Shakespeare's method reveals the approach distinctive of the dramatic artist, a limitless sympathy with man acting and suffering. Because of this sympathy, the passion, thought, and poetic imagination which inspire all artists are, in the dramatist, determined towards the distinctive dramatic method, the direct revelation by those who themselves act and suffer. And when these primal forces of art are so determined they infuse the principle of life that trans- mutes convention and transcends limitation, preserving the art from sterility and renewing it phoenix-like from age to age.

When we apply our minds to the understanding of a character in a great play, attempting to enter into it with our imaginations as a great actor does in preparing to act it, what is it that we find? We find that the dramatist has so wholly imagined his character that what he has revealed within the framework of the play seems to be only a part of what he knows, just as what a man reveals of himself in any one series of his actions is but a part of what he is. We are accustomed to say that the dramatist has identified him- self with Agamemnon, with Oedipus, with Agavé, with Macbeth, with Hjalmar Ekdal. We can, if we will, amuse ourselves by transporting the character to other periods or situations, back into childhood or away into some other series of events and actions, and this frivolity is not without its use if it teaches us something of the fullness of that original imagining. We find, by degrees, that we can do this most often with the characters of Shakespeare's plays, for it is his practice to give us hints, not so much of events as of formative influences in the lives of an Edmund, an Iago, a Hamlet, even of so early a figure as Richard III. And so, returning to our study of the actual content of the play before us, we may trace the processes of the mind, as the actor must and does, through scenes in which the continuum of speech is interrupted and find again that the guidance given us is enough because Shakespeare's understanding of the mind was whole. We can, if we use our imaginations faithfully in the interpretation of the clues that are given us, follow the thought of Bolingbroke through the scene before Flint Castle and the deposition scene, in both of which, but for a brief speech or two, he is silent through long periods; just so we may divine the links between the broken phrases in Lady Macbeth's speech in the sleep-walking scene, and relate each utterance to some moment in the foregoing action, the memory of which now calls it forth. All this we can do with the central figures in Shakespeare's plays as with many other dramatists (for some who are not the greatest treat in this way their central figures).

But can we now, disengaging Shakespeare's work again from the matrix of great drama we have been studying, discover anything more? What if the actor or the reader change his part from Macbeth to Lady Macbeth, is not what we have said still true? Obviously it is. Then is it true also of Duncan, of Banquo, of Macduff – even of the unfortunate Malcolm, encumbered as he is by the third scene of the fourth act? We must, I think, agree that it is. And are there not two murderers, men who appear but for a brief moment or two to plan with Macbeth the assassination of Banquo? Are we not given just enough indication of the world they live in to arrive at a momentary understanding of the springs of their motives and to remain convinced that though only a slender arc of each personality enters the frame of the play, the circle is complete beyond it, living full and whole in the poet's imagination? And so we might pursue the investigation through all the authentic plays of Shakespeare's maturity. In all of them we find this imaginative sympathy, this identification of the poet himself with every character in his drama.

But this is not the end. We said a moment ago that the thought of Bolingbroke in certain scenes of *Richard II* (II. iii and IV. i) was potentially revealed to us even in those passages where he is silent and other men are speaking, and that we, while they speak, can continue to identify ourselves with him. And we can, if we wish, make each of these other men in turn the centre of our attention and then, when they in their turn are silent, their thought will similarly be revealed to us while others speak. It is not a matter merely of Shakespeare's identifying himself with each in turn, with each man as he comes to life in speech, but with each man's momentarily hidden life for so long as he is within the framework of the play and, if necessary, beyond it. The self-identification with each and every character is not only whole but simultaneous. This, I submit, is the genuine dramatic mode of thought, the fundamental quality which reveals the innate dramatic genius, and it is this, I believe, which distinguishes the essentially dramatic from all other kinds of genius. How rare this is, a moment's reflection will assure us.

If this is true, then we have in Shakespeare not only a dramatist but *the* dramatist, the only one in the great company of dramatic poets who is wholly and continuously dramatic. The only one, that is to say, in whom there are to be found, in the highest degree and uncontaminated with other modes of thought, both the generic powers and differentiating qualities of dramatic genius, and a resultant art whose mode and whose methods are wholly dramatic.

The artistic experience of the essential dramatist thus differs from that of other artists at a point very near its roots, and the response of human beings of many races and of most recorded ages indicates the depth of the relation between common human experience and the best-loved of the arts. For the paradox inherent in the dramatist's attitude to man, his subject, is also the source of his power. In his vast, impersonal sympathy lies one solution of the problem so long familiar to mystics: 'Teach us to care and not to care.' And the dramatist having, like the great mystic, in some measure solved this problem, speaks as one having authority.

For the communication thus made is distinguished from that of the imperfectly dramatic by a factor whose significance it is almost impossible to over-estimate. 'This even-handed justice', this universal sympathy which has at once the balance of impersonal detachment and the radiance of affection, gives to the record made and to the reading of life implied a power of assurance byond that of any utterance short of the affirmation of the mystic. Convinced at once of the depth and the range of Shakespeare's experience through his imaginative understanding of the passions and thoughts of men, we are convinced no less of the truth of his perception through this single quality, the universal sympathy of the genuine dramatist. For it is this which, operating without bias, reveals in the mind of a man the shadow of the divine attribute of simultaneous immanence and transcendence. The confidence felt by generations of men of many races in the reading of life implicit in the total body of Shakespeare's plays depends in the last resort on the fact that not merely did he know what is in man, but that he knew it as a dramatist. 'If this is true', it was once said of a concerto of Bach, 'all is indeed well'. Because, in the man whose genius is wholly dramatic there is no prepossession, no prejudice, no theory, because no matter of common experience is left out of the account, his ultimate assumption, still implicit because still dramatic, will carry the same assurance as the revealed vision of the mystic, and will carry it in times and in the places the mystic does not touch. This is the supreme function of the dramatist. That Shakespeare has fulfilled that function beyond all others is only to say in another form that he, beyond all others, is wholly a dramatist.

NOTES

[1]The Annual Shakespeare Lecture of the British Academy, 1948. A typewritten draft of this lecture, under the title 'The Essential Dramatist', has been compared with the printed version. One passage, added in manuscript, has been restored, in square brackets, in note 6. The draft opens with three paragraphs differentiating dramatic and epic poets from other poets and artists. These are partly based on Lascelles Abercrombie's *Towards a Theory of Art* and *The Principles of Literary Criticism*.

[2]Oed. Col., 1225-8.
μὴ φῦναι τὸν ἅπαντα νικᾷ λόγον· τὸ δ'ἐπεὶ φανῇ
βῆναι κεῖθεν ὅθεν περ ἥκει
πολὺ δεύτερον, ὡς τάχιστα.

[3]I am partly indebted for this phrase to Mr C. Day Lewis, who, in his recent work *The Poetic Image* (1947), discusses in Chapter V the function of poetic logic, referring back to the use, by W.P. Ker, of the term 'poetical logic'.

[4]On the relations between the choric ode of Aeschylus with the form on the one hand and the theme on the other, see H.D.F. Kitto, *Greek Tragedy* (1939).

[5]See C. Day Lewis, *The Poetic Image* (p. 58).

[6]This is extremely rare in drama, even in comedy. (It is not to be confused with what is extremely common in most dramatists below the greatest, an imperfect distribution of sympathy, so that some of the characters, but not all, are treated objectively.) Middleton alone appears to preserve this attitude in tragedy and that only in the main plots of his two major tragedies. [Nor should we perhaps accept the appearance without inspection. For Middleton's pictures of the travelling mind lost upon a strange and sinister road of experience convey into the imagination of the reader the terror and the pity which do not come by chance but only from the operation of deep, if hidden, emotion. Middleton, like Swift, appears not to feel; but inasmuch as each stirs in reader or audience a powerful and painful response, the sympathy of the writer cannot be doubted.] Ibsen occasionally seems to achieve it, but this is generally found, on closer inspection, to be either a momentary failure of

sympathy in one direction or the result of a deceptive concealment of an underlying but passionate sympathy.

[7] Here the modern convention of dramatic plausibility may be partly responsible. Certain of the Elizabethans, who were not subject to the naturalistic convention, though poets of great dramatic force, availed themselves of the relative freedom of their dramatic form to use the equivalent of brief choric commentary without undue regard to the characters to whom it was assigned. Webster is adept at inducing his reader to accept this without realizing it.

[8] The spatial aspect of structure and the relation between spatial and temporal form in drama are discussed in detail in G. Wilson Knight's *The Wheel of Fire* (1930). 'A Shakespearean tragedy is set spatially as well as temporally in the mind. By this I mean that there are a set of correspondences which relate to each other independently of the time-sequence which is the story (p. 3). (The theory is developed in the first chapter, 'On the Principles of Shakespearean Interpretation'.)

[9] This use of what may be called the dramatic overtones, though it is as old as dramatic art itself, being akin on one side to irony and on another to the significant use of silence, is peculiarly skilful in some modern plays. The French *Théâtre de Silence* depends in part upon it for its effects; in Thornton Wilder's *Our Town* it is, if I am not mistaken, the principal vehicle of the theme.

[10] I assume here the distinction between artistic and aesthetic experience drawn by Lascelles Abercrombie in *Towards a Theory of Art* (1926), and now generally accepted, the artistic experience being that involved in the act of artistic creation.

II

The mode of the dramatist

Our conclusions suggest that the most direct way to an understanding of
the nature of drama may be in the study of character and that it is the
dramatist's approach to and universal sympathy with his characters that
leads him to those methods of communication that distinguish his art from
all others. It may be that after considering this we shall find confirmation
from other aspects of a work of dramatic art (such as the plot, or arrange-
ment of the incidents) and of the dramatists' technique as it is here
revealed. For we remember, too, that Aristotle says plainly that the plot is
the first essential.[1] But though Aristotle's claim may be true of the initial
inspiration, of which some critics believe him to be speaking here,[2] the
common reader's response to the resultant work of art appears to reverse
this order and approach instinctively through character. Perhaps the
present generation of readers is particularly ready to take this road; given
our prepossessions, our immediate tradition in Shakespeare criticism and
the habits this has bred, the most familiar way into the understanding of a
play is by what we call character. This happens to be the gate near which
the greater number of us dwell.

What then is 'character' in drama and what do we understand when we
talk of its functions? What is the relation, for the ideal reader, between
what he meets in life and what he meets in drama, life being, after all, the
material from which the dramatist's image of an action derives and upon
which it works?

Just[3] as a work of art differs as a whole from the raw material which is its
source, so much its various parts or aspects differ from the corresponding

aspects of that material. In that particular branch of the art of literature which we call drama, plot or action, for instance, is not identical with a series of actual events, though it has a special relationship to it; nor is dialogue identical with actual conversation, however cunningly it may contrive to appear so; nor 'character' with character. That aspect of a play which we may, if we wish, abstract from the whole and think of as a 'character' has travelled a long way from the original source of inspiration. It took its rise, in the dramatist's imagination, from his experience of and not-necessarily-conscious interpretation of human motive, emotion, thought, and action, as they appeared to him in life and at a particular moment. It was resolved, by the artistic process, into a conception or form held, unexpressed, in his mind. Next, or it may be half-simultaneously, this was transmuted into communicable form in terms of certain conventions, conventions mysteriously potent in their operation upon the imaginations of the recipients – in this case readers or audiences – communicating to them a proportion of the poet's original experience, the proportion varying, of course, in any given conjunction, in accordance with his power to communicate and theirs to receive.

From this it follows that we must not demand, when we approach dramatic character, too limited or too immediate correspondence with character as we meet in life. We do the artist wrong when we apply the test of superficial resemblance and use that as our criterion of his fidelity to truth. The revelation of character, like any other branch of dramatic technique, should not, properly, attempt to deceive us into believing that what we have before us is fact itself or a direct deduction from fact. Yet this must not be taken to imply that it is illusion, if by illusion we mean something incapable by its very nature of leading us to truth. Dramatic character, like dramatic plot, is an image on the grand scale, and it is the function of imagery to evoke in our minds certain perceptions, realizations, emotions, which are themselves aspects of an underlying reality, not to present us with a scientific statement of fact, an abstract from that perceived reality.

This is, of course, a commonplace of aesthetics, but its truth has some-times eluded critics, largely perhaps because certain dramatists have them-selves denied it in practice and in their theories, misleading dramatic criticism, not so much about their own experiment as about the real nature of this aspect of dramatic technique. For drama occupies a some-what anomalous position among the arts in that it appears at first glance to be inherently representational, and the habit of certain of its weaker practitioners in the recent phase of its history has confirmed this impres-sion in the minds alike of audiences, critics, and subsequent dramatists.

Fidelity to surface appearance, in character as in other branches of dramatic technique, has been given, in popular and in critical opinion, an honourable estate as a mode of presentation to which the evidence does not, I think, entitle it. A host of honest, workmanlike dramatists of the second rank have practised it assiduously and with the best of artistic intentions; one at least of the first rank seemed for a time to set his seal upon it. But drama, which, because it is transmitted to us in the theatre through impersonations by living men and women, appears to come nearer to the actual than any of the other arts, is in fact debarred by certain fundamental laws of its nature from any sustained attempt to present surface appearance. Its brevity alone would make this impossible, even if the deeper-lying demands of passion and thought did not add their weight to the swift momentum. We are thus confronted with another of those paradoxes that beset dramatic aesthetics. The art which in its proper sphere of the theatre seems the most nearly immediate of all is forced, in obedience to the law of concentration without which it would not seem immediate, to present action, character, and even speech itself in terms which, upon investigation, turn out to be profoundly unrealistic.

The attempt to deny this fundamental necessity of drama, which is, properly, the basic dramatic convention, is of very recent growth. Without the weighty authority of Ibsen, it is doubtful whether the diligent output of the everyday dramatist of the mid-nineteenth century would seriously have disturbed our acceptance of the grand, ancient technical tradition of what Aristotle classed as tragedy. But in a few of his plays (and how hard it is to persuade our generation that they were only a few!) Ibsen did in fact appear to lend his genius to an experiment the results of which bewilder our judgements to the present day. Some half-dozen sinister accidents then combined to make the small group of plays from *Pillars of Society* to *Wild Duck* his most influential in those countries whose own influence was to count for most in twentieth-century dramatic criticism. Small wonder that the early work of Dumas *fils* seemed to be confirmed in its implications, or that the Galsworthies and the Brieux of the twentieth century followed. A revolution occurred and it seemed for a time that major drama could be written in terms of everyday life, whether of action, character, or speech. And this meant in the domain of character that the brevity of drama must now be circumvented in a new way, not as before by offering an image of the hidden reality at the roots of life, but by an abstraction from it, a statement of conclusions drawn from it by a deductive process and presented in terms of diagrammatic or self-explanatory character. The great artists do this with consummate cunning

and Ibsen offers us a long line of characters in whom this procedure is justified because they have been forced by temperament or circumstances to
think about themselves, sometimes to know themselves, but always to
become lucid and facile in explaining themselves. Brand, Karsten Bernick,
Lona Hessel, Nora Helmer, Mrs Alving, Pastor Manders, Oswald
Alving, Regina Engstrand, the brothers Stockmann, all have this capacity
for self-examination and in each it seems at the worst plausible, at the best
inevitable. But the great hinterland of the unknown self to which the
Greeks and the Elizabethans had access, the domain of great poetry and of
the poet or the mystic in the common man, was closed. The counter-
revolution which Ibsen himself began in the late plays with the studies of
Solness, Hilda Wangel, Rosmer, Rebecca West, and John Gabriel
Borkman is not yet stabilized; we have lost our way, as W.B. Yeats long
ago realized, to the sources of the living imagination in drama. We are confronted with what appear to be two valid and alternative ways of revealing
character, the expository and the evocative, but in fact the first of these is
not valid and cannot lead to full, profound, or poetic revelation. Like the
lovers in Yeats's story we have attempted to put our knowledge of a
mystery into 'common words' and have lost our vision and the memory of
the way to the hidden country to which our real selves belong. In our
nostalgia we blame a multitude of causes for this century's failure to
produce great drama, but we seldom reflect that one of the roots of our
predicament is the denial of the poetic process, a denial that strangles the
poet in our dramatists. Nowhere in dramatic technique is this more
disastrous than in the technique of portraying character.

One of the odd corollaries of this false theorem is the application to the
whole body of the traditional drama behind us of the conclusions from the
practice and theories of the last hundred years. We accuse the great dramatists from Aeschylus downward (but principally Shakespeare, because
more of us study him) of perpetrating an illusion in their presentation of
character. The naturalists, in attempting to persuade us that a character in
a work of art is a character in nature, lost touch with the deep, hidden wells
of reality from which imagination draws its life, and the shallowness of
their resultant rendering has at last forced itself upon our notice. And from
this we unjustifiably conclude that 'character' in drama must always and
necessarily be illusion, theatrical effect only, that will not bear
investigating; and that the character-work of the great poetic dramatists,
because it lacks even superficial likeness to everyday events, is more
deeply guilty of illusion even than that of those naturalists. And so the
serious investigation of the characters of Shakespeare's plays becomes at

best a piece of venial day-dreaming, at worst a dangerous heresy. Whereas, in fact, it is the great poetic dramatists whose sure, unerring technique alone makes character revelation possible, because it alone finds anything to reveal, and the one thing that their presentation needs to assure us of this is investigation.[4]

I should like, with your permission, to illustrate what I mean at this point by reference to two specific passages. It must, of course, be understood that nothing less than the consideration of the total presentation of a character throughout a play (and preferably, of all the characters) could justly illustrate the technique of revelation. Extracts as brief as those which I must now use can do nothing more, even if they are passages of great significance, than illustrate the function of speech in a brief dialogue. What depends upon action, in so far as that can be distinguished from speech, is necessarily omitted and we lose further the cumulative power which the interrelation of action and speech gives to both and that further potent effect which the successive phases of the revelation derive from their place in the total action. But I am convinced that what is true of these passages is true one-hundredfold of the total effect of the play and that the distinction I am attempting to draw becomes more, not less, apparent as we pursue it further.

I choose for my first passage a short extract from the second Act of *Ghosts*, one of the few plays of Ibsen whose claim to the title of tragedy can hardly be denied under any definition, ancient or modern. It is the passage in which Manders and Mrs Alving speak face to face after years of silence and strip away one by one the veils that have hidden their past. It is a scene charged with passion, the stored-up bitterness of fruitless sacrifice, and yet it is as lucid as a logical or legal analysis, because the speaker, a woman of fearless and powerful mind, has subjected these injuries, and the moral code that caused them, to a slow, pitiless, and scientific examination through long years of solitude. It arises with the perfect naturalness of a mountain peak from its massif, for these two lovers who for years have been enemies are confronted with a situation which suddenly releases the pent-up thinking of a lifetime.

Mrs Alving. Let me tell you what I mean. I'm timid and half-hearted because I can't get rid of the ghosts that haunt me.

Manders. What do you say haunts you?

Mrs Alving. Ghosts! When I heard Regina and Oswald in there, it was as though I saw ghosts before me. But I almost think we're all of us ghosts, Pastor Manders. It's not only what we have inherited from our father and mother that 'walks' in us. It's all sorts of dead ideas, old lifeless beliefs, and so forth. They have no vitality; but they cling to us all the same, and we can't get rid of them. Whenever I take up a newspaper I seem to see ghosts gliding between the lines. There must be ghosts all over the country, as thick as the sand of the sea. And then we're all of us so pitifully afraid of the light.

Manders. Ah! here we have the fruits of your reading! And pretty fruits they are, upon my word! Those horrible, revolutionary, freethinking books!

Mrs Alving. You're mistaken, my dear Pastor. It was you yourself set me thinking. And I thank you for it with all my heart.

Manders. I?

Mrs Alving. Yes. When you forced me under the yoke you called 'Duty' and 'Obligation'; when you praised as right and proper what my whole soul rebelled against, as against something loathsome. It was then I began to look into the seams of your doctrine. I only meant to pick at a single knot; but when I'd got that undone, the whole thing ravelled out. And then I realized that it was all machine-sewn.

Manders (softly, with emotion). And was that the upshot of my life's hardest battle?

Mrs Alving. Call it, rather, your most pitiful defeat.

Manders. It was my greatest victory, Helen – the victory over myself.

Mrs Alving. It was a crime against us both.

Manders. When you went astray, and came to me crying, 'Here I am; take me!', I commanded you, saying – 'Woman, go home to your lawful husband.' Was that a crime?

Mrs Alving. Yes, I think so.

Manders. We two do not understand each other.

Mrs Alving. Not now, at any rate.

None of us would deny to this scene, thinking of it in its place in the drama, its cogency, the intensity of its passionate thought. It impresses us; almost it moves us; certainly it rivets our attention. Two minds are in conflict upon a moral issue. A life-history is revealed, lucidly, painfully; its case is pleaded before us, like a case in court. We listen intently, we sympathize, as step by step, actions are explained by motive and motive in turn by freshly interpreted fact. For in this court we are the judge and the plaintiff pleads her own case before us in this reinterpretation of fact and motive. But there is a fatal limitation in this function of judge that is forced upon us. For what kind of response does it call out in us? We should, of course, have no difficulty in describing the outstanding traits of the two people before us; there is no failure to define their characteristics. But what is there, in this clear self-analysis and self-defence, of the deeper movements of character, what sudden disclosure of the vast unexplored territories of the mind, seen suddenly as through parting mists, such as, in a single line of Aeschylus, reveals to us a human soul akin to the unknown or half-known soul within ourselves?

οὐδεὶς ἀκούει ταῦτα τῶν εὐδαιμόνων.

(Alas, none that is happy knows the word.) (*Ag.* 1303)

In that line Cassandra, at the crisis of her tragedy, discovers and lets fall one of those great truths whose perception changes the habit of a mind, transforms its reading of life. What communication have we, in the noble elucidation of Mrs Alving's motive and behaviour, with the region of the spirit from which such knowledge as Cassandra's comes? And yet can we really be said to have tragic character when we are cut off from these intimations, when we are restricted to the conscious, reasoning operations of the mind, which are the best we can hope for in a play in which the characters must perforce explain themselves if they are to be known at all? And is this technique, the inevitable result of his commitment to naturalism, ultimately worthy of the genius of Ibsen, however closely his architectural power interlocks the parts of the action, down to the smallest detail, however strongly his passion, held prisoner within that flawless and unbreakable design, throbs through the hard, clear dialogue? 'Je ne reconnais plus l'auteur du *Misanthrope*'; we miss the poet of the fifth act of *Peer Gynt* and of the death of Gabriel Borkman.

But if we turn back to Shakespeare we meet a technique that wastes no time or strength in trying to persuade us that a play is not a play or that the words that lie before us on the page are an exact reproduction of those of everyday life. The great poetic dramatists are mercifully delivered from this temptation by the traditional forms of their lines; no one has, I believe (not even in the criticism of the last hundred years), contended that the Elizabethans habitually spoke blank verse, the citizens of Athens iambics, or the audiences of the Hôtel de Bourgogne alexandrines. And, in this matter of dramatic technique, to be committed in advance to a great traditional convention, even if it govern no more than the vehicle of speech, is to be delivered from a host of misconceptions as to the relation between the truth (or reality) to be communicated and the medium through which it is transmitted. If our characters cannot speak the rhythms of everyday life, we are protected against the assumption that they can be made to sound as if they were living their outward lives before us. If we are guarded thus against the temptation to present those actual, outward lives as themselves an aspect of reality, we are free to use our brief dramatic span to reveal the enduring, the universal, the inward experience of man. But to do that, in so brief space, we must use, boldly, another technique – a technique that is not afraid of (has not indeed regarded) its unrealistic mode; a technique that indicates character by touches, by silences, by omissions, but by touches of such rare significance that their presence in those silences evokes in our imagination an ever-growing, living organism, a whole that is a character. To use language thus to indicate and evoke characters is not to practise illusion, any more than do those few brief words in which the mystic images a part of his experience and evokes a corresponding under-standing in those who can receive them. In the technique of revealing character in drama, it is, I repeat, the only way to achieve a revelation of validity and scope.

> *Macbeth.*   Two Truths are told,
>   As happy Prologues to the swelling Act
>   Of the Imperiall Theame. I thanke you Gentlemen:
>   This supernaturall solliciting
>   Cannot be ill; cannot be good. If ill,
>   Why hath it giuen me earnest of successe,
>   Commencing in a Truth? I am *Thane* of Cawdor.
>   If good, why doe I yeeld to that suggestion,
>   Whose horrid Image doth vnfixe my Heire,
>   And make my seated Heart knock at my Ribbes,
>   Against the vse of Nature? Present Feares
>   Are lesse then horrible imaginings:
>   My Thought, whose Murther yet is but fantasticall,
>   Shakes so my single state of Man, that Function
>   Is smother'd in surmise, and nothing is,
>   But what is not.

The turmoil and mystery of man's unknown self is released by this passage as great music releases it. It is a series of potent images that drop like deep shafts into the hidden wells of man's being to reach a strange and terrifying reality. If we were to examine it word by word, each phrase, each image, each suggestion would serve to lead us into speculation, into knowledge the total expression of which in explicit terms would demand a volume of writing no less in extent than a whole play (supposing, which is clearly impossible, that such explication could be conceived in dramatic

form at all). For it works upon us not through our judgement but by direct
appeal to that vast, hidden imaginative self which it alone can reach. In the
whole passage no sentence has the form of normal speech, except that in
which Macbeth breaks away for a moment from his preoccupation in the
brief 'I thank you, Gentlemen'. We may ask ourselves, 'What does this
tell us of character?' And the answer at first may seem to be 'Nothing', for
such moments are the meeting-grounds of passion and inchoate thought
that overwhelm characteristics and resolve the individual man into the
eternal, the universal, the generic. It tells us little of those superficial traits
and characteristics by which we so readily sum up character as it appears to
offer itself in the everyday commerce of life and in the drama that attempts
to work in terms of that commerce. But there is, after all, ample time for
such indication of those features as we shall need in the play, by a casual
reference here and there, by the juxtaposition of speech and action. What
we have here is the deep working of half-hidden and half-articulate motive
such as, in ourselves and other men, seems to overwhelm individuality,
that 'drowning of the dykes', that 'perishing into reality' in which Yeats
found the essential tragic experience. Yet, when we look more closely,
whether it is at the 'character' Shakespeare has called Macbeth or
at similar moments in our own experience, we know that this is not all;
that in this evocation of mysterious forces, this exploration of unknown
depths, the individuality is not utterly obliterated. Riding the torrent
it cannot stem, it survives into a measure of choice, and what follows,
in its action and thought, will have a power withheld in art or life from
the 'character' that is rooted in its own consciousness. Put the limitless and 'still-breeding' implication of this brief indication of the
hidden world of Macbeth's mind beside the limits that Ibsen, at the
stage of *Ghosts*, deliberately sets to the definition of his problem, and
dare we do otherwise than reverse the popular verdict of our day? It is the
technique of Ibsen's four realistic plays, and more still that technique as
practised by dramatists of lesser genius, which makes the presentation
of character in drama an illusion. It is the evocative and non-realistic
technique of Shakespeare and the poetic dramatists that leads us to
reality. Indeed, as Blake said: 'Improvement makes straight roads, but
crooked roads without improvement are roads of Genius.' Only by abandoning the apparent safeguards of verisimilitude can drama, especially
in this branch of its technique, become the vehicle of the deepest-hidden
truth. Ibsen's characters live the examined life commended by Plato:
ὁ ἀνεξέταστος βίος οὐ βιωτὸς ἀνθρώπῳ (*Ap.* 38A); but
Shakespeare's art, like all great poetry, depends on another

mode of being, commended in another place: 'Amen, amen dico vobis, nisi granum frumenti cadens in terram mortuum fuerit, ipsum solum manet; si autem mortuum fuerit, multum fructum affert', or the hidden life without safeguards which is the life of the mystics and of the great ideal poets.

We might very well have reached our conclusion as to the relative validity of these techniques by a different road, and I shall attempt in the space that I have left to indicate this. Ibsen and Shakespeare, like all artists, faced the inexorable task of selection. Even the realist cannot escape this, but it is the dramatic realist's misfortune that he must often pretend to do so. We can watch Ibsen at work and see something of the magnificent sureness with which he selects and re-combines, of the architectural economy that doubles and trebles the significance of every part or fragment by the relating to it of every other. But life does not select, and the need to hide the fact that the artist does taxed to the uttermost even Ibsen's powers, while the verisimilitude of lesser dramatists broke down, even as verisimilitude, in the effort to appear to use only the actual when one aspect of that actual is precisely a mass of detail that could in no circumstances be used. And so the nature of the selection the dramatist makes becomes the governing factor in his presentation of truth, in character as in all other branches of technique. Nothing can save him from this law, and his peril is his glory. He will be aware (consciously or unconsciously – or both) of event and character as a continuous stream of what for brevity's sake we will call experience, and his task as an artist is to dip into that stream and draw from it, now here, now there, small quantities which can never, by the very nature of the artistic process, be more than a minute proportion of the whole, disconnected, isolated from each other, and to sacrifice the rest of that vast continuum which is the material of inner and outward experience. Nothing can save him from disastrous errors of omission and wrong emphasis that would give a lying picture of reality except that gift of divination which is genius and the hidden, fundamental, and mysterious operations of its power. If he trusts instead to the operation of the intellect working upon observation, however acute, of the surface of life, he cuts himself off from the sources of power and of illumination.

I have spoken so far of the method by which the dramatist may transmit his perception of reality in character, as in other branches of technique, but in doing so I have made two obvious assumptions: that there is a reality to transmit and that the great poet is one of the channels for its transmission. I do not want to end without indicating my meaning here, since the test of technical validity depends upon a relation between technique and content.

For the purposes of this argument, I will merely say that I take truth, which the great artist communicates, to be a part or parts of a complete and irreducible reality, such as might be discerned by an unerring and all-including intelligence, which some of us find it briefer and less cumbersome to call God. I consider further that the spiritual universe affords the means for the knowledge of this truth; that it is part of its nature to do so. I believe this knowledge to be possible under certain conditions to human faculties, to such faculties, for instance, as are possessed by the great poets and the great saints. I believe, that is to say, that in this continuum of experience, of which we have spoken, it is possible to either of them to discern certain significant elements, unnameable perhaps by either and for the artist certainly better undefined, which so work upon the imagination as to produce awareness of form, of the presence of intention, of the operation of underlying law. Provided, that is to say, that the poet has within his power the means of transmission (and it has been my object here to discuss one particular aspect of his choice of those means), he is capable of transmitting truth, and that truth is there to be communicated.

But the distinction between the presentation of character in terms of statement and its indication by means of the evocative technique remains within the province of dramatic aesthetics. Since, as we have demonstrated, the technique of statement cannot reveal so much or so profoundly as can the evocative technique, the method, even in the hands of Ibsen, is a hindrance to drama, and, so far, undramatic. It appears to present reality, only to provoke the accusation that 'character' imagined (and in part transmitted, despite the technique) is an aspect of imaginative truth. But in the great poetic dramatists, who proceed by evocation, there is, rightly understood, no attempt to present a likeness to the surface of character. Speeches, phrases, single words even, are all indications, leading the imagination on to awareness and comprehension for which the intelligence has no words, to comprehension of processes of emotion, of hitherto unperceived depths and complexities of character which the dramatist himself has discerned. The touch which disengages these is the ultimate test of the genuine dramatist; the dramatist's technique when it is supreme is wholly evocative. Free to work, then, in terms of their great, traditional evocative technique, and using only so much of surface resemblance (and a very little is in fact needed) as will serve to stimulate the twin sympathies of pity and fear, the great dramatists speak, through their characters, from the depths of their own poetic experience to the depths of man's nature. And their reward is that the 'characters' they create will speak for ever, or for so long as human imagination survives to hear them.

NOTES

[1] *The Art of Poetry*, 6. 11.

[2] An interesting comment on the probable order of imitations in the process of communication will be found in Lascelles Abercrombie's *Principles of Literary Criticism* (1932), pp. 100-1.

[3] The remainder of this chapter was printed as 'The Nature of Character in Drama with special reference to Tragedy' after being delivered as a lecture at a Conference at Oxford, 1951.

[4] There follows, in the draft, a passage which was used, in a revised form, in 'Ibsen and Shakespeare as Dramatic Artists'.

III

Shakespeare and the dramatic mode

For nearly a century and a half now Shakespeare has been generally admitted to be one of the greatest of the world's dramatists and for nearly two hundred years certain of his readers have believed him the greatest of all. For in his mature work he seems to stand alone in fulness of achievement. This belief is undoubtedly due, in the first place, to his supreme possession of all the essential qualities or powers that belong to a great dramatist; the passion, the thought, and the sympathy with human experience that characterize the true dramatic imagination. And no other writer seems to have so full and unflawed possession of all these simultaneously. He stands supreme, not simply as the greatest writer using the dramatic form, but precisely because he is a dramatist. Being in all things the essential dramatist, his greatness is commensurate with the essentially dramatic quality in him; the quality constitutes the greatness. Or, to put it rather differently, it is precisely because he is more profoundly and more fully dramatic than any other that he is supreme.

If this is true, if it is the essential dramatist that is the essential Shakespeare, we may expect to find in his writing, as a part of the revelation of his powers, some correspondingly distinctive mode of dramatic expression; some way, that is, of transmitting his perceptions, something in his revealing of character or his articulation of structure which is distinctive precisely by reason of its service to dramatic ends. Here again, we should not expect to find him in sole possession of this secret, but we might discover that his continuous possession of it set him apart from all but a few of the greatest, and perhaps that the failure of others in respect of this peculiar artistic skill helped both to explain their relative failure as dramatists and to define, even more clearly, the wholly and supremely dramatic nature of Shakespeare's art.

The peculiar feature of his art that I have in mind, and that I venture to consider the distinctive mode in dramatic writing, is to be found in his way of revealing the profound movements of character or the hidden logic of event. His readers receive so nearly direct an impression of these that the immediacy, which is one source of the theatre's compelling power, is undimmed in the transmitting. We remain continuously immersed in the character's experience; we never cease to be Macbeth; we are never invited to observe him. This is in fact the essential difference between 'Guilty creatures sitting at a play' and those sitting at a sermon.

Many critics have, of course, been aware of Shakespeare's habit of writing from the depths and of a wholly different way of going to work on the part of certain other dramatists. In England, in the late eighteenth century, Lord Kames denounced the type of play in which description of experience was substituted for its revelation and, nearly simultaneously, Maurice Morgann gave us the unforgettable sentence, 'Shakespeare contrives to make secret impressions upon us'.

The difference depends, in the first instance, upon the depth to which the dramatist's perception has carried him, on his understanding of hidden motive and the hidden relations of events. But it is manifested in his power to make us in our turn aware of these hidden movements by means, as Morgann puts it, of those 'secret impressions', whereby we come into imaginative possession of realities beyond the reach of our conscious understanding. And it is the faculty which enables some dramatists so to communicate to the imaginations of their audiences all the truths learned from their own imaginative explorations, while still using only the medium of speech and action common to all drama, that distinguishes them in respect of mode. A poet's knowledge of man's experience and of the obscure movements of event that make up his destiny may be profound, but when he attempts to communicate this in a play he must so use those technical resources of speech and action, as to evoke in his audience an imaginative response at a depth corresponding to that of the imagined experience of his character. The transmission is necessarily made through the medium of words and actions, which themselves constitute the visible surface of life: this is a primary law of drama, since immediacy of impression is there a necessity. But in the greatest drama it is so made as to be simultaneously the clue to those hidden processes which the surface in no way necessarily resembles. All great poetry makes its communication at a level below the surface meaning of the words; depth speaks to depth in line after line of Wordsworth's greatest passages. But the dramatist, working only in terms of the speech and action of imagined characters, has a task of peculiar difficulty and a reward, if he surmounts it, of peculiar glory. At the summit of its achievement, as in the greatest plays of Shakespeare, of Aeschylus, of Sophocles, this art conveys at once the reality of depth and the immediacy of direct presentation.

And now appears the paradox we have already suggested, for the surface of life in most societies differs from its underlying cause more often than it resembles it, being, in fact, rather an indication of its presence than an exact reflection of its form. Thomas Hardy, in a poem called 'The Slow Nature', once isolated this simple truth with great clarity and with an analytical precision denied to the dramatist, who must not make his own comments. A countrywoman, in this poem, receives the news of her husband's sudden death with seeming apathy. The only thing that appears to concern her is that the house is not yet in order and the beds not yet made. The neighbour who breaks the news is shocked at this evidence of an unfeeling heart, this preoccupation with unimportant details. But it was not an unfeeling heart that caused that first reaction; hers was a slow nature and the passage from inner experience to outward expression was a long and devious one. A fortnight later she began to droop and soon after she was dead herself. There had been no obvious evidence, in her first bewildered response, of the mortal shock that had already laid hold on her; the surface conduct utterly belied the truth that was later proved. Now, Hardy sets out explicitly this relationship between depth and surface; he isolates this particular sequence of cause and effect by making of it a brief work of art; he picks out, if not always for comment, at least for emphasis and for juxtaposition (which almost constitutes comment), the main points in his story. A dramatist can do few of these things, though he may know as well as Hardy that the story is true and that the recognition of such truth is essential to the understanding of human nature in life or in drama. But he is here at the heart of a paradox of dramatic art, compelled to reveal the unseen through the seen, which offers no dependable image of it and may even at times be in flat contradiction. He must, in a sense Polonius never intended, 'by indirections find directions out'; and his 'indirections', his 'assays of bias', are sometimes little less than the total content of the play. So at least it is with Shakespeare in the fullness of his powers: Cordelia's behaviour, in the first scene of *King Lear*, offers a surface utterly at variance with her deep-lying motives; her knowledge of them is by no means as full as is Shakespeare's or even as ours must attempt to be. A modern dramatist, Pirandello, attempted to meet this paradox by demonstrating schematically the surprises that await his imaginary investigators as they proceed, with an orderliness seldom permitted to the average observer, to examine level below level of truth or reality, only to find a succession of contradictions, something, at each step, different from the appearance that had covered it. Each appearance, in such plays, is at once a fact in its own right and the sign of a deeper-lying fact which it misrepresents while yet deriving from it. A long recession of such reassessments is implied, each leading to another which appears in turn to invalidate it, although Pirandello only analyses the first few terms of the series. We know that neither life nor great drama is as neat as this, but the truth to which Pirandello and Hardy point us, which they in fact so precisely isolate for our inspection, is of the first order of importance when we consider the nature of drama and its relation to the multiform evidence that it takes for its material.

The dramatist's mind, that is to say, and the drama he creates, must move not merely in a two-dimensional world, cause and effect, motive, action and reaction being enacted and observed upon a single plane, but also in a bewildering series of planes, each with its own related world of cause and result, each obscurely related with, yet different in kind and in form from, those above and beneath. In this three-dimensional world, this ocean of experience, he is guided by intuitions of depth and distance; but he is bound, by the nature of dramatic art, to reveal his perceptions in terms of the end-product of the process he has discerned, in terms of that efflorescence upon the surface which is made up of the words and deeds of his characters. Only by so disposing these that, simultaneously with their outward and recognizable surface forms, there are revealed also the varying depths from which they took their origin, can he hope to reveal also what he has divined, either of those depths or of the mysterious relationship. Moreover, again because of the nature of his art, he must, out of the great complexity even of this surface take only a few fragmentary details, mere hints and indications of the vast movements, currents and powers, of the infinite variety that lies below, having, after all, for the instrument of his expression, only the words contained in some 3000 verse lines.

This is why I have suggested that it is precisely in revealing his apprehension of these relations, surface to surface, depth to depth and each to all, that the dramatist discloses the measure at once of his spirit's capacity and of his strength as an artist. Unless he has transcendent capacity of soul, he cannot explore the ultimate depths the knowledge of which will alone give the stamp of verity to his expression. If he has not great strength as an artist, the tyranny of the dramatic form, even it may be of specific conventions in a specific age, will force him to misrepresent or pervert such reality as he has perceived. For the tragic dramatist, as for all major artists, the cost of his knowledge is no less than a descent into hell, and in this journey only the greatest travel far: they are with Dante and with Wordsworth, with Beethoven and with Michelangelo. But no imaginative artist can avoid some part of the experience and so all dramatists are committed to the attempt, whether they will or no.

It is evident, moreover, that, in the process whose nature I have attempted to indicate, there are many ways of failing. And it may be that, by turning aside for a moment to examine some of these, we may arrive at a clearer notion of what constitutes, in the work of Shakespeare and those nearest to him, what I have called the dramatic mode and learn something of the way by which he touches the imaginations of his readers.

In passages which represent the speech and conduct of people in moments of intense experience or in the grip of sudden crises, it is clearly laid upon the dramatist to reveal strong and it may be conflicting emotions. But since, as we have already noticed, certain dramatists attempt to do this by methods which are in essence undramatic, we may consider now a passage in which a dramatist, abandoning, as it seems to me, his function as a dramatist, sets one of his characters to speak, in a moment of emotional crisis, not as a human being doing or suffering, but as an onlooker describing the effects of an emotion. I am going to choose a passage from Corneille's *Polyeucte*, not because I think it representative of Corneille's art as a whole, but because his mode is often of this kind, in the last analysis an essentially undramatic kind, and because the passage, which could readily be paralleled in much European drama of the seventeenth and eighteenth centuries, is precisely what we need to make the extreme position clear. It comes from the first scene of the second act, in which Fabian meets Sévère to break to him the news that Pauline, his betrothed, has been forced during Sévère's absence to marry another man. The speech of Sévère which immediately follows the reception of Fabian's news is characteristic of what I mean by an undramatic mode, for Corneille's character gives us a lecture on his emotional condition – not a very good lecture, at that – instead of becoming the channel for its communication.

Fabian. Je tremble à vous le dire; elle est . . .
Sévère.   Quoi?
Fabian.   Mariée.

Sévère. Soutiens-moi, Fabian; ce coup de foudre est grand,
   Et frappe d'autant plus, que plus il me surprend.
Fabian. Seigneur, qu'est devenu ce généreux courage?
Sévère. La constance est ici d'un difficile usage;
   De pareils déplaisirs accablent un grand coeur;
   La vertu la plus mâle en perd tout vigeur;
   Et quand d'un feu si beau les âmes sont éprises
   La mort les trouble moins que de telles surprises.
   Je ne suis plus a moi quand j'entends ce discours.
   Pauline est mariée!

Truly, of this and similar passages, we may say with Voiture 'On ne debite pas les lieux communs quand on est profondément affligé'. And truly, again, in Corneille's own medium of drama, Shakespeare will afford us the contrast. We all remember the third scene of the fourth act of *Macbeth*, in which Ross, who hates and bungles the task laid upon him, breaks to Macduff the news that his wife and children have been killed by order of Macbeth. We remember the young and as yet unfledged Malcolm playing a part somewhat like Fabian's in Corneille's play and endeavouring to rally Macduff's courage. But Macduff's reply, though it conveys a truth that is itself more profound and subtle than any of Sévère's abstract generalizations, comes in the language of drama, not of the lecture-hall. We overhear Macduff's mind, as it stumbles towards the realization, now seeming to grasp it entire, now faltering back into incredulity, then as suddenly meeting the shock of some fresh implication. The emotions themselves are tumultuous and entangled: grief, rage, the tenderest pity and self-reproach; the vivid colours interlace but do not mingle. This is the image of a mind as yet in chaos, not of the resultant that we shall find when the forces have come into equilibrium. (That comes where it belongs, at the end of the fifth act.) The duration of the chaos is brief, because this is the portrait of a man trained to action and decision, with the habit of a soldier and a commander; but while it lasts it is a vivid picture of the tumult of the soul. Macduff thinks aloud and intersperses his half-unconsciously uttered thoughts with questions that now leap ahead, now double back over the track he has covered: he no more knows what is happening to him than a man with concussion and he is no condition to explain it to the audience or to anyone else. He tells us nothing, but he reveals everything.

Now if we look back again at Sévère, we realize afresh how incredibly prompt is his diagnosis of his own state of mind. The blow has barely fallen when he is in full command, if not of his emotions, at least of their explanation. With one step he becomes an onlooker, a commentator, instead of a man taken in the toils of an experience. There is half a line of genuine dramatic speech and then lucid exposition. It is magnificent, but it is not drama.

Nor is the speech of Félix to Albin in the fifth scene of the third act dramatic, in the sense here implied. Beginning with the pronouncement, 'On ne sait pas les maux dont mon coeur est atteint', it proceeds rapidly to rectify the deficiency through some seventeen lines of analytical description. There is no revelation there; we do not accompany the mind of Félix upon a journey. Still less are we aware, as we often are in the speech of Shakespeare's characters, of looking into a further depth of experience below that the character himself perceives. We listen with respectful interest to a lecture on a state of mind delivered by the patient himself; but our thoughts stray to the prayer of Claudius in *Hamlet*, or to Angelo's tormented communion with his soul.

> *Félix.* On ne sait pas les maux dont mon coeur est atteint;
> De pensers sur pensers mon âme est agitée,
> De soucis sur soucis elle est inquiétée;
> Je sens l'amour, la haine, et la crainte, et l'espoir,
> La joie et la douleur tour-à-tour l'émouvoir;
> J'entre en des sentiments qui ne sont pas croyables;
> J'en ai de violents, j'en ai de pitoyables;
> J'en ai de généreux qui n'oseraient agir:
> J'en ai même de bas, et qui me font rougir.
> J'aime ce malheureux que j'ai choisi pour gendre,
> Je hais l'aveugle erreur qui le vient de surprendre;
> Je déplore sa perte, et, le voulant sauver,
> J'ai la gloire des dieux ensemble à conserver;
> Je redoute leur foudre, et celui de Décie;
> Il y va de ma charge, il y va de ma vie.
> Ainsi tantôt pour lui je m'expose au trépas,
> Et tantôt je le perds pour ne me perdre pas.

In this speech the expository manner is indeed more nearly justified, for its subject is a debate in the mind and not the reception of a sudden and overwhelming shock. But the soliloquy of debate has its own laws in drama and though these are of ample scope, there is a clear distinction between the enunciation of conclusions and the revelation of exploration and discovery, themselves accompanied by profound emotion. This is clear when we pass from Félix's speech to such a soliloquy as that of

Angelo at the beginning of the fourth scene of the second act of *Measure for Measure*. He too might claim justifiably that no one can gauge the misery of his soul, but the difference is that, in Angelo's case, he cannot understand it himself and that a large part of our experience in reading his speech is precisely our experience of his own dismay:

> When I would pray, and think, I thinke, and pray
> To seuerall subiects: heauen hath my empty words,
> Whilst my Inuention, hearing not my Tongue,
> Anchors on Isabell: heauen in my mouth,
> As if I did but onely chew his name,
> And in my heart the strong and swelling euill
> Of my conception: the state whereon I studied
> Is like a good thing, being often read
> Growne sere, and tedious: yea, my Grauitie
> Wherein (let no man heare me) I take pride,
> Could I, with boote, change for an idle plume
> Which the ayre beats for vaine: oh place, oh forme,
> How often dost thou with thy case, thy habit
> Wrench awe from fooles, and tye the wiser soules
> To thy false seeming? Blood, thou art blood,
> Let's write good Angell on the Deuills horne,
> 'Tis not the Deuills Crest:

Many kinds of technique intermediate between the undramatic and the wholly dramatic may obviously be found. In some, as in Dryden's best plays, a mixture of expository with evocative speech takes us a step nearer to the world of great poetic drama whose mode is wholly evocative. More subtly, in others, as in Corneille's *Le Cid*, the nature or habit of the characters goes part-way to justify their behaviour. Just as, in Ibsen's *Brand*, we recognize Brand's long, self-examining soliloquies as a process habitual to that mind and meet with sympathy the evident faithfulness of the expression, so, in Corneille's *Le Cid*, debates on points of principle come the nearer to dramatic revelation, simply because the characters so evidently have the habit of them. They are educated to constant conflict between their primal impulses and a military code of honour, noble in itself and so passionately held. Such men do not stop to think, because they know their responses by heart; they have been trained to expect conflicts between their code and their passions and so meet an onslaught on their emotions as a problem in dynamics: they simply balance the forces and arrive at the resolution without doubt or undue dismay. Corneille is justified here, as Ibsen is later, and for the same kind of reason. His characters speak eloquently, like Brand, because, like Brand, they are on familiar ground. 'L'honneur est un devoir'; and they are accustomed to apply their minds vigorously to balancing the claims of opposing duties.

> *D. Rodrigue.* L'honneur vous en est dû, je ne pouvais pas moins,
>   Etant sorti de vous et nourri par vos soins.
>   Je m'en tiens trop heureux, et mon âme est ravie
>   Que mon coup d'essai plaise à qui je dois la vie;
>   Mais parmi vos plaisirs ne soyez point jaloux
>   Si je m'ose à mon tour satisfaire après vous.
>   Souffrez qu'en liberté mon désespoir éclate;
>   Assez et trop longtemps votre discours le flatte.
>   Je ne me repens point de vous avoir servi;
>   Mais rendez-moi le bien que ce coup m'a ravi.
>   Mon bras, pour vous venger, armé contre ma flamme,
>   Par ce coup glorieux m'a privé de mon âme;
>   Ne me dites plus rien; pour vous j'ai tout perdu;
>   Ce que je vous devais, je vous l'ai bien rendu.
> *D. Diegue.* Porte, porte plus haut le fruit de ta victoire:
>   Je t'ai donné la vie, et tu me rends ma gloire;
>   Et d'autant que l'honneur m'est plus cher que le jour,
>   D'autant plus maintenant je te dois de retour.
>   Mais d'un coeur magnanime éloigne ces faiblesses;
>   Nous n'avons qu'un honneur, il est tant de maîtresses!
>   L'amour n'est qu'un plaisir, l'honneur est un devoir.

Out of this Corneille makes something vivid that reminds us of Hotspur's 'easie leap, To plucke bright Honor from the pale-fac'd Moone'. Something, indeed, is revealed in this high state of excitement, brilliant with passion and torment and the high vitality of youth. But the evidence of the play as a whole belies the evidence of some single noble speeches of Rodrigue or of Chimène. Rodrigue is not Hotspur, because he is immaculate; and this is only another way of saying that Corneille allows us no glimpses of the confused or imperfect human being that Shakespeare ever and again suffers his Hotspur to disclose. And this means that he is in fact denying to us that communication with the depths of the character without which a play may be a brilliant effect of balanced stresses and forces, but will not be drama. The oratory of the pulpit or of the senate-house is not the speech of the theatre when that is in intimate relation with the profound activity of the poetic imagination.

But rather than Hotspur, we may choose another soldier to put beside those of *Le Cid*; a man as valiant, as deeply imbued with an honourable and aristocratic code; a man caught, as Rodrigue is here, between two conflicting duties, called upon to balance two rival claims within the code; a man less eloquent than Rodrigue, except in the language of his specialized, chivalric code, but no less vehement and as glorious in achievement. Does Shakespeare, bringing before us a situation not utterly unlike those in some of Corneille's plays and a group of characters raised in traditions not wholly unlike those of Corneille's soldiers, afford us any further insight into the depths beneath such surfaces?

Let us look for a moment at the third scene of the fifth act of *Coriolanus*. Coriolanus, outlawed by the Roman mob, has gone over to the enemy camp and is leading the Volscians to the gates of Rome. He has bound himself by oath to the Volscians and so his honour as a soldier is engaged to them, and not to his country which had rewarded his services with banishment. But the headlong career of his passion for revenge is checked by the arrival of his mother, wife, and child and by the sudden uprising of another group of emotions which Volumnia deliberately brings to life again.

> *Coriolanus*. My wife comes formost, then the honour'd mould.
>   Wherein this Trunke was fram'd, and in her hand
>   The Grandchilde to her blood. But out affection,
>   All bond and priuiledge of Nature breake;
>   Let it be Vertuous to be Obstinate.
>   What is that Curt'sie worth? Or those Doues eyes,
>   Which can make Gods forsworne? I melt, and am not
>   Of stronger earth than others: my Mother bowes,
>   As if Olympus to a Mole-hill should
>   In supplication Nod: and my young Boy
>   Hath an Aspect of intercession, which
>   Great Nature cries, Deny not. Let the Volces
>   Plough Rome, and harrow Italy, Ile neuer
>   Be such a Gosling to obey instinct; but stand
>   As if a man were Author of himself,
>   And knew no other kin.
> *Virgilia*.   My Lord and Husband.
> *Coriolanus*. These eyes are not the same I wore in Rome.
> *Virgilia*. The sorrow that deliuers vs thus chang'd,
>   Makes you thinke so.
> *Coriolanus*.   Like a dull Actor now,

I haue forgot my part, and I am out,
Euen to a full Disgrace. Best of my Flesh,
Forgiue my Tyranny: but do not say,
For that forgiue our Romanes. O a kisse
Long as my Exile, sweet as my Reuenge!
Now by the iealous Queene of Heauen, that kisse
I carried from thee deare; and my true Lippe
Hath Virgin'd it ere since. You Gods, I prate,
And the most noble Mother of the world
Leaue vnsaluted: Sinke my knee i'th'earth,
Of thy deepe duty, more impression shew
Then that of common sonnes . . .
                                    O Mother, Mother!
What haue you done? Behold, the Heauens do ope,
The Gods looke downe, and this vnnaturall Scene
They laugh at. Oh my Mother, Mother: Oh!
You haue wonne a happy Victory to Rome.
But for your Sonne, beleeue it: Oh beleeue it,
Most dangerously you haue with him preuail'd,
If not most mortall to him. But let it come:
Auffidius, though I cannot make true Warres,
Ile frame conuenient peace. Now good Auffidius,
Were you in my steed, would you haue heard
A Mother lesse? or granted lesse, Auffidius?
Aufidius. I was mou'd withall.
Coriolanus.   I dare be sworne you were:
And sir, it is no little thing to make
Mine eyes to sweat compassion. But (good sir)
What peace you'l make, aduise me: For my part,
Ile not to Rome, Ile backe with you, and pray you
Stand to me in this cause. Oh Mother! Wife!
Aufidius (aside). I am glad thou hast set thy mercy and thy Honor
At difference in thee: Out of that Ile worke
My selfe a former Fortune.
Coriolanus.   I, by and by;
But we will drinke together: And you shall beare
A better witnesse backe then words, which we
On like conditions, will haue Counter-seal'd.
Come enter with vs: Ladies you deserue
To haue a Temple built you: All the Swords

In Italy, and her Confederate Armes
Could not haue made this peace.

Now here is a man analysing his own feelings, and doing it for the most part with the incompetence of people who mistrust the process even while indulging in it; here is seemingly description instead of revelation; here apparently is what Lord Kames condemns in the tragedies of his age, 'a cold description in the language of a bystander', a thing no more excusable in Coriolanus than in Sévère or Félix, Almanzor or Rodrigue. Furthermore, the restless brilliance of Rodrigue's speech is wanting. But is this in fact the thing that seizes our imaginations? We have read or watched the play, we have already been immersed during four acts and a half in the passions of Coriolanus and the entanglement of those passions in the fortunes of Rome and of the Volscians. We no longer accept as the poet's intimation of the truth what Coriolanus says about himself. But we are profoundly concerned with the fact that he says it. Self-explanation in Coriolanus is not a dramatist's clumsy substitute for revelation; it is the profound and tragic disclosure of the nature of a man who 'hath euer but slenderly knowne himselfe'. This underlying nature, deep buried and hidden more successfully from himself even than from those who surround him, has been gradually communicating itself to us by 'secret impressions' throughout the play. We may not at this point know precisely what that nature is, perhaps we never apprehend it clearly; but we know by now that it is utterly unlike what he himself here believes it to be. He has been subjected, under terrific pressure, to a heroic ideal as dangerously divorced from normal humanity as that high code upon which Rodrigue was nourished. But Shakespeare's figure is not, like Corneille's, the walking embodiment of a code; he is a recognizable human being bearing about him evidences of the cost of such a process. He speaks of a conventional language as fluently as does Rodrigue, but the image of himself that he sees and proclaims is a vast, inhuman thing:

Like to a lonely Dragon, that his Fenne
Makes fear'd, and talk'd of more then seene . . .
                              Ile neuer
Be such a Gosling to obey instinct; but stand
As if a man were Author of himself,
And knew no other kin.

The inflation of his imagery is there to point the way to our discovery, and if the imagery failed (which it could not) the rhythm of the lines would do

the work. Coriolanus explains himself. Yes: and the explanation is a fig-
ment so fantastic that its presence testifies, as nothing else could do, to the
tumult of a soul denied its primal rights of sane and normal growth.

In this scene, where the potency of the conflicting forces is greater than
in any other, some faint shadow of the truth seems about to reach him, like
intimations in a dream. The imagery of acting runs through the scene,

> Like a dull Actor now,
> I haue forgot my part ...

and not least of the terrible ironies in this scene is the fact that he speaks
such lines half-jestingly; lines that contain the clue to the tragedy of his
spirit.

This, briefly, is the difference between the undramatic technique of
which Lord Kames complained and the true dramatic mode. Never is the
difference more clearly illuminated than when a genuine dramatist, while
serving his own dramatic purposes, shows that he too perceives it.

Finally, we may consider the third scene of the first act of *Hamlet*, in
which Shakespeare's way of disclosing the movements of a mind and the
nature of a character is finely and subtly revealed, the scene in which
Ophelia's brief speeches explain so little of what is happening beneath the
surface of her mind that a dramatist of the expository school would doubtless have given her long passages of expostulation, of distress, of self-
analysis, passages that would have been utterly foreign to the impression
Shakespeare so surely and so 'secretly' makes upon us.

Polonius. What ist Ophelia he hath said to you?
Ophelia. So please you, somthing touching the Lord Hamlet.
Polonius. Marry, well bethought:
   Tis told me he hath very oft of late
   Giuen priuate time to you; and you your selfe
   Haue of your audience beene most free and bounteous.
   If it be so, as so tis put on me;
   And that in way of caution: I must tell you,
   You doe not vnderstand your selfe so cleerely,
   As it behoues my Daughter, and your Honour.
   What is betweene you, giue me. vp the truth?
Ophelia. He hath my Lord of late, made many tenders
   Of his affection to me.
Polonius. Affection, puh. You speake like a greene Girle,
   Vnsifted in such perillous Circumstance.
   Doe you beleeue his tenders, as you call them?

Ophelia. I do not know, my Lord, what I should thinke.

Polonius. Marry Ile teach you; thinke your selfe a Baby,
   That you haue tane his tenders for true pay,
   Which are not sterling. Tender your selfe more dearly;
   Or not to crack the winde of the poore Phrase,
   Running it thus, you'l tender me a foole.

Ophelia. My Lord, he hath importun'd me with loue,
   In honourable fashion.

Polonius. I, fashion you may call it, go too, go too.

Ophelia. And hath giuen countenance to his speech, my Lord,
   With almost all the holy vowes of Heauen.

Polonius. I, Springes to catch Woodcocks. I doe know
   When the Bloud burnes, how Prodigall the Soule
   Giues the tongue vowes: these blazes, Daughter,
   Giuing more light then heate; extinct in both,
   Euen in their promise, as it is a making;
   You must not take for fire. From this time Daughter,
   Be somewhat scanter of your Maiden presence;
   Set your entreatments at a higher rate,
   Then a command to parley. For Lord Hamlet,
   Beleeue so much of him, that he is young,
   And with a larger tether may he walke,
   Then may be giuen you. In few, Ophelia,
   Doe not beleeue his vowes; for they are Broakers,
   Not of that dye, which their Inuestments show:
   But meere implorators of vnholy Sutes,
   Breathing like sanctified and pious bawds,
   The better to beguile. This is for all:
   I would not, in plaine tearmes, from this time forth,
   Have you so slander any moment leisure,
   As to giue words or talke with the Lord Hamlet:
   Looke too't, I charge you; come your wayes.

Ophelia. I shall obey my Lord.

Now here, taken as it stands, we seem to see the portrait of a submissive
and rather characterless young girl; what was once called an 'unformed
character'; a being without vivid interests or enjoyment, strong or eager
impulses; content to do as she is told in lazy dependence upon the wills and
plans of those in authority. We notice that Shakespeare gives Ophelia only
six speeches, none of them more than two lines in length; in all, seven
lines-and-a-half, as against a total of forty-eight in the whole dialogue. The

first two are plain and obedient replies to her father's questions, the third is the simple confession, 'I do not know, my lord, what I should think', the next two, faint attempts at justification, immediately quashed by Polonius's long and vigorous exhortation to discretion, and the last, a half-line of complete acceptance. Whatever she feels or fancies she feels about Hamlet is apparently removed from her mind as easily as chalk is rubbed off a blackboard. Jane Austen, we may remember, once made a full-length study of just such a soft and compliant character in Harriet Smith in *Emma*; Harriet obediently falls in love and out of love, makes friends and gives up, as Emma directs her. Such it would seem is the account of herself that Ophelia gives us in this scene; such are her words as they meet us on the surface.

But what relation does this bear to what is going on in her mind? Either the one we have already suggested, in which the brief speeches, with their prim, conventional phrasing, do in fact mirror faithfully the movements of soul from which they derive, or a relationship of contradiction and concealment. Perhaps we should suspect, beneath the formal statements, some conflict or confusion, less tumultuous than that to which the language of such a character as Coriolanus would point us, but not less fatally at odds with demeanour of the surface.

If we look back to the beginning of this scene, we find Ophelia alone with her brother, bidding him farewell. There is evidently some genuine affection between them; Laertes' grief in the later part of the play, even if it is too voluble for depth, is sincere in its kind. And so Ophelia is frank with him; gay, almost talkative, showing some eagerness of apprehension and some good sense. She accepts his lesson on self-control and the problems of public life soberly but without signs of distress. She calls it 'this good lesson', which on the whole it is, being in that respect utterly unlike the cheap and cynical shrewdness which Polonius recommends to each of his children in turn. Laertes sees Hamlet's position with sympathy and respect; he touches the situation with more profundity and generosity than his father – though perhaps it would be hard for any man to do so with less. And Ophelia recognizes a certain wisdom in him and responds with frankness and a touch of genuine maturity. Already, we may observe, she 'has heard there are tricks in the world', though the conventional imagery of her references here, while she is still sane, contrasts sharply with the directness of this actual phrase, spoken later, in her madness, and shows her knowledge to be as yet but general and theoretical.

I have dwelt upon this short introductory passage, because it is the only one in which we see Ophelia as she was before the action of the tragedy engulfed her and because the sudden contrast of her gay but sane little conversation with her brother is in strong contrast with what immediately follows. She next listens to Polonius's advice to Laertes, that shrewd advocacy of ungenerous reserves and skilful façades, with its absurd and flat contradictions to its own cautions, and immediately upon this follows the dialogue in which Polonius applies his policy to the case of his younger child.

Something, it would seem, then chills her suddenly. It may be the respect due to her father, with whom she is not on as familiar terms as with Laertes or as many of Shakespeare's daughters are with their fathers. It may be an inarticulate, undefined, but none the less profound recoil from Polonius's coarse-grained, rule-of-thumb estimates of human motive, in conflict not only with the deference habitually paid to him as her guide, but with the deeper intimations of her own instinctive recognition of Hamlet's nature. All this, and perhaps some dim awareness that Laertes' going has robbed her of the only sympathetic counsellor she has known, are undoubtedly at work in her. It is enough that Shakespeare, through his intimations in the first part of the scene, has given us impressions which determine in us at unawares our hidden responses to her subsequent speech. Knowing also, in fact, what follows, the madness which is to testify to deep and inarticulate emotions, to the pressure upon her of forces whose values she cannot estimate and the conflict of faiths which she cannot share or express, we no longer have warrant for believing her indifferent or untouched. True, she is no Juliet whose inner confidence in the rightness of her passion makes her way straight. She is no Helena whose intellectual clarity determines and assess her conduct. She lacks the native endowments of these, but she does not lack depth. Moreover, by ironic cruelty of circumstance, she is isolated with her own inexperience as neither of these more active natures was. Here is no friar to countenance and abet a secret marriage, no Countess of Rousillon to sympathize and support.

Bringing back then to the passage before us this legitimate knowledge from earlier and later scenes in the play, we see her moving in bewilderment through this dialogue, which now takes on the highest significance as the beginning of the process that is to lead her to madness and death. Now the colourless speeches begin to yield evidence of something moving beneath the surface, something agonized, bewildered, utterly at variance with their prim and meaningless form. Step by step, through the faint and easily strangled protests, to the final, numbed acquiescence that follows her long silence, we trace the process of a mind on whom the gates of fear and ignorance are closing until in truth it 'cannot tell' what it 'should think'.

Here then, again, as Morgann demonstrated in his analysis of Shakespeare's method with Falstaff, is a world of 'secret impressions' contradicting the surface evidence of words and actions, yet only to be discerned through what that surface can disclose, and each, both surface and hidden depth, derives a tragic and ironic meaning from the relationship between the two. Here, as throughout the plays, is the true dramatic mode, in which utterance proper to human reactions as it would appear in life itself, is yet, by the height of dramatic art, induced to reveal what lies beneath, as life itself often refuses to reveal it.

Every play of his maturity will reveal the same way of going to work, whether Lear is talking to the Fool in the fifth scene of the first act, or Lady Macbeth to Macbeth after the banquet. It is most frequent in the tragedies and in them most potent in moments of high spiritual tension, precisely such moments as most often fail in the work of the dramatists who attempt the technically easier but ultimately fatal method of laying upon their characters the responsibility of describing to us what their circumstances or condition would never permit them to perceive.

In one passage, and I think in one only, does Shakespeare show us the underside of this pattern, suffering us thereby to recognize at once the source from which each utterance is derived. We dare not say, even here, of what kind the connections are or by what process the spoken words derive from the hidden depths, but we come nearer to it than in any other passage. In the first scene of the fifth act of *Macbeth*, Lady Macbeth, speaking aloud though asleep, reveals through this special medium, the turmoil of soul of which only a bare hint had been given earlier. And there is not a word in her speeches which cannot be traced to an earlier moment in the play or found to be implicit in the action, a moment which, when it occurred, was met with a demeanour as firm, as clear and as effective as this is haunted and tormented. The existence of this scene is not necessary to our perception of the nature of Shakespeare's mode, but its presence should have left no doubt in our minds of the fact that that mode is an essential part of his art. And it is perhaps permissible to infer that not only is it essential to Shakespeare's art, but that it is itself the distinctive mode of all supreme drama.

We suggested at the end of Chapter II that the habit of identifying himself with every character wholly and simultaneously was closely related to the dramatist's use of an evocative and essentially dramatic mode. For only if he maintains that sympathy with all his characters, and with all of them simultaneously, does he so know them, in silence as in speech, in the intervals between events as in contributory action, as to know in each the image of a living creature and to know it far beyond the purposes for which the surface of the play uses it. But this knowledge must be communicated to the reader and audience, or at least potentially communicated, to the limit of their powers of reception. And no art, let alone the brief art of drama, could make this communication in explicit terms or in words whose function was no more than their connotation. Only the technique of evocation, with its 'generation of still-breeding thoughts' will allow this. Only the secret impressions at work in the imagination will serve the genuine dramatist for full communication.

IV

The nature of plot in drama

If we approach the play by way of plot instead of by way of character, we shall reach similar conclusions. For since character, plot, imagery, language, verbal music are only aspects of the indivisible whole which is the play, whatever we discover in one of them to be essential to the whole will reveal itself also in others. We separate them by virtue of an agreed convention. But in relation to the whole and to each other they are inseparable; each may in fact appear at times to be an aspect of another, since their territories are ultimately indivisible. And just as what drama presents to our imagination as character differs from what life presents, so is it with plot, which is not identical with a series of actual events or even with the groups of events that sometimes seem to emerge in life. Each has a similar relation to its counterpart in what we call the actual world in that in each the artist's imagination has selected from the raw material on which his inspiration worked and revealed a pattern inherent in it. And the nature of this imaginative selection is determined by the mode of the dramatist, so that in every aspect of the technique we may trace a corresponding pattern in harmony with the form of the whole to which it contributes. Each aspect of the technique, then, plays its part in revealing the dramatist's apprehension of life, but plot may fitly follow character here since they merge naturally into each other through the continuous interplay between individual character and even within a given play.

Plot, indeed, whether simple or complex, single or multiple, may be said to have two aspects, the spatial, which is concerned with character-grouping, and the temporal, which has regard to the order and relation of events.[1] The first, like a picture or a statuary group, may be thought of (if we adopt Lessing's distinction)[2] as static in time and extended in space and in studying we consider the characters not in terms of their experience or of their effect upon the plot, but in terms of the illumination we receive from their juxtaposition and their relative positions in the composition. The other approach to plot shows it as extended in time and gives us the ordered sequence of causally related events. This again appears, upon closer inspection, to have two strands, the inner and the outer plot or drama, both moving continuously forward in time, both intermittently revealed and inseparably related.[3] The differences in mode that we have already observed may be traced in both these aspects of the plot and in both levels of the second.

Thus, in the spatial aspect a dramatist of one kind will use a design which itself seems to demonstrate some theme or argument, a logical, expository grouping that constitutes an explanation or furnishes a key to some problem, reminding us sometimes of the Victorian narrative school of painting in which the picture 'told a story'. Another, having no demonstrable theme, problem, or thesis, having no palpable design upon his drama and no purpose but the artist's fundamental purpose of making a work of art, will reveal wholly different implications through the composition of his picture.

The first will present a carefully planned range of characters that balance each other as in Ibsen's *Ghosts*, where the five are so selected that each contributes to the central idea of the play one part of the final, composite effect. The dead hand of convention and obligation has subdued to its purposes Pastor Manders, who has thus become its vehicle and its exponent, but it has driven Mrs Alving to rebellion and so to emancipation of thought. Modifying the contrasted positions of these two are three others who show the workings of the compulsion upon related, yet differing, types of mind and character. Each is a variation on the central theme and the whole group indicates the salient effects and in representative proportions: Regine has rebelled without thought or heart-searching and has suffered the degeneration that comes of rejecting the good and the bad alike in a given social code; her 'father', Engstrand, as immoral as she but more shrewd, has cunningly observed the workings of the system and found his account in playing upon its victims; Osvald has escaped psychological harm only to be destroyed by the physical consequences from which nothing could save him. Each bears mute or articulate testimony to the weight of this dead hand and their relationship demonstrates the operation of the curse; a Laocoon group, figures still imprisoned or too late emancipated to maintain valid life.

But another dramatist may relate his characters in such a way that, instead of a close-locked group, itself the image of the operation of a force, with each member sustaining an essential part of the whole in strict relation of contrast and likeness to the others, we find characters widely differing as individuals or as groups, and so placed that our imaginations are induced to supply, it may be at unawares, intermediate and background figures or moods that complete a harmony of wide range and complexity, suggesting to our minds not a clear-cut image or a dominant theme, but the breadth of life and of humanity. We recognize that without such subtlety of relationship between the figures in the picture there would be no harmony, but only a scattering of portraits, vivid it might be and even varied, but giving no significance to the content of the play. Somewhere in the dramatist's way of relating them lies the stimulus to which our imaginations respond; here we may find secret impressions conveyed by the grouping itself. Shakespeare in as early a play as *A Midsummer Night's Dream* already prompts us by the spatial aspect of his plot alone to the 'generation of still breeding thoughts' by which we 'people this little world'.

And what a range this world has! Our first glance shows us princes and their subjects, townsfolk, peasants, and craftsmen; lovers, parents, and children; the wide variety of personality which ranges from the judicial magnanimity of Theseus to the crabbed Egeus, the unmoral fairy world, the childish egotism of the young lovers and the hearty freedom of the peasants. But delicate threads of relationship join these figures or groups into a more complex and subtle pattern. Theseus and Hippolyta are princes, but so also are Oberon and Titania; even Bottom is the born ruler of his village community. Hermia, Helena, Lysander, and Demetrius are lovers after one fashion, but so, after another and a better, are Theseus and Hippolyta, and so in their strange way are Oberon and Titania. Not only are there the human relations of parent and child, lover and lover, but also a wide range of age, from the old Egeus and the mature Theseus to the four young lovers, all made significant by the constant presence of the ageless, immortal fairies. At the centre still is Theseus, the responsible father of his people, at once submitting to and upholding the social order of his dukedom; but the individualists Bottom and Puck are there too, each absorbed, in delighted preoccupation, with fantasies humdrum or exquisite of his own creating. And so the network spreads, linking, each to each, characters in all else disparate and seemingly unrelated. Each figure in a play whose spatial structure is of this kind is like an illuminated point, independent and set at a distance from each of the others; yet seemingly endless patterns now suggest themselves by linking each to several others and the central figure to all. There is here no palpable intention of suggesting by the disposal of the characters the multitudinous complexity of life, still less of laying upon each the task of sustaining its share of an emergent idea. But the imaginary line that flashes from one corner to another of the picture passes through (and gathers up by its passing) many who are not present in the play. Prince, townsman, peasant, craftsman, reveal when we link them the invisible presence of intermediate 'occupations' and 'trades'. And the fairies, creatures of yet another kind, set off and illuminate by contrast the human groups and their organisations. Age, maturity, youth suggest between them the span of human life, but the ageless fairies reveal by their timelessness the significance of time which determines human life. And what our imaginations receive is an impression not of a theme or of an idea but of a world and a life in which every individual is essentially itself and not primarily a part of a thematic design, but in which, nevertheless, each is related to others by contrast or likeness of age, sex, function, or temperament, so that none can be thought of for long in isolation. But it is the secret impressions that have given us the sense of this; the imaginary lines which linked light to light and drew out from their background of invisibility those hidden figures whose momentary and imagined presence made up the world in which the people of the play lived and were at home. The function of the dramatic mode here is to enrich, fill out, and if need be modify the image of the world that surrounds and reveals itself through the characters.[4] Just so, when we considered these as individuals, it was seen to reveal the fuller world within each character.

At an earlier period of dramatic history the genius of Aeschylus evokes in like way an image of a play's world by the placing of its characters. Agamemnon is a prince, like Clytemnestra; an Argive, as are the chorus and all the other characters except Cassandra; he is linked with Clytemnestra by marriage and parenthood; with Aegisthus by blood relationship and the common heritage of the Thyestean curse; with the soldier who announces his homecoming by the ties of profession and the long experience of the siege of Troy; with the sentinel, who is his faithful servant, by Argos; and with Cassandra again by the common background of the Trojan war and of princely birth. Clytemnestra, too, has other links not only with him, but with Aegisthus as her lover, as a home-dwelling Argive and finally as fellow-murderer. Cassandra alone stands in an isolation which links her by very contrast; no longer a prince but a captive, the only Trojan among the home-keeping Argives and the returning

Argive army, young in a world of the mature and the old, cut off even by her foreign speech, yet driven by Apollo to join her fate with Agamemnon's. By these six characters and the lines that link them we are made aware of three worlds: the Argive polity, its inheritance, and its doom; the fallen greatness of the Trojan civilization; and the darkly triumphant Argive army that has lain ten years encamped before Troy. Each of the characters sustains a share, not in the disclosure of a theme (that task is laid upon the chorus), but in revealing and suggesting the fates and history of one or other of these three worlds of men. And thus our impression of the immense scope of the play derives simultaneously from the choric comments and from awareness of wider worlds evoked by the lines that link the characters by contrast and likeness.[5] This is true also of the other plays of Aeschylus, of Sophocles, and of Euripides. Even in the more primitive *Supplices*, where the clash of two civilizations is the evident substance of the play, the links, though less subtle, bear still an essential part of extending the scope. In the *Bacchae* of Euripides at the other end of the period, we discern the same net-work of lines with the same functions as in the late work of Aeschylus, but approaching now nearer to the multitudinous evocation of Shakespeare's structure. And so we find the evocative technique of the essential dramatist at work in the spatial structure of his plays, while it is deliberately replaced by another mode in the corresponding structure of a philosophical dramatist such as Ibsen. In the Greek drama and that derived from the Greek as is Racine's, the characters are few and, except for an occasional subsidiary figure, are spread across the foreground; the design imposed on the production by the shallow Greek stage thus finds its analogue in the positions of the characters in the spatial design of the play.

But in the plays of Shakespeare's maturity, we perceive a third dimension, akin to the depth given by perspective to a painting; in dimensions and tone alike the characters retreat successively from the foreground towards a background where they reach a virtual vanishing point.[6] In the play of *Antony and Cleopatra* the magnitude of the issues, the grandeur of the chief characters, the multiplicity of figures and events witness to the vastness of its design and the cosmic imagery leads the imagination on to a universe beyond, into which the immediate world of the play seems limitlessly extended. The spatial structure too plays its own, considerable part in this final impression. The spatial relations of the characters may be traced as they were in *A Midsummer Night's Dream* and the amplitude of the later play is then seen to embrace the whole known world. But just as in a painting the sense of vastness may be given not only by the spread of the foreground, but also by depth and distance,[7] so, in a play, the relative proportions in function and the relative vividness in personality complete that impression of extent already made upon us by greatness of scope, character, and event. In the greatest plays, moreover, distance itself gives prominence to the chief characters; the attention of the subordinate agents is focused upon them, investing them with significance which draws some of its potency from their spatial relations. A whole universe, it seems, is intent upon the action of those foreground figures and their power in turn reaches to the uttermost bounds of the world, to figures upon the very border of invisibility. The dramatic function of perspective in *Antony and Cleopatra* is to evoke, by this secret impression, the sense at once of vastness, of coherence, and of significance.

When we attempt to group in the mind's eye the figures in this play, we are struck at once by the operation of a simple law; those that are most vivid in personality are also those that have the most important functions. A character of relatively minor importance who makes a brief appearance in an early scene and with no evident or immediate promise of a greater part to play later, yet stirs the imagination and remains vividly in our minds, will almost invariably appear again in a later scene when his function will be graver or weightier. The marks of such a character may be of various kinds; the language he speaks, his imagery, or a noticeable habit of syntax; the attention he draws to himself from other characters; a peculiar relation to one of the main characters, even if it is only our own emotional response to him; some light thrown upon him by the attitude of that other or by some comment drawn from him. This, which we may describe as the colour or tone initially given to a minor character, will be found to correspond, when the whole play is before us, with the function assigned him, with his ultimate position in the plot. Characters, on the other hand, whose initial speeches seem curiously colourless in view of the number of scenes in which they promise to appear, turn out to have in fact little function beyond that of frequently standing on the stage; they do not speak much or contribute much; they are found to be as limited in their ultimate function as they are in their initial colour. There is thus, it would appear, a consistent relation between what, reverting to our pictorial image, we may call colour and size and as scene succeeds scene in the temporal plot of the play it tends to reveal the same tonal relation between the characters in it as does the total spatial plot.

Setting aside then the main characters, whose prominence no one proposes to question, we may fairly expect to discover continuous regression in the spatial grouping of the minor figures. And it is upon continuity in regression that a great part of the depth of the play's focus depends. Behind the first ten or twelve figures, who themselves recede and diminish in size and colour from Antony and Cleopatra to Maecenas, Agrippa, and Alexas, come those of further diminishing proportions, Scarus, Dolabella, Menecrates, Mardian, Canidius, with behind them again, Ventidius, Thyreus, the clown, the Soothsayer, Dercetas, Diomed. In all these, function and colour, though growing ever slighter and fainter, are still distinct, while behind them range a number of figures, growing steadily less distinct, servants, messengers, soldiers, guards, some thirty-five or -six of them, the ultimate horizon being represented by the virtually invisible Taurus (of III. viii. 21) whose total contribution to the play is the line 'My Lord?'

Now it is somewhere within this range, from Scarus to Taurus, that the principle of continuous regression in character grouping will finally be revealed, for it is these minor figures who between them define the furthest depths of the scene. Scarus appears in three scenes (III. viii, IV. vii and IV. viii) though he only speaks in the first two and has only ten speeches, some twenty-five lines, in all. But the five speeches in III. viii are full of rich and memorable imagery, part comic, part poetic, the vehement language of syntax of wrath and abuse. We recognize the clear colours of the character; an experienced officer involved in a defeat, a brave, high-hearted soldier. He stands out at once from the background of soldiers, guards and messengers who appear once and then disappear and in the second and third scenes his function grows to match the vividness with which his character was first drawn. He supports and encourages Antony helping to turn the tide of war, and is then drawn forward out of the background by the warmth and understanding of Antony's words to Cleopatra. The sharpness of colour which caught the eye in the first three or four short speeches was, then, a true index of his position and of a function ultimately greater than we should have expected.

Behind him again are more figures who belong to the ever receding background and mark its depth by their ever decreasing colour and magnitude. The soldier who bears the news of Enobarbus's desertion (IV. v) has but five speeches so brief that they total only about seven lines; something of his character is allowed to appear, sturdy, loyal, uncompromising, even provocative. And this degree of individuality is warranted by his function; he is the means of revealing the gentleness of Antony on the eve of a great battle and calls forth the expression of the General's generous understanding of Enobarbus. The slight figure of this soldier is thus so placed and so coloured that it illuminates one side of Antony's character.

Of corresponding dimensions and tone are the soldier who in III. vi bears Enobarbus's treasure to him from Antony, the messenger of I. iii and Silius in III. i. And close to them in the grouping, but diminished and paler, are the soldier of III. vii and Diomed in IV. xii and V. i.

At a little further distance we come upon figures such as Seleucus, the Messenger of I. ii, the two servants of II. vii, and the guard of V. ii. The few lines of Seleucus (he has only three, divided between three speeches) contain more colour than their brevity might suggest, but the function of the disloyal servant has a moment's sharp significance and so the colour of his speech, for the moment too matches it, slight though both are.

We are approaching the vanishing point now, where Taurus disappears with his two-word speech, but to the very edge of visibility the figures maintain their simultaneous diminution of function and tone. The four soldiers who in IV. iii listen to the mysterious music on the eve of Antony's defeat, being charged with the function of heightening, in their short scene, the effect of anticipation and of revealing the perilous psychological balance of Antony's troops, have yet just enough individual tone to be distinguishable from each other and the first, with nine short speeches contained in seven lines, is the leader; he can hear the music and shows some initiative in investigating it. The second, more imaginative and apprehensive, hazards an interpretation. The anxiety of the third only echoes the other speakers point by point and the fourth shows a steady if imaginative optimism. The last three share between them fourteen speeches in about as many lines, but the faint indications of character can still be seen. Behind them and fainter yet are Varrius, the second and third soldiers of IV. ix, the three guards of IV. xii, the messenger of I. ii, Demetrius, the Egyptian of V. i, and the messenger of III. vii. The last two are as nearly colourless and functionless as it is possible to be while yet serving some purpose in the background of the play and are only slightly removed from the invisibility of the vanishing-point. But their function is nevertheless indispensable, for they define the last positions in that continuous regression which has given depth and distance to the spatial aspect of the play and completed the impression of its magnitude.

If we look at the temporal aspects of that ordered sequence of events that we call the plot, we find that this also is affected by the mode of the dramatist; one will present a logically articulated series and the other reveal what the poet has divined by inducing a continuing or developing experience in the mind of reader or audience. The first is the counterpart of the self-explanatory characters and the demonstrative spatial plot that we have just described. The other is associated with the process that reveals or modifies character by half-hidden signs and plots by leaving our imaginations to supply (it may be all unawares) the events needed to complete the full graph by linking together crucial events or scenes.

The coherence given to the first kind of plot by the logic of event serves a philosopher dramatist to emphasize his underlying idea and is indeed almost separable from his mode of writing. It is found in its finest form in the middle work of Ibsen, where the architectural power of the master building governs the relation of events, the indication of cause and effect by a precise articulation of the details of the plot. Each episode, each piece of setting, each section of dialogue, by its content, by its timing and by its placing, contributes directly to a design whose purpose is to set before us an interlocking series of events such as shall leave us no conclusion but the one Ibsen intends us to draw. The opening passages of these plays often fulfil four or five functions simultaneously, all directly or indirectly connected with the elucidation and the disengaging of the theme. This flawless, economical integration of the parts with the whole and with each other gives its own impression of inevitability; the sequence of events constitutes a demonstration. This is the natural way for him to use structure to demonstrate his theme. A usual but not inseparable consequence of this compact and coherent plotting is the brevity of its dramatic time. The ultimate causes of the events presented to us lie far back in the past and Ibsen must bring them before our eyes by some form of recollection or reminiscence, but the occasion or immediate cause of word, deed, or event within the play is followed closely by its consequence and the final stages of the demonstration are before us in detail. So full is this detail that it may mislead us into thinking that the dramatist has given us the fulness of life itself.[8]

This logical and coherent ordering of the sequence of events, though only used in the drama of high seriousness by the philosophical dramatist has been understood from relatively early times by dramatists with other purposes. Even if the dramatist has no theme for the demonstrative technique to define by the three means we have already described, he may yet take a purely artistic delight in its design. The relations of cause and effect within each subsidiary plot and more still the relation between them, take on, in the hands of some dramatists of superlative skill, the beauty that always belongs to subtly related rhythms and curves of movement, such as those of a corps de ballet or a flock of seagulls in spring. In such cases, the content of the play is usually comic; the finest comedy of intrigue is of this kind and Terence and Plautus mastered it long ago. Sometimes a mind of musical or it may be of mathematical bent will design a complex plot the intricate relations and variations of whose curves are themselves a delight to us and, we must presume, to him. Perhaps no dramatist has ever touched Ben Jonson in this special domain. He did not use it in his tragedies, but in the near-tragedy of *Volpone* and in the bitter satire of *The Alchemist* we find a comedy whose rhythms hold strange commerce with 'The laws that keep The planets in their radiant courses.' But there is no theme here to be served and the only 'precepts deep' we are like to meet at the hands of Ben Jonson's rascals are curiously congruous with those of Praed's worthy vicar. The strength, swiftness, and precision of Ben Jonson's draughtsmanship carries the technique of this particular kind of plot to achievements it does not usually reach, except in the process of demonstrating a theme. But it must be admitted that in the humbler domain of farce many a play has been saved from worthlessness by the taut, athletic movements and the logic (it may be fantastic) of its plot; by a strict disposal of the relations of cause and effect the more noticeable perhaps in that this is the only kind of artistic virtue farce is free to practise.

Now Shakespeare's mode which reveals the character of Coriolanus and the magnitude of the spatial design in *Antony and Cleopatra* by secret impressions made upon our imaginations makes an utterly different disposal of the ordered sequence of events that constitute the temporal aspect of the plot. These are not now compact, nor, on the plane of actual event, closely coherent. There are wide gaps in the sequence, to be leapt by the imagination, and these spaces or intervals have not a merely negative but a positive function. This becomes clear when we consider what is in fact omitted in some of the greatest of his plays from the material he might have used, material that a lesser dramatist would have considered suitable or even highly effective in its theatrical or rhetorical effects.

If we look at some dozen of such potential scenes that find no place in *Macbeth* we notice at once that not only is the logical continuity of event set aside in some cases but that it is superseded in order that a profound reality may thereby have the greater power to evoke an imaginative response. At the risk of seeming to speak frivolously, I will name some of these, because I think that each one on my list would have been seized on as valuable theatrical material by some Elizabethan dramatist (even if we have to go as low as Chettle to find him), and that some of them have counterparts easily recognized in the work of the major Jacobeans. Some of these could take the form predominantly of spectacle, some of poetic or rhetorical soliloquy; some again could be built into effective episodes presented through the dialogue.

Shakespeare gives us nothing of the turbulent emotions that must have occupied Macbeth's mind during that ride from Forres to Invern⟨e⟩ (between I. iv and I. v) when, with murder in his heart, he rode ahead provide for Duncan's coming; nor of Lady Macbeth's when, a prey to t⟨he⟩ same nightmare thoughts, she presided at the supper of Duncan betwe⟨en⟩ I. vi and I. vii. Shakespeare does not present the murder of Dunc⟨an⟩ between II. i and II. ii, nor the coronation of Macbeth between II. iii a⟨nd⟩ III. i. Nor, though he makes clear that there is an interval, does he give any episode to illustrate the first stages of Macbeth's assumption of pow⟨er⟩ any soliloquy in which Macbeth should decide upon the murder of Banq⟨uo⟩ (that crucial decision which separates him from Lady Macbeth), nor th⟨e⟩ other soliloquy which would have disclosed Macbeth's growing sense ⟨of⟩ insecurity, so clearly acknowledged in III. i. We have no scene in which ⟨he⟩ orders the murder of Lady Macduff, comparable to III. i in which ⟨he⟩ arranges that of Banquo. And when we pass into the later part of the pla⟨y⟩ we find that we have seen nothing of the many further incidents ⟨of⟩ Macbeth's tyrannous and uneasy reign which are commonplaces ⟨to⟩ Malcolm and Macduff in IV. iii. Neither have we any picture of La⟨dy⟩ Macbeth's mental progress between the banquet of III. iv and th⟨e⟩ sleepwalking of V. i; during three scenes she has not appeared at all. The⟨re⟩ is no record of the mustering of the English forces between IV. iii an⟨d⟩ V. ii, nor of the simultaneous rising of the Scots, and again no revelation ⟨of⟩ Macbeth's inner experience between IV. i and V. ii, when during thre⟨e⟩ scenes he himself does not appear.

Now I submit that none of these are impracticable in the theatre. Th⟨e⟩ Elizabethan soliloquy was equal to the revelation of any thought ⟨or⟩ emotion and though certain of the scenes suggested would have repeate⟨d⟩ the form of others already in the play, there are contemporaries ⟨of⟩ Shakespeare who would not have been deterred by this from a fine piece ⟨of⟩ theatrical effect; any skilled dramatist knows how to vary his repetition⟨s⟩ and even to snatch a cumulative effect from them. Furthermore, five a⟨t⟩ least of these are scenes that few working theatre-men who were not grea⟨t⟩ artists would have been likely to resist: the murder of Duncan, th⟨e⟩ coronation of Macbeth, the haunting of Lady Macbeth's mind by th⟨e⟩ crimes she has known or guessed at, the mustering of the English army and the rising of the Scots to join them. It would have been a strangely di⟨f⟩ferent play if we had had these instead of or as well as what we have. But i⟨t⟩ is evident that the scenes that are there must have some superior power ⟨of⟩ carrying the action from point to point so as to stimulate our imagination to conceive the whole.

The art of the dramatist has been engaged not in presenting a closel⟨y⟩

locked and logically coherent action that points irresistibly to a certain deduction, but in selecting those fragments of the whole that stimulate our imaginations to an understanding of the essential experience, to the perception of a nexus of truths too vast to be defined as themes, whose enduring power disengages a seemingly unending series of perceptions and responses.

It would seem that the imagination of audience or reader is thrown forward, by the immense impact of such scenes, upon a track of emotional experience, to come to rest upon the next scene, at the moment in its curving flight at which it can alight without interference or loss of momentum, to be projected again upon another movement, there to be similarly received, diverted, and flung out again upon its track of discovery. And this proceeds with economy and harmony as do the forces of gravitation at work upon the movements of the bodies in a solar system.

May we attempt, despite the presumption of the act, to consider, by looking at what goes before and what follows, why Shakespeare does not give us the murder of Duncan? Our imaginations have been engaged first by the fortunes of Macbeth through the initial meeting with the witches and his rapid rise to favour and power and then by the terrible conflict in his mind as temptation lays holds upon it and the vision of murder 'shakes so [his] single state of man that function is smothered in surmise'. From this point we identify ourselves with Macbeth; we have looked into his mind by one of those shafts of illumination which are the glory of the evocative technique in the revelation of character. The meeting with Lady Macbeth at once releases and directs the full force of those elemental powers of evil which lead him forward towards the crime he dreads and desires. From the moment at which he sees the air-drawn dagger he is in a state of suspended life in which time and place and fact have lost their customary relations, in which he sees only 'the future in the instant'. In that world of his imagination, and of ours identified with his, the murder is already done; the act itself is a piece of automatism, a kind of sleepwalking, the mere embodying in deed of what his will and resolution had already accomplished. There is no interim between this and the revulsion and horror which follow immediately after it; almost we may believe that that recoil would have followed if the deed had been imagined only and prevented of actual achievement. In this flight from one point of experience to another there is no room for pause; the presentation of the deed itself would have been a disastrous and irrelevant interruption, breaking the curve of the essential experience. For the act itself which is for Macbeth a timeless interim, a suspension of the faculties, could not have been so for us, the audience. We should have had perforce to subject our imaginations to that scene and in so doing change the swift forward movement of our minds. Even if the dramatist had presented to us a Macbeth who himself moved like a sleep-walker, it would still have been a fatal interruption. And in fact he could hardly have done this if he had lifted the scene into the dominant position it must occupy if it is to be presented at all. For Macbeth in this trance-like frenzy of resolution to have spoken would have been impossible; the silence of suspended consciousness does not speak, even in soliloquy. And yet no such scene as this could have been trusted to dumb show. All other possible stage treatments our fancy can devise lead us but to the same conclusion, that the essential, inner experience which is the essence of the play's action here must move swift as thought from the moment when the bell invites him to the moment when he heard 'a noise' 'as [he] descended'. From the middle of I. iv to the end of II. ii is a 'hideous storm of terror' from which there must be no respite for the audience until, dazed and horror-stricken, we come to rest to hear the intrusion of the everyday world as the porter grumbles his way to the door on which the knocking still resounds.

Such, I would suggest, is the process at work as the action of great poetic drama is embodied in a sequence of events ordered not by demonstrative but by poetic logic. So great is its evocative power that our imagination can bridge a gap which in lesser drama and in common life would contain the crucial event of Macbeth's career. This or a like process will be found to indicate not merely the gaps and the omissions but the functional relations of the moments by which the artist leads us, from point to point, to an apprehension of the essential action of the play which the presentation of outward fact not only could not give us but would in certain instances destroy.

This seemingly arbitrary selection of crucial situations was the customary foundation of Elizabethan drama; the finest tragic dramatists, Marlowe, Webster, Middleton, Ford, all seem to be feeling their way to the same kind of plot as we find in Shakespeare and sometimes triumphantly if intermittently achieving it. The succession of disconnected crises that we sometimes find even in the major and usually in the minor dramatists points to a failure of artistic imagination in them, and imperfect hold upon the action (in Aristotle's sense) by whose direction Shakespeare's plots were unfolded.

*

We spoke at the beginning of this chapter of the inner and outer aspects of the plot and though the distinction is dangerous if it is used arbitrarily, it has a certain value. Some of the events in the plot belong to the surface and we are aware of them at once as deeds or speeches that visibly determine its direction. If we could imagine a sequence of outer events that formed a coherent series in a play we could speak of an outer plot, and if we could be made aware of the corresponding sequence of inner events we could similarly speak of the inner plot. In fact we cannot do either, for we cannot imagine a series sufficiently coherent to form by itself a plot or a strand of a plot, but it is evident that the two processes are at work in every play which is a work of art and that their relative proportions and the interplay between them go far to determine the nature of the play. A play which discloses the deeper levels of experience in the minds of the characters is to that extent concerned with an inner level of plot and one which shows us principally the effects of these experiences is concerned primarily with an outer plot; if Kyd's *Hamlet* had survived (always supposing it to have existed) it would, we may suppose, be found to have treated the story in such a way that the proportions and relations of these two aspects of its plot were like those of *The Spanish Tragedy*. But these are not the proportions or the relations of Shakespeare's *Hamlet*.

A plot which leaves upon our minds the impression that it is logical, argumentative, or demonstrative will be found to be so at its outer as its inner level and a play whose structure is evocative will be so at both levels also. I have already suggested that in *Macbeth* an event or series of events may evoke in our imaginations other intervening events, so that we pass from one to another without the sense of hiatus or space and end with a sense of the continuity of the whole, ordered sequence. Just so, the revelation of inner event may proceed in this way, whether by soliloquy or by dialogue. Macbeth's soliloquy 'If it were done when 'tis done', although it begins as an attempt to think out his position, is filled with thick-coming fancies and terrifying images that seem to leave his argument where it began. But we who have heard him know that a long phase of experience has been lived through and the very pauses, changes of direction, or inconsistencies have but shown us the journeying mind coming momentarily into sight. They have evoked in our imaginations the experience through which he has travelled; but it is an experience of which much is left undescribed, even in soliloquy. So it is with Hamlet when he sets out to debate whether to be or not to be. Our imaginations leap the gaps with his. The inner plot here uses its own special medium of revelation, the soliloquy itself. The progress of a mind intent upon its inner experience may be revealed to us by just such a stirring of our imaginations when Lear speaks to the Fool in Act I, scene v. We no longer see the same man at the end of that short passage of dialogue as we did at the beginning; we have followed the slender but sufficient clues through a wilderness of experience and self-discovery.

In the same way, we may recognize the contrary mode; the logical treatment of plot that we find in *The Alchemist* or *Strife* may be discovered also at the inner level whenever the experience of a character is revealed systematically, step by step; so that, whatever its relation to the events that belong primarily to the outer aspect of the plot, we recognize a piece of continuous disclosure or self-discovery going on beneath that surface. This is comparatively rare in drama, but we may find it in Racine's *Bérénice* or *Athalie* and we find it again in Ibsen's *Rosmersholm* or *John Gabriel Borkman*. Rebekka West, like Mrs Alving, has made a great part of her pilgrimage before the play opens, but *Rosmersholm*, unlike *Ghosts*, is mainly concerned with the final stages of her interpretation, with her assessment of her past conduct, and her deliberate translation of her final decision into action. And her mind, despite the strength of her emotions, works as clearly upon the true meaning of her past and the dilemma it has created in the present as if she were examining the motives and conduct of another person. Our imagination is required to follow her steps, but not to leap chasms with her.

Some indication of the variety possible to the inter-relations of these different levels of plot may be seen when we look at Ibsen's play bearing in mind such a play as *Hamlet* where also the inner aspect is concerned with exploration, a measure of self-discovery and integration. In *Hamlet*, the events in the world that surrounds him continually affect and are in turn affected by his inward progression; neither escapes for long the influence of the other. But in plays such as *Rosmersholm* the events that make up the surface become a mere vehicle for the significant succession of inner events. Moreover, this drama arises primarily not from the effect of tragic or catastrophic event upon the surface level of the play or from entirely new experience offered by this to the character, but from exploration and revaluation of the past in the light of these events, of fresh situations and changing relations. The material for an Elizabethan domestic tragedy does indeed lie behind the play; a long history of mingled events upon both levels, of interesting deeds, thoughts and decisions has brought the characters to the point at which they now stand. But the substance of the play itself is the recollection of that history and the re-assessment both of it and of the present to which Rebekka is prompted by the slight and relatively colourless surface events of the play.[9]

Some relation between these levels, between that which lies upon the surface and that which lies at varying depths beneath it, reveals itself then as surely in a play's structure as in the dramatist's revelation of character. But equally surely the mode of the essential dramatist distinguishes itself in both from that of the philosophic dramatist. And the mark of the evocative mode is, even here, its generic power, while the mark of the other is its logical demonstration. Even in so great a play as *Rosmersholm*, where the poetry of Ibsen's thought creates high imaginative drama, the logic of inner event is still to be found in the process of the mind which is revealed at the inner level of the plot.

From the linking and proportioning of these two levels comes, as I have suggested, the balance of the play's content. From their separation many significant implications derive. One of these in Elizabethan drama is the impression of the fluidity of time and of the different nature which it may assume at different moments. Our sense of multiple time-schemes within a play such as *Othello* comes in part from this difference of the tempo, the inner life proceeding with a swiftness perfectly consistent with common experience, the succession of outer events occupying meanwhile a brief space of solar time. The systole and diastole of many plays may be traced to the same cause; two separate and equally true ways of measuring time, implied by the two different levels, may reveal at the heart of a play a hint of the mystery of the two lives led by every man, of the mystery, that is, of incarnation.

NOTES

[1]The intimacy of the relationship between character and plot again becomes clear when we consider that the grouping of characters may be regarded either as the structural aspect of character or the spatial aspect of plot. Upon the spatial aspect of plot, see G. Wilson Knight, *The Wheel of Fire*, Chap. I.

[2]See *Laokoon* Chaps XV-XVIII. 'Es bleibt dabei: die Zeitfolge ist das Gebiet des Dichters, so wie der Raum das Gebiet des Malers.' (Chap. XVIII.)

[3]The relations of these two levels of plot within the time continuum admit obviously of wide variety in kind and spacing.

[4]The nature of this kind of spatial structure becomes clearer still if we set beside it yet another play of Ibsen, *The Pillars of the Community*, whose character grouping might appear at first glance to resemble that of *A Midsummer Night's Dream*. The relations between the many strands of action and the direct links between the numerous characters reveal to a careful inspection the fact that the most seemingly detached of these strands are related to at least three or four others. But there is a

palpable purpose behind this only less evident than that behind the statuesque grouping of the characters in *Ghosts*. Again, the characters are related to certain problems and responsible for revealing them. They are so placed not so much to imply a world of men as to contribute to a balance of forces. Through them all runs the dominant theme of Bernick's conversion, the progress of his soul through crime and punishment to redemption. Ibsen gathers up and puts into Bernick's hands all the threads of the plot and consequently all the responsibility. We assist throughout the play at an inevitable progress to a triumphant demonstration. But the function of the spatial aspect is to contribute to our understanding of the emergent theme, rather than to extend the implications of the play.

[5]The same function of spatial relations may be traced in the work of that later poet who is, by discipline and devotion, chief heir to the Greek dramatic genius. In some seven at least of the plays of Racine the few characters extend the scope of the drama by drawing into the spatial plot a wide range of worlds or associations. This is perhaps most clearly seen in *Andromaque* and *Bérénice*, but it is at work also in *Mithridate*, *Iphigénie*, *Phèdre*, *Esther*, and *Athalie*.

[6]This technique in painting is, of course, common and elementary knowledge. But even at the risk of offering a naïve comment, I should like to describe those aspects which appear relevant also to the study of drama. This footnote should obviously be passed over by those who know the elements of the technique of painting and, even more obviously, by those who paint.

The familiar ways of conveying the impression of distance are by the perspective of line and of colour; in line by diminution of size in identical objects and in colour by diminution of tone or change of line. Thus, both in nature and in painting, we observe fewer distinctive characteristics as objects become more distant and, as a corollary, they make less claim on the attention. This does not imply that they appear less real. A tree at a distance does not normally appear unreal; it is merely, by reason of its position, less individualized than a tree in the foreground. We can see the pattern of the window-curtain in the house across the road; we cannot distinguish even the windows in a farm near Calais seen from Dover Beach. But we accept both as houses. Moreover, in both the trees and the houses, loss of size has been accompanied by loss of tone (or brilliance of hue). When the atmosphere does not contribute a colour of its own, grey, blue, purple, increasing in proportion to the distance, we are able to observe pure loss of tone with distance. This can conveniently be done in, for instance, the Painted Desert of Arizona, where objects eighty miles away will be found surprisingly to retain some of their colour, but to retain it in diluted form. This may perhaps be regarded as a case of pure colour perspective, since nothing has been added by 'veils' of atmosphere. Even when atmosphere does interfere, there is still a true relationship between line and colour perspective, though it may sometimes take a fantastic form; when one is painting a tree in a London fog, the furthest branch may be reduced to a pale grey, while the nearest is dark and vivid and hardly any linear perspective is noticed. The law is ultimately the same: with increasing distance there must be both reduction of size and dilution of colour; though the one may have its maximum effect and the other its minimum, in any given scene there must be a consistent relationship between the two. What is essential is the diminishing potency of the object in the picture. The loss of tone also accounts for the loss of detail; the main patches of colour are themselves diluted, the shadows grow paler, the highlights dimmer until there is, at a sufficient distance, no distinction between the three. Anyone who attempts to paint mountain or desert scenery recognizes this regressive loss of tone, its contribution to the sense of distance and the relative inability of linear perspective to achieve this by itself.

Just as certain painters (Cuyp, Van Goyen, Capelle, Hendrik Avercamp) achieve the effect of great distance and depth of scene by continuous and simultaneous perspective of line and colour, so, too, certain dramatists use a corresponding technique in the spatial structure of their plays.

Nor, as we have said, does this recession from the foreground of the play rob the characters or episodes of reality, but only of distinction in detail. The essential reality of the minor figures remains up to the verge of visibility (at which point a sentry's only speech may be 'My Lord?'). Here, admittedly, it is hard to find individuality and it would be an ill-constructed drama in which we could, for a dramatist, though aware of the reality of even the least of his minors, will nevertheless reduce him to an almost invisible figure if his function in the play sets him in the far distant background.

[7]Frith's *Ramsgate Sands* is a long, crowded ribbon of figures that gives little sense of distance, but Hendrik Avercamp's *Winter* (a far smaller canvas) is a wide and melancholy plain of ice, its distances defined by diminishing figures, progressively smaller and fainter. The element of continuous regression, found in many Dutch landscapes with figures, is of vital importance to the impression of depth and distance.

[8]This specific artistic discipline was one that could be learnt by Ibsen's successors and its influence may be traced in the work of Galsworthy and Granville-Barker in England and of Brieux in France. Few clearer instances could be found than Galsworthy's *Strife*, a play in which the addition of symmetry in the two subsidiary plots which combine to form the whole plot gives an almost euclidian finality to the demonstration. Barker's *Voysey Inheritance*, though less economical and less compact, belongs to the same family. It continues to appear in varying degree in many of the dramatists concerned with social problems; *Hindle Wakes*, *Chains*, and *Jane Clegg* all appear to owe something to it.

[9]The unfailing tact of the Greek drama leads to its special rendering by the aid of the Chorus of the relationship between the levels of event. The disclosure of the characters' motives and reflections gives us the origins of their actions, but the acts themselves are banished from the stage. Thus we have a drama which lays emphasis upon the inner aspect of plot in the midst of tragic and catastrophic outward events. These events are withdrawn into the background and the causes and responses within the human soul are given their true supremacy.

V

Communication in thought

We have looked first at a dramatist at work upon the revelation of character and on the ordered sequence of events that make the plot because these
are the aspects of the play to which we turn first when we are thinking
about the dramatic mode. They make up the greater part of the play's
content; the greater part – but not all. There remains the language itself,
forming yet another aspect of the play's technique and as evidently bringing its own contribution to the total effect; the sound or the immediate
sense of words considered singly or in small groups, perhaps afterwards to
be related together in their proper and continuous pattern, words in their
own right, distinguishable from their function as mediators of the content.
All this will be found in a work of art to be in harmony with the mode
already discovered in the treatment of character and plot. There remains
above all the imagery, which is a special part of this and sometimes, as in
the visual imagery called for by settings, almost a separable part and self-
contained.

But between them, at this point, there comes into sight another factor,
neither wholly a matter of character nor wholly of plot and yet not defin-
able simply in terms of the language which clothes it and them, difficult to
define and still more difficult to name and yet undoubtedly playing its part
in great drama (an agressive part in some) and again claiming consideration in its own right. There are speeches whose function is not solely that
of furthering event or revealing character or even both of these; speeches
which sometimes reveal, in our final image of the play, too consistent and
too continuous a nature of their own to be judged merely as an element of

the plot or the property of any one character. Their contribution to the play appears to be a part, but not the whole, of what Aristotle called *dianoia*; under due safeguards it is possible to speak of it in English as thought.

When Ulysses in *Troilus and Cressida* describes at length in the Greek camp the nature of 'degree' or of the hierarchical state (I. iii. 83-134), when Hector a little later (II. ii.) debates with the Trojans the nature of value, the form of the dialogue is an argument, the subject-matter is an idea or a group of related ideas, the force which makes speech vivid and vehement is a passionate absorption in the experience of thinking; the passages contribute less to the ordered sequence of events in the play, for indeed neither passage affects the immediate movement of event, than to the revelation of the ideas, preconceptions or assumptions on which the play rests, the intellectual motives which were part of the characters' passion from the beginning, part of the initial action of the play. Thinking, for such characters, is passionate experience and we recognize this when we respond to these scenes as to any other essentially dramatic passage or episode. We meet the same kind of material in the English history plays, and especially in the two parts of *Henry IV*, and something akin to it in the comparatively rare instances of serious debate in soliloquy such as those of Claudius and Angelo. Wherever we find this emphasis upon argument or self-examination, upon the process we speak of as 'thinking it out', we meet in effect an emphasis laid upon one side of human experience; and if a large proportion of the play's content is of this kind (as in *Troilus and Cressida*) we find an exceptional grouping or selection of characters who are themselves prone to or apt for that experience. This proneness to thought (or 'thinking'), when, so far from being out of character, it is of the very essence of the characters' natures and part of their passionate experience, is undeniably dramatic and it is what we mean by 'thought' in drama. After what we have already said [in previous chapters] we shall be prepared to find that, in the various dramatists' treatment of this element of the play, there is room again for diversity of mode.

We have been using the word 'thought' until now without strict definition, but it is advisable to bear in mind the most frequent connotations of the word in a dramatic context. If we begin by speaking of a single character, we may mean by his thought the process or method of this thinking, revealed as part of his experience (and so fit matter for drama).[1] Or we may think of the conclusions he draws, at whatever level of consciousness, from this process and this too will be part of his experience and so again fit matter for drama. But we may, if we wish, think of the characters collectively instead of individually and here again we shall need the word 'thought' to describe the effect on the tone and mood of the play of the thinking contained in it, of the total activity of thinking, of the sum of all the characters' experience of that process. And again, as with the individual character, we may mean by 'thought' the total body of ideas expressed, the sum of the conclusions of all the characters. For certain dramatists and in certain plays, we may add a fifth and a sixth connotation, using the term 'thought' to mean the process of thinking or the resultant conclusions of the dramatist himself. When this is made unmistakeably clear, when, that is to say, we hear the voice of the dramatist in addition to that of his character, when we recognize the ideas of Chapman extending beyond or even conflicting with those of Byron or Bussy, we are disconcerted and perceive that we are no longer assisting at a play. We have emerged momentarily from the dramatic into some other mode. This is not Shakespeare's way, nor that of any wholly dramatic writer, for it is as unnatural (and as unnecessary) for him to present his ideas as abstract principles within his play as for the painter or musician to resort to words instead of to his own medium. We may, it is true, apprehend something of his underlying ideas about life from the total body of his art or even from a single work, but we make this abstraction ourselves and the process is a complex one. No single character, not Ulysses, not Henry IV on his death-bed, gives us Shakespeare's idea of the nature of kingship or government, for each gives us strictly and dramatically his own inference from his own experience. That the experience of each of these comes near to Shakespeare's imaginative experience of the same situation we may conjecture, but that neither coincides precisely with the implications of the total body of the Histories we may see for ourselves if we make the empirical test of taking either speech as a gloss upon that whole body. The individuality of the speaker deflects it at one point or another; it is no true epitome of the thought that underlies all those plays, from *Henry VI* to *The Tempest*, which contain characters concerned with this theme.[2]

But there are, as we have said, certain plays in which the element of thought, while being essentially dramatic, forms a large part of the content and others again in which we suspect that its intrusion is not entirely dramatic. In the first case, we find a drama in which thought preponderates to such a degree as to outweigh or to threaten other interests suggesting a different kind of drama from anything we have hitherto considered. In the second, we shall probably find that the play falls short of the essential dramatic mode. And in both we must be prepared to distinguish its functions in relation to character and to plot.[3]

The most interesting plays thus weighted with thought are found in modern drama, from that phase, that is to say, which begins with Shakespeare and leads up to Ibsen and his successors, not because thought is alien to Greek drama but because the presence of the chorus there alters the balance of distribution.[4] The most evident speeches of this kind are perhaps those which present conclusions; adjudications, summaries of a position reached at the end of a process of thinking which is not itself presented. They are such speeches as are made in everyday life by a judge or a chairman of a board, and often contain a statement of relevant theory or a definition of policy. The sequence of the parts or the shape of the argument is, as a rule, undisturbed by emotion; the speaker's emotion, if any, is controlled and that of the hearers is revealed chiefly by implication in the preceding or following speeches and events. Such is the speech in which Claudius addresses his court at the beginning of *Hamlet* (I. ii. 1-39), a state-speech, a public declaration of policy, a ministerial report. Such, too, though delivered in the form of soliloquy, is Prince Henry's comment on his Eastcheap associates (*I Henry IV*, I. iii. 217-39), a piece not of thinking but of recapitulation, whose conclusions are clear and definite and evidently long familiar. So, too, in the main, is the deathbed speech of Henry IV (*II Henry IV*, IV. v. 180-218), which, despite the controlled emotion which gives it power, is essentially reminiscent of earlier thought, a distillation of the wisdom brought by bitter experience and endorsed 'like deep harmony' by the tongue of a dying man. And such again is the speech of the Lord Chief Justice later in the play (*II Henry IV*, V. ii. 73-101), the definition at once of his position and his creed, an orderly exposition undisturbed either by his own underlying emotion or the tension of the situation. We may add to these Ulysses's speech (*Troilus and Cressida*, I. ii. 83-134) on the hierarchical State and the consequences of the Greek neglect of degree, a long and masterly statement of a theory of government applied to a specific crisis. His thoughts do not arise in his mind as he speaks: they are the fruit of long-considered policy, prepared beforehand and delivered, as they should be, with vigour but without confusion. All these are essentially dramatic because, though not a revelation of passionate thinking, they are the consequences in one form or other of thought that has been evoked by passion and because they are either the cause or consequence of passionate event. They rightly have the appearance of impersonal deliveries because they are spoken by men trained by office to deliver impersonal judgements upon momentous occasions and led or forced to do so here by the surrounding events. We may add to these one or two other speeches, conceived and delivered in the same mood in response to the same demands: Athena's verdict at the end of the *Eumenides*, the judgement of Tullius at the end of *Horace* (V. iii), or Cinna's speeches (*Cinna*, II. i. 145-67, 215-306) on the nature of the Roman nation and its government. The list could be extended.

When we come to consider the exchange of thought in discussion, we are on rather different ground. The same laws govern argument or debate as govern all revelation of thought in drama, but the process of thinking appears side by side with the results in the speeches of at least some of the characters and, if the issue be vital enough to be fit matter for drama, emotion is likely to find its way into expression. Much of such dialogue is like the speech of counsel rather than the judge's summing up, the cabinet debate rather than the ministerial pronouncement. It attempts to reach a conclusion or to convince its dramatic audience and it is more usually a passage of dialogue than a single speech.[5] Such are the debate on war policy in the Trojan council chamber (*Troilus and Cressida*, II. ii), which resolves itself into a close discussion of the nature of value or the rougher and less keenly analytical discussion of conduct and policy between Westmorland, Mowbray, and the Archbishop of York (*II Henry IV*, IV. i). Such also are, in effect if not in fact, three scenes in which the form of a discussion is maintained and in two of which passionate concern is simulated, though in fact the underlying purposes of the disputants are quite other. The first is Henry V's discussion with his advisors on the interpretation of Salique law (*Henry V*, I. ii. 1-114), where the actual and perhaps the dramatic audience suspects that his intention is not so much to discover the truth as to provide himself with an excuse, and the discussion lacks urgency because the conclusion is predetermined. Another and subtler use of an argument concealing rather than declaring the intentions of the debaters is that in which Richard of Gloucester stages his mock-refusal of the crown and his hypocritical capitulation (*Richard III*, II. vii. 116-72). Some close and cunning argument is here reproduced both by Richard and Buckingham, but the scene derives its dramatic power less from the passion with which the argument is pursued than from the continual conflict between the debating points adduced and the known intentions of the two chief characters. The apparent debate, in which the processes of thinking are simulated, is well-enough reasoned to give it dramatic interest, but that interest is heightened by the irony and by passions that move not within the thought but beneath its deceptive surface. Not unlike this is the opening scene of the second act of *Cinna*, where the debate on imperial rule between Augustus, Cinna, and Maximus has also two levels of meaning. But here the arguments for and against

Augustus's policy, though clearly enough worked out, are hardly urgent enough to hold our interest. Nor can they be, for, not only are they again simulated argument, but we are much more deeply engaged upon a series of more urgent questions as to who is in fact deceiving whom and whether or not some sudden disclosure is to be made. But all these scenes are built out of thought and out of the preoccupation of the speaker with their own thought whether revealed or concealed, and in all of them we watch the process of thinking, at one or at two levels, and the thinking and the thought are the dramatic substance of the scheme.

Of a different kind again is self-examination as often as this takes or attempts to take the form of a debate in the mind of the speaker; the process then is that of thinking out his position or intentions and not an expression of feeling alone. The normal form for this is soliloquy which, at least among the Elizabethans and in some degree until the coming of naturalism, represents, by an agreed convention, the unspoken thought of a character. It is indeed possible for a character to conduct his self-examination in a speech or speeches which are made to another person and yet primarily précis of genuine thinking aloud. But such speeches are in fact extremely rare, as is indeed the situation in which they could occur.[6] Nor can we include in this group all soliloquies for not all soliloquies reveal a process which reaches by argument a conclusion, valid or false, upon which action is or is to be based. The diversity within this group is very great, for here the whole range of the mind may be revealed, its individual process of thinking followed without constraint; there is no dramatic audience for the speaker to persuade or convince and to whom he must adapt his expression and the steps of his reasoning. Moreover, in this kind of speech, the relationship between emotion and thought becomes more intricate. Thought itself may be of passionate intensity, it is true, but it is also true that in many soliloquies, even where thought is dominant and the thinker determined to organize his experience to reach a conclusion, the very depth of his concern with his thinking may itself interfere with the process; the emotions which arise at each step may cross it and disturb the orderly procedure that was his intention. In Claudius's prayer (*Hamlet*, III. iii. 36-72), in the two passages of Angelo's self-examination (*Measure for Measure*, II. ii. 161-87 and II. iv. 1-17), there is hardly a trace of the detachment maintained by Henry IV or by the Lord Chief Justice, even in the midst of tension. In such self-communing the 'whirlwind of passion' contends with the stillness of ordered thought, but not to its complete disordering. This is essential to any faithful and dramatic revelation of passionate thinking in soliloquy and Shakespeare's characters, from Proteus (*Two Gentlemen of Verona*, II. v. 193-215 and II. vi. 1-43) to Prospero (*The Tempest*, V. i. 33-57), confirm this truth. For if, in any comparable situation, the logical form and the detachment is preserved that was proper to character and situation when Ulysses spoke or Henry IV, we are uneasily aware of something which is not a revelation of human experience in the mind of the character before us, but a summary of conclusions which could only have been reached at some psychological distance from the event; the thought has been unnaturally rescued from the turmoil of emotion and set out as an ordered sequence whose very brevity and coherence put it outside the world of the drama before us and constitute a narrative summary of a part of its inner plot. This convention, for a convention it sometimes is, is the reverse of that by which soliloquy admits us to the inner thought of a character; instead it puts us at two removes from his experience of the moment and gives us the likeness of that experience, robbed of its immediacy, as it may perhaps be destined to appear to him at some later date or in a future beyond the play. Such doubts extend to many impressive speeches in the plays of Corneille; to Emilie's in the opening soliloquy of *Cinna*, to Pauline's at the beginning of the third act of *Polyeucte*, to Félix's in a passage already spoken of a little later in the same act (III. v. 12-28). But when the characters of Racine, on the other hand, set themselves to think out their problems, they so think and feel that the very process of their thinking and feeling rises, as does that of Shakespeare's characters, before our eyes.[7] Among the dramatists of the nineteenth century none has this secret more surely than Ibsen, whose Brand, a man whose profession compels self-examination as an exercise, carries us with him step by step through his agonized progress to conclusions which are but half-truths.[8] And beside him, in at least one speech, is Bjornson's Paul Lange.[9]

It has already been implied that among the dramatists I have instanced, it is Corneille who appears to work in another and perhaps less dramatic mode in this matter of revealing the process of thinking and in the relation in his works between the process and the resultant thought. And since thought, both as thoughts and as thinking, is a great part of his subject-matter, it is clear that he presents us with something which must either distinguish him from most other dramatists or lead us to revise our conclusions. For one could no more dispute the importance of argument and debate in his dialogue and soliloquy than one could deny the predominance of characters in his plays whose minds are alive with thought and who reflect its habit in the very rhythm and syntax of their speeches and in their compensating paucity of imagery.

The glory of Corneille's drama lies precisely in this, that it is a drama of thought. The characters exist to express it and the structure to sustain it. It is found in its most stirring form in the plays in which the characters deliberate least, in which thought or thinking is less a matter of reflection than of swift balancing of conflicting codes or duties and of equally swift decision rapidly calculated from the results of a parallelogram of psychological forces. The pace and the passion of drama are to be found in the clash between love and hate on the one hand and iron discipline of an accepted code of honour and conduct upon the other. Provided only that this is the kind of code that human beings may create and that they know their responses by heart, one does not question the process of their thought or the mode of revelation. One knows them only too well. Their codes may be primitive but they are clear and they are gallant. And the type of character, above all others, to whom this is natural is the soldier.

When, therefore, Corneille fills his plays with soldiers and the women bred in the tradition of the services, he gives us a play that satisfies our instinctive demands upon drama and will prove upon examination to satisfy such dramatic laws as we are able to discern. It is not for nothing *Le Cid* has entranced readers and audiences of many races who are slow to respond to certain of his other plays. For a soldier's honour is a real thing and a part of everyday existence wherever survival depends upon the valour and the power of leadership that only unflawed honour can give. This play lives by virtue of the mood of high excitement, brilliant with passion and torment and the supreme vitality of youth. And so long as the play is filled with the very people, the young and the men dedicated to the military code, in whom such swift and passionate action is native in response to their code, so long is the play dramatic. They are men for whom 'it were an easy leap To pluck bright honour from the pale-faced moon', and had Shakespeare written a play peopled only with Hotspurs and Sewards, it might have resembled this. Only, Shakespeare would never so have peopled his play. And this indicates a gulf between the two dramatists which may be found to reach to the foundations of dramatic art. Moreover, his Hotspurs are maculate and imperfect beings while the Rodrigues must of necessity be as immaculate as Galahad; one sees the shining of the silver armour and hears the high, clear clash of its movements as the noble lines ring down upon the stage.

But where, when we have admitted this, is the thought in that stricter kind which is characteristic of Cornelian drama? The characters even here think out each position as it confronts them, balance the alternatives, reject one with passionate regret but select and act swiftly upon the other.

And in doing this they explain their motives or that part of their motive which has been indoctrinated in them by the code. And their explanation is a calculation of conflicting claims natural only to a certain military caste trained so to calculate and to decide by established criteria without reference to and if necessary in defiance of the deep-lying instincts, of the promptings that rise from the inner experience or the total consciousness, and so affords us perhaps the only instance possible of a self-explanatory character which is yet a mediator of drama. When all is said, these men search not their hearts but the code which tells them how to act without reference to the heart. This may afford a noble theme, but it is not in effect a part of common human experience; it is so far from universal that what is distinctive in it is scarcely human, though it may be universally accepted as the superhuman achievement of dedicated men. In short, in the one play in which Corneille writes what is indubitably drama in a widely accepted kind and creates that drama out of thought, he does this precisely by specializing the type of character and the type of thinking within extremely narrow limits. Within these limits he has succeeded, to the extent of one play, of making the reasoned debate the substance of his play and that substance dramatic. He appears to leave us face to face with the astonishing paradox that only men of action, in action, can reason dramatically.

It is his other plays then that afford us what we are seeking, a drama in which the characters reason and debate with each other and with themselves at the crucial moments of the plot, in which there is a continuous attempt to reveal their inner experience to us largely in terms of deduction and self-explanation. It is a drama, in which the reasoning process seems to be idealized as at once the object of aspiration and the means of moral achievement. Such a drama is naturally peopled with beings for whom reason holds a high place in the scale of aids and means to virtue, who seek to solve perplexity by reference not to the hidden depths of their being but to the clear and burnished surface of consciousness. It is habitual with such persons to approach a crisis with a clear intention to think out where they stand before they go further: 'Settle thy studies, Faustus, and begin/To sound the depth of that thou wilt profess.' But neither they nor Faustus at this point of experience do in fact sound those depths, for the intention in both cases is to pass in review the conflicting desires or purposes and to act upon a deduction that follows from that survey. We are not concerned here with the question of whether persons with a persistent habit of self-explanation and self-analysis may exist, but with the question of whether, if they do, they are fit subjects for drama. If their reasoning is other than a swift and vehement comparison of conflicting codes and an equally swift and soldierly choice between them, then it is likely, as we have suggested, to be the result of a fixed habit of inward, philosophical debate. And if the process and demeanour which properly result from this are suffered to determine the form of their expression at moments which the dramatist claims to be those of intense emotion, then either the emotion is not in fact intense, in which case their philosophical demeanour can well be a faithful picture of human conduct, or he has falsified their experience by causing them to display a philosophic demeanour impossible to passionate men in the grip of their passions. In the first instance the character, being predominantly dispassionate, is unfit matter for drama and in the second the falsification of character, together with the remoteness superimposed upon its expression, destroys the cogency and the immediacy of drama. We are driven to conclude that conditions such as those of *Le Cid* are the only ones in which self-expression in the form of reasoned exposition at the moments of emotional crisis can appear natural to 'man doing and suffering', and that in conditions that lack the peculiar kind of urgency and pressure proper to this play, the habit appears to misrepresent the normal processes of human behaviour.

This leads us immediately to another question. Have we in fact grounds for concluding that the matter of thought may itself be so treated by one dramatist as to be essentially dramatic and by another as to be in certain respects undramatic? Is there in fact a dramatic mode of revealing thought and an undramatic mode of presenting it? Does Corneille, for instance, fall into an undramatic mode by the unnatural completeness of expression that he imposes on the characters?[10]

What holds our attention, then? In what is it that we are interested, in the characteristic Cornelian drama, that drama in which thought is a high activity explicitly expressed and proceeding at the surface of the characters' minds? To answer this fairly we must look at passages which are part of the poet's intention, led up to by preceding scenes, placed and timed with precision and built into the play.[11] Such a scene is that, already referred to, which opens the second act of *Cinna*, where for some 250 lines, the three characters on the stage engage in a long debate on the advantages and disadvantages of imperial and democratic government, although the purpose of the argument is not in fact to arrive at a decision on that issue nor to lead on through that decision to some determining events in inner or outer plot. For this scene rests on a basis of irony and derives its suspense not from the direction or conclusion of the argument but from the direction and conclusion of a battle of wits to which this is a mask. At both levels it is an intellectual exercise and the fact that it is twofold does not alter the fact that our interest is in the astute, Machiavellian game of wits and not, as in the superficially similar scene in *Richard III* (III. vii), in the subtle study of hypocrisy and the imaginative dread which the ominous exercise of Richard's skill evokes.

Augustus has summoned Cinna and Maximus at the height of their conspiracy and as the scene opens we await in suspense, if we are reading the play for the first time, the answer to two questions. Has Augustus discovered the conspiracy or not? Will he or will he not have the two conspirators arrested and executed? These are followed immediately by a third question, as Augustus dismisses his guards and remains alone with the conspirators: will they seize the opportunity to kill him? As the dialogue goes on, our minds are further exercised by trying to discover whether he is in earnest when he asks for their advice on his proposed resignation or whether he is setting a trap for them which, like Henry V with Cambridge, Grey, and Scroop (*Henry V*, II. ii), he will presently spring. As the scene goes on, and it begins to look as though nothing is going to happen from Augustus's side, we give our minds more and more to the underlying ironies, which are themselves subject to doubt from our still unanswered questions. Supposing Augustus to be ignorant of the conspiracy, there is much irony in his asking advice on his position from precisely the two men who have sworn to assassinate him, in Cinna's well-argued assurances that his reign is beneficent, when we know that it is Augustus's seizing of the empire that is Cinna's reason for the intended assassination, in Maximus's equally well-argued entreaties that he should resign, when resignation would save him from their vengeance, in the lively and vigorous debate between these two conspirators who are sworn to agreement in a purpose opposite to their words, in the surprise which, though it is concealed until the following scene, we know that each must be feeling at the position taken up by the other. There is excitement in this and the suspense at first reading or hearing is intense; in later readings we must forgo the suspense and depend for enjoyment upon the neatness of the debate and the ironic undertones. But what are we to say of a key scene in which, in all subsequent readings, we are left to depend upon the cunning of the arguments and their ironic implications? That part of suspense which depends on our ignorance of event vanishes also after one reading of *Oedipus* or *Othello*, of any tragedy by a Greek or an Elizabethan dramatist; indeed this ignorance is for most of us like Ann Oldham's virginity, we cannot remember when we lost it. But with the Greeks and the Elizabethans, when that part of suspense is gone which was strictly the province of melodrama, we are left to our imaginative participation in that more terrible suspense which the characters themselves experience. We know how *Macbeth* will end, but that is nothing beside the fact that we are ourselves Macbeth and that he does not. It is the characters and their fates, and the significance of fate and character that engage us here. But Corneille is using certain of the methods of comedy in tragedy – a fact that no one knew better than he[12] – but they are of a specialized kind of comedy, of the kind that watches the manoeuvres of Face and Surface like the evolution of a well-known ballet, for sheer delight in the precision and virtuosity of the movements. It is not the comedy which holds its breath while Dogberry and Verges obscure urgent police messages or catches that breath when Beatrice cries, 'Kill Claudio!' The scene in *Cinna* that we are watching is no more the comedy of sympathy than it is the tragedy of sympathy and while comedy without good will is possible for a time (but not possible throughout, even for Ben Jonson or for Congreve)[13] tragedy which for any reason hinders the participation of the audience in the experience of the agents thwarts its own purposes. The reason for this is probably to be sought, as we have suggested, in the level of consciousness at which the characters enter upon the conflict. The drama which Kames denounced and about which even Voiture had his doubts[14] reveals, if only by its facility in debate, that we are not assisting at a conflict of the soul.[15]

Thought may indeed be activated by passion and it may then, as in *Le Cid* and in *Faustus*, sometimes become passionate thought, but the areas in which it can operate are extremely small and the boundaries of that area themselves serve to define the dramatic use of thought (always potential matter for drama) and the undramatic deployment of it in debate. For debate is, after all, a small part of total human experience, normal in unusual degree only to certain temperaments, professions, and situations, and though these themselves are as fit matter for drama as anything else, only the passionate part of even that thinking is fit. Mental conflict may indeed rise to the surface as mental debate, but an essential difference exists between the kind of drama in which mingled passion and thought result in mingled coherence and incoherence, in mingled deed and speech, and the kind in which the thinking and its conclusions, in perfect lucidity and poise, are the main activity of the speakers and the main interest of the hearer. We may attend a trial from concern for and interest in the contestants or we may attend in order to savour the skill of the pleading and of the judge's summing up; it is doubtful whether we can do both in the same instance, and this indicates the gulf between the two attitudes. The same distinction may be drawn between the drama of experience and the drama of debate, with this difference that the second of these attempts to merge prosecutor with plaintiff, defence with defendant; and if the issues are serious our common experience of human behaviour rebels against super-imposition of lucid detachment upon passionate concern. The drama of cabinet meetings, council chambers, lecture platforms, and pulpits (except in the rare instances where these issues are matters of life and death), where nothing is confused and little entirely secret, is separated by a wide gulf from the drama that depends upon secret impressions, where the hidden processes of the mind mingle with every stage of argument and help to determine every deed.[16]

Finally, to return to our original question, is it true to say that the thought which forms part of the tissue of a play's content may, like charac-ter, be treated in widely differing ways by different dramatists and those the ways of secret impressions upon the one hand and, at the opposite extreme, of less wholly dramatic and more explicit expression? To the first part of this we have already suggested an answer. What we have now to ask is whether thought, in the sense in which we have spoken of it in this chapter, can itself be the vehicle of secret impressions and serve the purposes of evocative drama? We may arrive at some conclusion by comparing Pauline's soliloquy, which opens the third act of *Polyeucte*, with those two in which Angelo finds himself 'that way going to temp-tation,/Where prayers cross' (*Measure for Measure*, II. ii. 161-87 and II. iv. 1-17).

Both are pictures of mental conflict, the first concerned with the conflict of others, the second with its own; but both are alike in recognizing confusion and turmoil, the first of hopes and fears, the second of the 'prayers' that 'cross', and in knowing that out of these some kind of order must be brought. At that point all likeness stops and the significant differences begin. Pauline recognizes the confusion and describes it clearly in lines whose syntax, internal rhythms, and rhyming couplets add pre-cision to every stage of her description.

> Que de soucis flottants, que de confus nuages
> Présentent à mes yeux d'inconstantes images!
> Douce tranquillité, que je n'ose espérer,
> Que ton divin rayon tarde à les éclairer!
> Mille agitations, que troubles produisent,
> Dans mon cœur ébranlé tour à tour se détruisent:
> Aucun espoir n'y coule où j'ose persister;
> Aucun effroi n'y règne où j'ose m'arreter.
> Mon esprit, embrassant tout ce qu'il s'imagine,

Voit tantôt mon bonheur, et tantôt ma ruine,
Et suit leur vaine idée avec si peu d'effet,
Qu'il ne peut espérer ni craindre tout à fait.

After these twelve lines of lucid and accurate psychological description, she turns to a sixteen-line examination of the problem which has caused her distress. What will happen when Sévère and Polyeucte meet, her affianced lover and her husband? She balances the probabilities as though it were a problem in dynamics, delivering a summary of the case for a quarrel in a way that would do credit to a historian or a psychologist defining a situation to a class. Then she illustrates the conflict described in the first twelve lines by changing her assumption and putting, more briefly this time, the considerations that may lead them to forbearance. She returns for another brief period to renew and add to the arguments for the first probability and ends with one line of pious, but obviously unfounded, hope. It is a brilliant speech; a vivid and compact piece of exposition, designed to show us (by what is admittedly a convention) a part of the background to the events of the play. But we cannot rid ourselves of the feeling that it would have carried more conviction in the convention of a messenger's speech. We are not listening to a soul in the grip of its own distracting torment, but to someone narrating another's experience. And it would have served better our understanding of the character and our acceptance of the tragedy if the narrator had not been that character itself. This superb speech is in every line a denial of character, of that hidden correspondence between depth and surface upon which character depends. Whether some effect equivalent to that of drama can be produced by this technique where spirited narrative takes the place of manifold and evocative disclosure is doubtful. What is certain is that Corneille, herein differing essentially from Racine no less than from Shakespeare, attempted to substitute coherent thought throughout his drama for the half incoherent revelation normal to human beings in extremity and in so employing his genius, demonstrated for all time the essentially undramatic nature of demonstration in drama.

NOTES

[1] 'Fit matter for drama' does not, of course, imply that the matter is necessarily used dramatically in any given passage or by any given dramatist.

[2] It would be convenient if we could say that 'thought', in so far as it is fit matter for drama, was covered by Aristotle's term 'dianoia', but in fact there is

overlapping, but no coincidence. To accept Butcher's assumption (*Aristotle and the Fine Arts* (ed. 1923) p.337, n. 2, quoting R. P. Hardie in *Mind*, vol.IV,No.15) that by 'διάνοια' Aristotle did in fact mean 'μίμησις τῆς διανόιας' , without providing this aspect of technique with a special term to delimit the relationship, as he did with μῦθος and πρᾶξις, is to exclude satisfactorily enough the directly revealed thought of the dramatist and to confine the use of the term to the first four connotations that we have suggested, to the thought, that is, of the character or characters. But even so, the last two of these would appear to fall outside the content of Aristotle's 'dianoia' (*Poetics*, VI, 6, 16, 17) and the first two (or, indeed, all four) to contain rather less than is required by *Poetics*, XIX, 2, or *Ethics*, VI, 2. We must therefore reluctantly abandon what looks at first like a convenient category and continue to lay the burden of differentiation upon our own overworked term, 'thought'.

Again, it may be questioned why Aristotle did not warn us against the danger of preoccupation with dianoia as he did against the danger of neglecting muthos for ethos. This answer is simply that dianoia is the active principle in character and ethos the passive groundwork of personality. So, while it is quite possible (see below) to find plays unduly given to 'thought' in the sense in which we are here using the term, a play unduly given to dianoia at the expense of muthos would be a contradiction in terms. This again serves to mark the distinction between dianoia and 'thought' (as used here) and between the aspects of dramatic content which they define.

[3]It is evident from the outset that no limit is set by the nature of drama to the extent to which thinking and thought may become part of the content of a play. For obviously no subject-matter can be inherently undramatic if it is possible to human nature to make of it a passionate experience.

[4]The Greek dramatists were for the most part able to transfer to the chorus the task of presenting the final impression of and conclusions from the thought of all the characters ('thought' III and IV), thus securing its presentation without laying this responsibility upon the dialogue.

[5]As a single speech we may instance that of the Bishop of Carlisle (*Richard II*, IV. i. 114-19). This stands alone simply because it is met not by a counter-argument but by his arrest.

[6]Most of these resolve themselves upon inspection into summaries of conclusions already reached or into debates in which the other character supplies from time to time opposition or encouragement and so gives a fresh direction to the thought. Self-examination in the presence of another character is not unspoken thought but confession and though there is nothing to prevent this being a process of 'thinking things out', the situation is rare in life and still more rarely part of a dramatic sequence of events. Ibsen probably brings us nearer to it than any other dramatist.

It is clearly among the moderns that we must look for it and there only in realistic drama. For wherever the soliloquy is an accepted convention, it is unnecessary and the use of it will probably reveal a mistaken conception on the part of the dramatist as to the processes by which the character could have explored his own mind. Corneille's *Polyeucte* seems to offer an instance of this, in the scene (III. v) in which Félix analyses in the presence of Albin the effects of an experience too recent for us to suppose that he could yet have reached clear conclusions upon it.

[7]As, for instance, the soliloquies of Antiochus (*Bérénice*, I. ii), Titus (ibid., IV. iv), Atalide (*Bajazet*, V. i), Mithridate (*Mithridate*, IV. v), to indicate only a few.

[8]See especially *Brand*, Acts I, IV and V.

[9]*Paul Lange and Tora Parsburg* (V).

[10]In so far as the reasoning being has full right to reason in a play, provided he does so with passionate intensity, we may instance many of Ibsen's people, notably Brand and Mrs Alving, in each of whom the habit is justified by circumstance or training. What Ibsen does not do is to fill his play with such characters on the one hand or to let them explain themselves in defiance of their nature and habits on the other. Given a world whose Autolycuses were reasonable and whose Dogberries lucid we should have to admit the universality of the reasoning habit. But we should still be free to maintain that that habit, dispassionately prevailing, did not afford to its poets matter for that form of art that we call drama.

[11]Not, that is to say, scenes which appear (as does *Macbeth*, IV. i) to change the tempo of the play, to arrest movement and to puzzle criticism by appearing as eddies or backwaters of the main-stream of the drama.

[12]See *Discours de l'utilité et des parties du poëme dramatique* in *Oeuvres* (1910), I, pp. 13-51, especially p. 30.

[13]Still less for Plautus or Molière, and less still again, for Terence. Corneille himself in his comedies comes nearer to it than any of the three, though a twinge of anxiety follows Dorante at his most difficult moments which is not given to the baser villainies of Ben Jonson's criminals.

[14]'On ne débite pas les lieux communs quand on est profondément ému.'

[15]Preoccupation with this facility may betray the dramatist into an imperfect relation between the conduct of a character and its effects as it does, I think, with Corneille's Félix in *Polyeucte*.

[16]A brief comparison with the methods of the Greek dramatists may help to clear up the distinction I have attempted to draw. A Greek dramatist had two ways of conveying the thought of his characters, in their own speeches and in the choric odes. The first is now used, as by the Elizabethans, to an extent and in a context normal and natural to 'man doing and suffering'. For the second, the Elizabethans had no resource but the soliloquy, except in a few passages where they lay upon certain characters, in defiance of dramatic probability, some of the responsibilities of a commentator; Webster and Chapman use most often this undramatic device. But Corneille, having little or no chorus, appears to have transferred this part of its function to the characters themselves, charging them indiscriminately with the burden of thought carried by the Greek chorus. This led to some astonishing results to the balance of character and the consequent veracity of the drama, for the characters must then reveal that part of their hidden reflections which the Greek chorus had revealed for the Greek dramatists. This lifts the hidden up into explicit

expression in an unnatural way and leaves the characters to reveal what they did not know and had no business to know and that in a way which can only be tolerated by the audience if it is revealed by means of a frank convention like the Elizabethan soliloquy and that only when the soliloquy represents thought as it would appear to an audience that could dispense with the medium of words. This constitutes one of the most fundamental differences between the mode of Corneille and the mode of Racine, in whose plays we meet again that tragic inevitability that we miss in Corneille's.

VI

The functions of imagery in drama

The plays or groups that we have already considered[1] have shown how seemingly incompatible subject-matter may be shaped into dramatic form, a supreme work of art winning a victory, where least expected, by transcending the normal limitations. But victory of this kind on the grand scale is rare, and there are less remarkable triumphs over limitation which are made possible by skilful and unobtrusive technique. These are almost all matters of detail rather than of basic structure and generally work by extending the scope through suggestion and implication without modifying the presentation of the matter. Imagery and prosody, together with certain bold conventions and even devices of setting, serve in various ways to overcome the disadvantages of that brevity which is essential to the concentration and immediacy of drama. A play in which any or all of these are richly used conveys an impression both of magnitude and of subtlety, while the dramatist who uses fewer of them must (like Ibsen in the social dramas) compensate the resulting austerity by some other means, such as the power and skill of the architecture. It is hardly necessary to point out that the average sound theatre play, whether of the present age or of any other, does neither; its potency is thus commensurate with its necessary dramatic brevity; it may be effective in the theatre, but it will not grow in the mind as will a great imaginative work of art.

Of these ways of deepening the imaginative significance of a play without increasing its length or bulk, imagery is perhaps at once the most simple and the most powerful.

In approaching this question we take almost inevitably as our point of departure the finest poetic drama; such as that of Shakespeare's maturity, in which the imagery seems to be entirely functional. Such imagery, that is to say, is an integral part of the play, just as is the theme or the structure; it is there, just as they are, because it is essential to the play, because it has a function belonging to nothing else but imagery, because without that imagery the play would be the poorer from whatever aspect we regarded it. At the other extreme from this there are admittedly plays (which perhaps qualify but doubtfully for the title 'poetic') in which such imagery as there is is wholly or partly decorative and not an integral part of the play. There are also many plays, probably the greater number, in which the relation between the whole work of art and the imagery occupies a position inter-mediate between these two, in which the imagery is at times an aspect of the whole and at other times only incompletely related. But unless we are concerned mainly with the historical side of the subject, with tracing the development of this relation, our interest will almost certainly turn first to those plays in which the functional value of imagery is most fully revealed.

When we speak of imagery in this way we generally find that we are using the term in that stricter and somewhat limited sense which recent writers have tended to adopt when considering Shakespeare,[2] taking it, that is, either as co-extensive with metaphor or at most with the figures closely allied to metaphor. This is, I believe, advisable, even though, in the special case of drama, there are sometimes reasons for extending it to include the frontiers of symbolism, description, or even, it may be, the setting itself, when, as in much modern drama, the playwright relies upon that to express a part of his intention.[3]

Can we, then, within these limits, describe what are or have been some of the functions by which imagery helps drama to overcome the limitations inherent in its brevity?

All imagery that has a functional relation with a play increases dramatic concentration. In common with all genuine metaphorical expression, it reveals a significant and suddenly perceived relation between an abstract theme and a subject closer to the experience of the senses in such a way as to transfer to the rightly apprehending mind the shock, the stimulus with which the union of these two stirred the mind of the poet himself. Strong emotional experience is stored in the brief space of an image, and its release illuminates powerfully the emotions, the reflections, the inferences which it is the purpose of the passage to evoke. There is thus an artistic economy in imagery hardly to be equalled by that of any other kind of verbal expres-sion, with the possible exception of irony; in each the potency comes from the high charge of implicit thought or feeling. Moreover, dramatic imagery tends to be the most strongly charged of all kinds; the concen-tration natural to drama impressing itself upon the imagery, just as the imagery in its turn enables the drama to increase its native concentration.[4]

A play which contains little or no imagery is not necessarily shorter than a play which carries a high charge of it. The concentration of imagery in a poetic play operates rather by enabling the play, without overrunning its brief form, to extend its scope and strengthen its texture. Lacking the leisure and the digressive privileges of the narrative and reflective forms, drama is sometimes in danger of poverty of implication or detail. This is true even of the finest type of drama, which maintains severely its proportioning and the magnitude of its theme. Even here, without the support of functional imagery, there is danger of thinness of character, absence of suggestive comment and lack of passionate significance in spite of richness of event. More often than we should readily believe, we find the presence or absence of imagery to be the immediate technical explanation of those differences in content, in fullness and in amplitude in plays otherwise similar in dimension, theme and structure.[5]

Imagery, as we have said, has certain functions which can compensate drama for the heavy liabilities inherent in its form. Without losing the intensity and compactness which is its virtue, the poetic drama of Aeschylus, of Shakespeare or of one of the modern poetic dramatists, such as Synge, depends largely upon functional imagery for its breadth and scope, for our awareness of a wider setting than that in which the actual events occur. Again, while still preserving its rapidity of pace, drama may, by virtue of the charge carried by its imagery, achieve some of the fullness and elaboration of detail in the revelation of character or of thought which, in narrative or reflective verse and prose, can be revealed at leisure by the descriptive method.

These several functions may be seen at work in the Greek drama as in that of the Elizabethans, at intervals in the drama of the Continent down to the present day and in England again since the revival of the poetic drama in the twentieth century.

Imagery, in such drama, often reveals the presence of a surrounding or accompanying universe of thought or experience which cannot otherwise be included, however essential to its poetic purpose, without forfeiting the rapidity and compression in which the artistic strength of drama chiefly lies. This is often also effected by symbolism, setting or incidental description,[6] but imagery, in the strict sense of metaphorical speech, is a more powerful means; more passionate than symbolism, more flexible than setting, more concentrated than descriptive disgression.

This function of imagery may be traced in many of Shakespeare's plays, where the vastness of the issues involved, of which the action that is shown us is but a part, is kept constantly before us by the imagery. As early as

Romeo and Juliet the vastness of love is illuminated for a moment by an image whose revelation remains with us throughout the sequent action:

> My bounty is as boundless as the sea,
> My love as deep.

Just so, the universal, all-enveloping horror of Macbeth's crime, its unutterable and inescapable consequence, is borne in upon us, not only by the pitiless relation of cause and effect revealed in the action, but by images that light up, by potent analogy, the nature of the deed:

> This my hand will rather
> The multitudinous seas incarnadine
> Making the green one red.

Macbeth's mind, in which 'function is smothered in surmise', is a microcosm of the 'state' whose ordered processes are, by the consequences of his deeds, as surely smothered. He thinks instinctively of 'the seeds of time' and 'Nature's germens', thus flashing before us in single images the surrounding universes of time and causality through which the events move.

In Timon's mind the themes of disease, misgeneration, and robbery image themselves in the elements; the earth, the sea, and the great process of nature. We are never long without this reminder of the universal nature of calamity and evil:

> The sun's a thief and with his great attraction
> Robs the vast sea; the moon's an arrant thing
> And her pale fire she snatches from the sun.

In *Troilus and Cressida* again there is constant reference out from the affairs of man, in which the action consists, to the surrounding universe of being to which they transfer and from which they derive their sickness. The polity of man mirrors the order or disorder of the cosmos, and universal disjunction and disintegration are there imaged with a rapidity and power that could not be compassed in long passages of descriptive analysis. Much of the tempest imagery in *Lear* has a like function.

In *Antony and Cleopatra* there is brought before us by the imagery first the world-wide power of Rome and of Antony, 'the triple pillar of the world', and later the presence of the infinity of time and space which dwarf that world. For Cleopatra there is

> Nothing left remarkable
> Beneath the visiting moon.

while, in the memory of Antony,

> His voice was propertied
> As all the tuned spheres.

Her longings are 'immortal', and Charmian has leave to play till dooms-day.[7]

If we look for a modern parallel to these we may find something similar in Synge's peculiar use of nature imagery, especially in his later plays, in which it suggests the world surrounding the action but not directly presented in it. This is especially noticeable in *The Playboy of the Western World*, where it reveals the background of the characters and their actions. Synge does not attempt, like Aeschylus and Shakespeare, to reveal a vast, surrounding world of being. He contents himself with using it (most precisely) to reveal an accompanying, but separate part of the experience of his characters.[8] Its presence is an essential part of the natures of the people and of their conduct. That they are, unlike the people in *Riders to the Sea*, unaware of the moulding power of the world outside Flaherty's shebeen, adds subtlety and significance to the functional power with which Synge invests their unconscious references and images. The dialogue is full of brief pictures, either in description or in metaphor, of the empty, isolated, and yet beautiful countryside of Mayo. Inside the bar are the drunken peasant farmers with their dreary lives and their starved but inflammable imaginations. The desolation of the country has crushed their enterprise, its beauty has kept their imaginations living. Out of the conflict comes their aptitude for intoxication, whether by the liquor of Kate Cassidy's wake or by the saga of Christy Mahon's heroic exploit. Synge has presented in the setting of the play the inside of the shebeen, only one of the two worlds they live in. He has thrown upon the imagery and allusions the entire function of revealing a world outside, by which this has been conditioned.

But these are only various forms of one function of imagery, that which reveals the relations between the world of the play and a wider surrounding world or universe. Far more frequent in poetic drama are those functions by which imagery enriches the content and implications that lie within the play itself. And of these perhaps the most frequent is that which reveals or keeps in mind the underlying mood. This not only knits the play together but emphasizes by iteration – and by iteration whose appeal is always to the emotions – the idea or mood which had guided the poet's choice of theme and shaping of form. It may be urged that this second function of imagery must always be at work in any poetic drama which has become a complete work of art; the main preoccupation of the poet's mind must be revealed in greater or less degree by all the aspects of a play that is the issue of that preoccupation. And it is true that iterative imagery, the peculiar function of which is to keep the dominant mood of the whole before us throughout the succession of parts, may be found, in some degree, in any work in which the poet's expression has issued in full artistic expression. But this, in special cases, becomes so clear as to form a continuous and recognizable undertone throughout the play; the under-tone of moonlight and woodland in *A Midsummer Night's Dream*, of light and darkness in *Romeo and Juliet*, of sound and movement in *Much Ado About Nothing*.[9]

The function here is clear. A play is fuller and richer in significance because we are continually in the presence of certain elements in nature, themselves the reflection of the mood in which the play is written. This kind of imagery is distinct from, though it may harmonize with, setting or its Elizabethan equivalent, incidental description. For though the subjects of the images may seem to reproduce the setting, as in *A Midsummer Night's Dream*, much of their potency derives from the fact that they *are* images, called forth not by the immediate need to represent a scene but primarily in response to the poet's perception of a fundamental identity between them and his theme. When Lorenzo exclaims, 'How sweet the moonlight sleeps upon this bank!' we recognize it as a direction to the Elizabethan audience to imagine the setting that could not be presented; it is perhaps hardly more significant than the finest of modern moonlight effects. But when Othello says,

> It is the very error of the moon.
> She comes more near the earth than she was wont
> And makes men mad,[10]

the passage is suffused with a spellbound bewilderment, half of enchant-ment, half of nightmare, like that which sometimes follows the awakening from deep unconsciousness into the strange radiance of moonlight. Othello's mind is revealed to us in one brief piece of metaphorical illumi-nation, the moon linking his vision of oncoming madness with the familiar, cognate physical experience in which it is imaged. In just such a way, the iterative imagery of moonlight in *A Midsummer Night's Dream* has, because it *is* imagery, the power to release associations of far fuller content than could be achieved by a long expository analysis. The picture of virginity, 'Chanting faint hymns to the cold, fruitless moon', illuminates with its implications and charged associations a play whose central action is a tangle of cross-purposes and apparent frustrations in love.

Closely related with this service, that of qualifying and enriching each part of a play by continually recalling the moon or preoccupation from which all derive, are certain functions whereby imagery helps to amplify, to make subtler and more detailed the nature or relation of events, the bases of character, the content or processes of thought, which might else suffer impoverishment from the rapidity and compression of the dramatic form.

In the opening scenes of a play in which events are to move swiftly we often find a kind of anticipation, not only of the mood of the subsequent action, but of the very events themselves; some hint, in the subject of an image, of the course of the action, which, though we may not notice it consciously, sinks into the mind and prepares us to accept more rapidly some series of events which is to follow. This is a genuine dramatic function; imagery, that is to say, which is thus used in drama is functional to a high degree.

One of the Jacobean poetic dramatists, John Webster, seems to have developed almost consciously this function of imagery; we may notice that the action of his plays is of precisely that copious and rapid kind which most needs such aids as this if it is to maintain depth and significance. In the first scene of his *Vittoria Corombona*, where the fate of Lodovico reveals in miniature the passions and forces at work on the main action of the play, the speeches are shot with imagery that is prophetic not only of those passions, but of the kinds of events which they may (and in fact do) draw down:

> Fortune's a right whore:
> If she gives ought she gives it in small parcels,
> That she may take away all at one swoop.

This is a not unusual Elizabethan image and it is only one of many that might have satisfied Lodovico's hatred of fortune, but it is not insignificant that one of the first words that rings out distinctly in this scene is 'whore', which is to be bandied to and fro around Vittoria through the rest of the play and sums up one interpretation of the main part of the action. And the swoop of destruction is the fit image of the sudden turns of fortune and of the final catastrophe. Fortune in the later part of this image has already become in part a bird or beast of prey. In the next lines Lodovico's 'great enemies' become 'your wolf', the fitting embodiment of the predatory and ruthless figure of Flamineo, who guides and twists the action to his ends, only himself to founder in swift-moving destruction. 'An idle meteor', Gasparo calls Lodovico, to be 'soon lost i' the air'; and we have another image of the later action, in the brilliant and blazing careers of Vittoria, Brachiano, Flamineo, which vanish into sudden extinction, 'driven I know not whither'. And the images from knives, swords, and daggers here, 'I'll make Italian cut-works in their guts', 'Great men sell sheep thus to be cut in pieces', point on with sinister precision to the details of the final havoc.[11]

Sometimes a still subtler form of this use may be found in Shakespeare's works. In the first and third scenes of *Cymbeline* there is a series of images connected with or spoken by Imogen, which unobtrusively conveys her isolation, her exposure to the pricks of malice and of evil eyes,[12] and does this more quickly and more fully than would much direct comment from other characters. By helping to convey her position, it helps also to convey the balance of the situation, the hostility surrounding her, upon which much of the subsequent action depends.

Closely akin to this use, though probably more usual and possibly more powerful, is the aid given by imagery to the rapid and significant revelation of character. How much more impressive and vivid are the brief imagistic summaries of character given at the beginning of *The Duchess of Malfi* than, for instance, Ben Jonson's lucid and often exquisitely balanced character analyses in *Cynthia's Revels*. How much deeper, indeed, than the impression made by these intellectual expositions is that of the imaginative picture of Ben Jonson's own Volpone?

> A fox
> Stretched on the earth, with fine delusive sleights,
> Mocking a gaping crow.

This, or some part of the picture called up by it, stays in the memory for the rest of the play and guides us, quicker than pages of character study, to the right interpreting of Volpone's character in the action which immediately follows. Just such is the function of the image, in the *Duchess of Malfi*, which introduces the Cardinal and Ferdinand; they are 'plum-trees that grow crooked over standing pools; they are rich and o'er-laden with fruit, but none but crows, pies and caterpillars feed on them'.

In all these the function of revealing character has fallen upon the associations of the subject in which it is imaged. But there is another and sometimes subtler use of image which occurs also in a large number of the Jacobean dramatists. In this the characters reveal themselves by their instinctive choice of subjects in which to image their thought and often also by the form of the image, by the relation, that is, between subject and theme. The work of Webster, Tourneur, and Shakespeare is full of imagery which has this profoundly dramatic function.[13] Shakespeare's later characters, and in some degree those of his middle period, have their individual imagery. It is related inevitably to the underlying mood out of which the play is, like the characters, generated, but is yet subtly distinguished, within the limits of that character's relation to the whole. Hamlet, Claudius, and Gertrude; Macbeth, Lady Macbeth, Macduff, Ross, and even the murderers have their own trend of imagery in subject or in form or in both; so again have Timon, Lear, Edmund, Antony, Cleopatra, Prospero.[14]

The imagery of Claudius and Gertrude furthers, without our necessarily being aware of the means, our understanding both of their characters and of their relationship. Indeed, certain of the 'problems' of the play might with advantage be referred to the findings of a detailed analysis of these two significant groups. A brief indication of their function may perhaps serve here to indicate the value of the direct and unobtrusive revelation of character which can be made by imagery. The imagery of Claudius's public speech differs from that of his speech in private, though there are some fundamental resemblances. On formal occasions it is brief, superficial, and commonplace; illustrating his statements in a clear, efficient way that is hardly ever imaginative. The subjects of the images are homely, drawn from everyday life, frequently from warfare or military life, and sometimes from the operations of justice. He seldom surprises us by revealing anything beneath this surface, though he can sometimes, as in endeavouring to conciliate Laertes, become inept.[15] In private life, when he is alone, with Gertrude whom he can deceive easily or with certain courtiers such as Polonius whom he deceives hardly less easily, it is more vigorous and reveals more and more of the obsessions against which he struggles. It is still simple and generally homely, the index of a mind that is astute and practical rather than speculative or imaginative. But it is no longer superficial or perfunctory. The disturbance and sickness of his mind betrays itself in ever-recurring images of pestilence, infection, poison, and disease, especially hidden disease that feeds on the 'pith of life', to reveal itself suddenly. The habit of concealment and the dread of discovery find their release in images of painting and false colouring like that of the 'harlot's cheek'; sin is 'rank' and 'smells to heaven'.

In Gertrude's speech there are remarkably few images, and those generally colourless and drawn almost entirely from commonplace themes. They have little vigour and hardly ever call up a vivid picture: the images of a mind that has never received sharp or deep impressions, that is, in fact, incapable of any imaginative effort. Some light is perhaps thrown upon the boundaries of these two natures and of the place at which they meet by even a cursory glance at the mental habits revealed by the images.

Most, as I have suggested, of the characters of Shakespeare's maturity will be found to have in some degree their native imagery. The contrast between that of Macbeth and Lady Macbeth is too clear to justify a brief examination; a full study of each character could, like Miss Spurgeon's picture of Falstaff, be built up from the images alone. Even in subsidiary characters or in those which closely resemble each other, some traces of individual imagery can be found, contributing, whether we recognize it or not, to our quicker apprehension of their distinctive qualities; in the speech of Regan there is a slight preponderance of images drawn from calculation, wealth contrasted with poverty; in that of Goneril a similar preponderance of images drawn from passion and the uncurbed experience of the senses. In the speech of Edmund, images from disease and maiming conflict (especially at the beginning of the play) and alternate with those drawn from the elemental energies of nature, and both are crossed again by others, from the exercise of skill, of adroit and successful manipulation. With him, as with Claudius, the native strain is stronger in solitude and subdued or disguised in public.

The same poetic revelation of character and mental preoccupation may be traced in dramatists of far more limited range than Shakespeare, who are also, within their limits, capable of nice distinctions in this field. One of the most consciously precise of his contemporaries is Cyril Tourneur, whose *Atheist's Tragedy* offers a group of characters all differentiated by this means. In spite of Tourneur's conscious psychological exposition, a great part of our understanding of the characters is actually due to our largely unconscious assimilation of what is revealed by their images. D'Amville's character, the most potent and virile in the play, is revealed in outline by his actions and his cogent and fiery commentary; but in the last analysis it is mainly to the subjects and the form of his images that we owe an impression of a character in which power of imagination has been deliberately balanced by the playwright against a scientist's approach to and treatment of fact. Brief but highly charged poetic images are followed by the lucid, often sustained illustrative or intellectual imagery in which Tourneur delighted.[16] In marked contrast with D'Amville's is the imagery of Sebastian in the same play; plain, pithy, and with excellent relating of theme to subject, but the imagery of a shrewd and energetic practical mind. In marked contrast again is that of Levidulcia, which, in addition to being voluble and commonplace, shows a loose linking of subject and theme, not in a single instance and to indicate a momentary uncertainty, as with Claudius, but so constantly that we realize it as the very habit of her mind. Her conduct throughout the play testifies to a slipshod mental process; the structure of her own images reflects it.[17]

This, which is one of the most important of the dramatic functions of imagery, is frequent in the Elizabethan drama. It can be traced in much other poetic drama, whether in verse or prose, but falls into abeyance, as does all living imagery of whatever function, in prosaic and naturalistic drama. It returns, as do those other kinds, with the revival of poetic drama in our own century, though the absence of live metaphor in the common speech of our time has an inevitable reaction upon the language of our drama and upon the playwright's choice of themes and characters. A conscious and deliberate use of imagery to fulfil this and other cognate functions is to be found in certain kinds of analytical drama, in expressionist drama, especially when this approaches surrealist technique, and in plays of specific psychological theme. But even in these it is less abundant, I think, than in the drama of the great poetic period; Strindberg, Kaiser, and O'Neill (to instance only a few) do not use it so amply as the Elizabethans.

There is yet another function of dramatic imagery which, though less usual than those we have already considered, is still of great service in giving fullness of content despite dramatic compression; that in which imagery does the work of argument or reflection. A discussion or process of deduction may appear full or complete without the tedious and undramatic dilution that we should at once observe if it were in fact complete. In Hamlet's soliloquies imagery, rather than abstract terminology, is generally the medium for the expression of reflection, and when he speaks of 'the native hue of resolution' as 'sicklied o'er with the pale cast of thought', we apprehend in two brief lines a condition of mind which would need many lines or indeed speeches were it to be expounded. And so, throughout the soliloquy, moods and states of mind are revealed by single images or groups and related to each other by the apposition of the images and the transitions from one to another. The effect of a long psychological diagnosis is thus given in one speech, without diluting the dramatic concentration.

In certain other passages in Shakespeare's plays[18] the way in which the images are placed in relation to each other implies a train of thought linking image with image which is, upon analysis, found to be itself an argument. The original train of thought is thus started afresh in the minds of an audience who can catch the successive implications of the images, so that at the end of the speech they have experienced the equivalent of a long argument in the compass of a relatively brief speech, simply by virtue of the power with which imagery is charged to stimulate and to illuminate the imagination. Almost the whole of the conversation between Achilles and Ulysses (*Troilus and Cressida*, II. iii) is of this kind; imagery is used by both speakers (but chiefly by Ulysses) not only to express single reflections but also to imply the relationship between a sequence of reflections. This is perhaps most clear in Ulysses' central speech (III. iii. 145-90), where the transition from image to image – from the oblivion caused by ungrateful Time to perseverance which 'keeps honour bright', from past virtue, which is 'to hang Quite out of fashion' to the fierce competition of the narrow way of honour – give by the shock of their juxtaposition, the stimulus which stirs the imagination not only to apprehend the image but to apply the inferences to which these deliberately contrasted images are designed to lead us. Though this function appears perhaps most frequently and most powerfully in *Troilus and Cressida*, that play is by no means alone in this respect. Parts of *Hamlet* and much of *Measure for Measure* on the one hand and of *Timon* on the other depend for their effect upon this function.

In reflective and in religious poetry we often find images used not only (as in Hamlet's speech) to express an idea, but also to reveal spiritual experiences which, it would appear, could not have been expressed (or not by that writer) in the language of abstract statement. When Wordsworth says,

> For I must tread on shadowy ground, must sink
> Deep – and, aloft ascending, breathe in worlds
> To which the heaven of heavens is but a veil,

we are in the presence of imagery of this kind. Sometimes, but not often, drama enters this territory, and when it does we often find that it is to imagery that the poet turns as the quickest and most potent – sometimes, it may be, the sole – means of expressing a thought impossible to convey in disquisition or in action unless these were intolerably and undramatically extended. When Chapman's Byron in the hour of death reflects that he is seated 'betwixt both the heavens', he takes leave of the world in a series of pictures which attempt to image the approaching disintegration of the mind in death, an experience which neither Chapman nor his hero would have found easy to expound or to analyse in abstract terms:

> Wretched world,
> Consisting most of parts that fly each other,
> A firmness breeding all inconstancy,
> A bond of all disjunction; like a man
> Long buried, is a man that long hath lived;
> Touch him, he falls to ashes: for one fault,
> I forfeit all the fashion of a man.
> Why should I keep my soul in this dark light,
> Whose black beams lighted me to lose myself?

Shakespeare's Troilus, revealing to Ulysses his conception of his state, uses imagery in the same way; his need is in fact even more imperative than Byron's, for, though our imaginations receive his meaning readily enough through the medium of the image, it is hard to give either a clear account of the subject apart from the theme or a statement in abstract terms of his precise conception of the relations between the various aspects:

> Oh madness of discourse,
> That cause sets up with and against itself;
> Bifold authority! Where reason can revolt
> Without perdition, and loss assume all reason
> Without revolt.

In just such a way as this Mr T.S. Eliot, in *The Family Reunion*, leaves to imagery the function of revealing much of the thought or of the spiritual experience which would else prove well-nigh inexpressible within the limits of dramatic form. But the function of the imagery here is even more vital than in either of the two other cases, for these thoughts and these experiences are the main stuff of the play, sometimes its sole action. Here, then, is a play in which this peculiar function of imagery is exercised so fully that it would be hard to find a parallel outside the narrative or reflective poetry of mystical experience; yet it is an integral part of the action and thus essentially dramatic in function:

> There are hours when there seems to be no past or future,
> Only a present moment of pointed light
> When you want to burn. When you stretch out your hand
> To the flames. They only come once,
> Thank God, that kind. Perhaps there is another kind,
> I believe, across a whole Thibet of broken stones
> That lie, fangs up, a lifetime's march. I have believed this.

This is not incidental description or commentary; it is the centre of the action because it is the central experience of the chief characters; it is the subject of the play.

The functions of imagery which we have here considered[19] are among the most rapid and potent means of deepening the imaginative significance of a play and thereby helping to transcend the natural limitations of the form. Metaphor, being almost inseparable from poetic expression, must find some place in poetic drama and thus, as the art matures, be drawn into closer and closer functional relation. The functions I have tried to indicate here will, I believe, be found to exist whenever poetic drama rises to a height in any way comparable with that of the Greek and of the Elizabethan. (Nor do I doubt that there are other functions that I have not yet discerned in the drama that I have studied and have been unable to experience in that which I have not.) Many, as I have suggested, are already reappearing today in the poetic drama of Europe and America, and their presence there appears to indicate the operation of a fundamental law of dramatic aesthetics.

Indeed, that this should be so is not improbable, since the history of dramatic form is in one sense a history of its conflict with its own inherent limitations. That imagery should be one means of circumventing these is, it would appear, as inevitable as that certain technical devices, to be examined in detail in the following chapter, should be evolved for a similar purpose. The conflict of dramatic form with its potential content calls into being the peculiar functions of imagery that have been indicated here. The conflict between content and medium leads to the various devices which must now be considered.

NOTES

[1] This refers to Chapters VII and VIII of this volume, and to one on '*Samson Agonistes* and Religious Drama'.

[2] This, as I interpret them, is the view of H.W. Wells, Middleton Murry, S.J. Brown, Elizabeth Homes, C.F.E. Spurgeon, G.W. Knight, and Wolfgang Clemen, among others.

[3] A familiar instance is the work of H. Lenormand in the present century.

[4] Moreover, as Mr Robert Nichols has recently pointed out to me, a high proportion of the imagery in Shakespeare's plays is dynamic and is distinct in this from that static imagery of the sonnets. Here again is reciprocity: action, which is characteristic of Elizabethan drama, is reflected as movement in the functional imagery of that drama.

⁵An example or two may help to make this clear. Ibsen largely (though by no means entirely) discards imagery (as distinguished from symbolism) in *The Pillars of Society* and the succeeding social plays. But he achieves strength of texture by that close interlocking of event and character that cost him so many revisions. Mr Eliot, in *The Family Reunion*, to take an opposite case, derives great extension of scope from a specialized use of imagery, Galsworthy's *Strife* appears to separate the two functions, obtaining a certain strength of texture by methods not unlike Ibsen's and a certain enriching of meaning by the images of a few of his characters. But in Shakespeare's work both scope and texture are served by imagery, and the plays would be knit together by it even if the structure were unsure.

⁶We may remind ourselves here of the recurrent symbolism of Ibsen, Strindberg, or Maeterlinck, the fragmentary allegory and personification in the early Elizabethans, and the dreams and visions in the work of some of the Jacobeans (notably of Webster and Tourneur); of the expressionism of Strindberg and the succeeding German school, represented in our own day by Toller and Kaiser; of the setting which itself becomes an image of a mental state in parts of *Macbeth*, *Lear* or *Timon*, or in such contemporary plays as Mr O'Neill's *Emperor Jones*, M. Lenormand's *Simoun*, *A L'Ombre du Mal* and, somewhat similarly, in *Le Temps est un Songe* and *L'Homme et ses Fantômes*. (A detail similarly used to excellent ironic effect in our own realistic drama is the firescreen at the beginning of Galsworthy's *Strife*.) We may finally notice how incidental description plays this part in many of the early Elizabethans, most gracefully perhaps in the work of Peele. All these fulfil the function of extending the experience of the reader beyond the actual events, passions, and thoughts presented in the play to include a wider experience equally necessary to a full understanding of what is contained within the play.

⁷These images are not incidental or scattered, as may be suggested by so brief an indication, but constant and frequent, forming, in all these plays and in many others, continuous motives or undertones. (C.F.E. Spurgeon notices, to take a specific case, that in *Antony and Cleopatra* there are no fewer than forty-two recurrences of the word 'world' in the imagery. See *Shakespeare's Imagery*, p. 352.)

⁸See, on Synge's nature imagery and its functions, my *Irish Dramatic Movement*, Chapter VIII.

⁹This has been revealed by the full and lucid analysis of Professor Caroline Spurgeon, to whom I am indebted for the summaries above. See 'Shakespeare's Iterative Imagery' (*British Academy Proc.*, 1931) and *Shakespeare's Imagery* (Cambridge, 1935), especially Part II, 'The Function of Imagery as Background and Undertone in Shakespeare's Art'.

¹⁰It may be questioned whether this is strict imagery. Whether it is or not must depend upon the extent to which we credit Othello with a literal belief in the influences of the heavenly bodies upon human destiny. If we assume in him the qualified belief common to many Elizabethans, the 'influences' would already have become half allegorical and the words therefore metaphorical. It is so that I take them.

¹¹These are only a few of the images that are, I think, charged with this power of

anticipating by pictures or associations the nature of the events that follow. The same functional use can be found in the opening scene of Webster's second play, *The Duchess of Malfi*, in both of Tourneur's (especially the *Revenger's Tragedy*) and, in an elementary form, as early as Marston's *Antonio and Mellida*. It was, I think, well understood (though not necessarily consciously understood) among many of the dramatists of the early Jacobean period.

[12]'Evil-eyed', 'tickle', 'wounds', 'hourly shot of angry eyes', 'gall', 'a pinch . . . more sharp', 'a touch more rare', 'needle', 'prick', 'sharp as any needle', 'gnat', etc.

[13]C.F.E. Spurgeon has made a detailed analysis of the imagery of Falstaff, showing in what ways and to what extent it reveals his character (*Shakespeare's Imagery*: Appendix VII). It will be seen in this examination that the character could be reconstructed from the images alone, with their revelation of the content of the mind.

[14]I have instanced here only a few out of many characters. Upon some of these, and upon others that I have not cited, see Wolfgang Clemen: *Shakespeares Bilder*, especially pp. 149-51, 176-9, 207-11, 222-4.

[15]   The great love the general gender bear him;
        Who, dipping all his faults in their affection,
        Would, like the spring that turneth wood to stone,
        Convert his gyves to graces. (IV. vii.)

This is the result of an over-anxious effort to persuade and convince. And Shakespeare had doubtless observed that this effort sometimes causes even so astute an intelligence as Claudius's to lose itself in words. Claudius seldom uses extended metaphors, and I know of no other passage in which he has constructed one whose two sides are not aptly related. The changing of wood into stone by a petrifying spring is a highly unsuitable picture of the transforming of Hamlet's punishment into additional grace or charm by the affection of the people. If it says anything, it says the opposite of what Claudius would have it mean – the inflexible stone replacing the live and flexible wood is a process the reverse of that by which the encumbering fetters add to Hamlet's graces.

I have examined this one passage in some detail because, taken in conjunction with the rest of Claudius's imagery in public speech – plain and straightforward as it usually is – this is a delicate indication of the fumbling uncertainty of his mind in this scene.

[16]Special reference may be made to certain passages: *The Atheist's Tragedy*, II. iv. 104-8, 203-4, IV. iii. 244-58, and V. i. 94-100. For a fuller analysis of Tourneur's imagery in a somewhat different connection, see my article, 'The Imagery of *The Revengers Tragedie* and *The Atheist's Tragedie*'. *The Modern Language Review*, July 1935, and for his use of imagery to reveal character, mood, and temperament see my *Jacobean Drama*, pp. 160-1.

[17]This culminates and is best illustrated in the soliloquy before her suicide, where the confusion between the various rivers, fountains, and oceans and their

relation to the passions and deeds that they are called upon to image defy elucidation. There is, of course, no question but that Tourneur's art here is conscious and deliberate.

[18]Upon a cognate but slightly different use of imagery as a general medium for reflection in Shakespeare see Wolfgan Clemen: *Shakespeares Bilder* (Bonn, 1936), Section II, 'Reflexion in Bildern'. 'Bilder', according to Clemen, 'werden mehr und mehr zu einer Hilfe der Gedanken der Menschen, zu einer bedeutsamen Kristallisation ihres Nachdenkens' (p. 105). And see also Section III, especially pp. 131-2, 149-51. Clemen's book was revised and translated as *The Development of Shakespeare's Imagery* (London, 1951).

[19]Like all students of this subject, I have a considerable debt to the clear thought and the imaginative analyses of Dr Clemen's study of Shakespeare's imagery. The functions I have considered are not always those to which he attaches most importance and my categories differ somewhat from his, while sometimes overlapping. For his interesting and exhaustive examination of Shakespeare's early imagery, the reader is referred to the first part of his book (*Shakespeares Bilder*), especially to pp. 30-1, 46, 50, 52, 57, 62, 71, 73, 82, 85-6, 105; for the analysis of the imagery of the great tragedies, to the later parts, especially Sections III and IV.

VII

Shakespeare's political plays

In the sequence of the history plays, Shakespeare, as I have suggested in an
earlier chapter, achieved a reconciliation of epic material with dramatic
form, somewhat as Milton, in *Samson Agonistes*, transmuted the matter
of religious experience into drama. In studying Milton's play, we were
drawn imperceptibly into describing its dramatic power; for the reality of
the religious experience was self-evident, and the question whether or not
the reconciliation had been achieved rested upon that of whether or not
the resulting work was dramatic. With Shakespeare's histories we find
ourselves, equally of necessity, approaching from the opposite direction.
We do not, at this point in Shakespeare studies, question whether
individual plays are dramatic, but we may well question whether or not the
series contains the material of epic. We may perhaps suggest in what ways
and by what means they have preserved the spaciousness and coherence of
their epic material as well as the concentration and immediacy of drama.

The spaciousness has been preserved by the fact that we have primarily
a group of four central plays supported by at least four or five more (one of
which is of unquestioned dramatic power), extending together over
several historical periods and introducing some two hundred different
characters. This, of course, does not in itself guarantee the effect of
vastness; it might merely guarantee chaos. But the balance and relating of
characters in Shakespeare's hands are such that we experience the multifariousness of life and not mere confusion. The presence of some element
of continuity between the plays of the main and even of the subsidiary
group[1] is, I think, less obvious; but it is this which ultimately gives

coherence to the wealth of material. In fact, it is precisely here that the challenge of epic form to dramatic material arises. For a series of plays on related themes, with a certain number of overlapping characters, though clear and ordered in their individual disposal of their material, might yet remain no more than a number of excellent individual works of art, illuminating each other, but affording no continuous and coherent image, no central, emergent idea. Now, in most epic material we find a central figure, some aspect of whose life and experience forms a theme to which, should an epic poem be written upon that subject, everything in the poem could be made to contribute. Each character, episode, or group of events could bear, that is, a necessary relation to this central figure or idea, illuminating and illuminated by it, while at the same time maintaining its own relation, in the spatial and chronological scheme of the poem, with the other characters, episodes, and events. Aeneas's wanderings are a naturally shaped sequence, and can be causally related in a work of art, provided that all that is included affects or illuminates his experience and purpose.

This complete cohesion is characteristic only of the epic itself; there is, as a rule, only potential cohesion in the raw epic material. But is there anything akin to this potential continuity of epic material in the series of Shakespeare's political plays? Can we distinguish in them something which relates what would else be isolated units, causing them to illuminate each other and to contribute, each in turn, some indispensable part of a whole whose balance would be impaired without it?

I think we can distinguish some such factor in Shakespeare's series but, as I have suggested, it will not be found in the generally prevailing mood of nationalism (and his attitude to nationalism passes through many phases between the writing of *Henry VI* and the writing of *Henry V*) nor in any single character. The central and continuous image in these plays, more specific than a mood, more comprehensive than a character, is, I believe, a composite figure – that of the statesman-king, the leader and the public man, which Shakespeare builds up gradually through the series of the political plays from *Henry VI* to *Henry V*. This figure recurs, in varying forms, through the greater part of Shakespeare's drama, for after the picture is completed in the political plays he appears to revise and reconsider it, studying it from a different angle in several of the tragedies and late plays. For the purposes of this discussion we are concerned with the political plays, and chiefly with those four in which Shakespeare achieves simultaneously the abundance of epic material and the cogency of drama. But I have permitted myself, in order to indicate the vastness and complexity of this image, to include some evidence of his later thought;

the revaluation, by reason of which he builds up a contrasting portrait, thereby making explicit and definite what had been implicit in that first portrait with which we are primarily concerned.

The portrait of the statesman-king is the result of a series of explorations, now the study of a failure, now of a partial success; a vast, closely articulated body of thought imaged always in terms of actual character, yet completely incorporated in no one character. The figure that finally emerges is not Falconbridge or Theseus or Henry IV or Henry V, yet it would be incomplete if any one of them were taken away; nor is it the mere opposite of Henry VI or John or Richard III or Richard II, yet it would also be incomplete if one of these were destroyed. These separate images are but statements or qualifications contributing to that vast image, no one of them in itself coextensive with the composite whole. It is this which gives coherence to the material of the history plays, which nevertheless remain individual works of art. If it is true that Shakespeare has thus subdued potential epic material to dramatic form, may we now consider in more detail certain plays, in order to see how the emergent figure of the king dominates and draws to itself the whole of the central series?

Of the figures who appear in Shakespeare's political plays, we need survey only a certain group – the men upon whom the highest offices devolve. Inevitably, with an Elizabethan or Jacobean writer, this means the office of kingship, or of leadership in some form very like kingship. The position may be reached by violence and usurpation or by peaceful inheritance; in the first place the man may be capable of maintaining it and so partly justified in his action, or incapable of what he attempts, and so lose it; in the second case he may lend himself willingly to the task or it may be thrust upon an unwilling or inadequate man. But in every case, from his earliest to his latest work, Shakespeare makes an imaginative exploration of the experience, adding something to the vast body of his comment on the figure of the statesman-king. Moreover, he is, broadly speaking, concerned in his Elizabethan phase mainly with what the office requires in the man, in his Jacobean phase with what the office does to the man. He passes, that is, from an interest centred chiefly in building up the picture of an ideal king or leader, to a study of the effect on the individual of the demands and privileges of his office.

Shakespeare's first explorations of this field seem to have been incidental to other work and to have led him, for the most part, to negative conclusions. The process by which he feels his way towards the centre of the experience is familiar to all his readers. The figure of Henry VI is the first which he is forced to consider (and at this early stage there presumably was an element of compulsion in the choice of the theme), and by his way of portraying the disasters of that reign Shakespeare shows clearly that he perceives some element of kingliness to be lacking. Henry is a pious, reflective man, by no means lacking in dignity, with a conscientious, but not necessarily intelligent, sense of his position. In an age when kings must be equally competent in peace and war, he is too simple for a politician (much less a statesman) and too ready to trust to conciliation to be a soldier. He lets his wife and his supporters fight his battle while he sits upon a hill alongside the field and laments that he has not been born a shepherd; yet at his death he claims in all good faith that he has loved his people and is convinced that they have no cause to desert him. A good man, a conscientious man, admirably suited for certain kinds of private, or, better still, monastic life; but neither firm, intelligent, shrewd, nor capable. A figure that tells us clearly that Shakespeare has already marked and inwardly digested the admonitions of the seventh chapter of Machiavelli's *Prince* and sees that ruthlessness is sometimes merciful and that a 'dangerous lenity' has no place among the 'king-becoming graces'.

Nor, for the matter of that, has a pure self-seeking individualism, and this type of leader he unhesitatingly despatches at the end of *Henry VI* and in the course of *Richard III*. What may be briefly termed the Tamburlaine-Hotspur-Essex-Byron figure that fascinated Chapman, the great lawless sixteenth-century nobleman whose purpose was his own glorification, had short shrift at Shakespeare's hands. Actually Richard III receives less consideration as a type of leader than almost any other figure. He stands, in the group of Shakespeare's kings, as a crude but highly coloured specimen of the Tudor adventurer, storming his way to power, possessing the kingdom by violence, but unstable both on account of the violence of his passion and of some weakness inherent in the act of usurpation itself.

Indeed, it is this attitude of possessiveness that Shakespeare seems next to notice as one at least of the factors in the downfall of many leaders, and, as he defines it more clearly in *King John*, there forms behind it the shadowy suggestion of an opposite quality which comes, in the end, to be the essence of Shakespeare's positive ideal of kingship. The kings and rulers in *King John* all talk of their countries in terms of possession; the country is their property, they are landlords whose responsibilities go no further than treating it well enough to get a good yield from it; being men of sense, they preserve or protect it so that it does not depreciate, but there is no glimmer in their minds of any other feeling. Only in the mind of Salisbury, which misgives him at the thought of bringing civil war among the people he should protect, and in that of Falconbridge, who sees that the king is responsible for putting courage and good heart into his people, is there anything further. In Falconbridge we have a positive, if simple, ideal of service, a positive picture of kingly bearing and, incidentally, certain attributes that reappear in all Shakespeare's later successful kings; tenacity, resourcefulness, and shrewdness.

It is at this point that Shakespeare pauses to sum up, in a somewhat unexpected place, the positive findings of these first four political plays. The findings have, we admit, been up to now mainly negative – it is easier to write dramatically about disastrous reigns than about calm and prosperous ones, and there were more on record in the late sixteenth century. A king must not be submissive, conciliatory, and retiring (like Henry VI), however pious and conscientious; still less must he be a self-indulgent sentimentalist like Edward IV. But neither must he be a marauding egotist like Richard III, nor a landlord of his country like John, Philip, and the King of Austria. All these bring disaster with them and themselves end in disaster, because, however else they may differ, they are all at bottom individualists who have not sunk their individualism in their office of leader. It matters little to Shakespeare, at this stage and in this connection, whether the individualism take the form of withdrawal from the world or of rapacious assault upon it, whether the natural habitat of the mind be a monastery or a battlefield. Both alike fail to meet the demands of sixteenth-century kingship because they do not think primarily of their office as a demand.

And it is here that the other figure to which I referred is interposed, that short study of a king who is indeed kingly; firm, just, even-tempered, possessed of a broad humanity and the characteristic Tudor love of his people, which, while it will no longer regard them as counters in an international gamble, yet knows precisely how to make a discreet display of that humanity and that love, so as to rivet unshakably the affections of those people. In the consciousness of the political value of these affections, no less than in the already slightly cynical realization of the manipulation needed to keep them at their height, Shakespeare has made a long step forward from the group of early historical plays.

Theseus. What are they that do play it?

Philostrate. Hard-handed men, that work in Athens here,
   Which never labour'd in their minds till now;
   And now have toiled their unbreathed memories
   With this same play, against your nuptial.

Theseus. And we will hear it.

... What poor duty cannot do, noble respect
Takes it in might, not merit.
Where I have come, great clerks have purposed
To greet me with premeditated welcomes;
Where I have seen them shiver and look pale,
Make periods in the midst of sentences,
Throttle their practis'd accent in their fears,
And, in conclusion, dumbly have broke off,
Not paying me a welcome. Trust me, sweet,
Out of this silence yet I pick'd a welcome:
And in the modesty of fearful duty
I read as much as from the rattling tongue
Of saucy and audacious eloquence.

This, it may well be contended, is not Theseus speaking, but, rather, a greater than Theseus, the last and greatest of the Tudor monarchs, who had 'the heart of a king and of a king of England, too'. But, what is equally significant for our purpose, it is already an anticipation of one of the dominant voices from the next group of plays, the group of the major histories, whose task is to build up the positive figure of kingship, to which the group of minor and preliminary histories have so far contributed only negative suggestions. The ground, then, has been thoroughly cleared by the time Shakespeare reaches the great tetralogy (*Richard II, Henry IV, I and II, Henry V*), and a few positive suggestions have been made.

The portrait of Richard II defines more clearly what is already implied, the fatal weakness of self-indulgent egotism, even though it be accompanied by private graces or virtues. But it adds, far more strongly, a picture of the fatal blindness that arrogates to itself the privileges of kingship while disregarding the responsibilities on whose account alone the privileges exist. Shakespeare's effective leaders, Falconbridge, Theseus, Henry IV, Henry V, Claudius, all see with perfect clearness the essential reciprocity of these two, and the last three at least have no sentimental illusions about either. Richard, in whom the sense of privilege amounts to megalomania, serves to define the extreme of that position, just as his immediate successor, Henry IV, defines the extreme position of the man oppressed by the sense of responsibility. (Here, as in so much else, it is Henry V who achieves the balance and reconciliation of the two.)

Not all the water in the rough rude sea
Can wash the balm from an anointed king;
The breath of worldly men cannot depose

The deputy elected by the Lord:
For every man that Bolingbroke hath pressed,
To lift shrewd steel against our golden crown,
God for his Richard hath in heavenly pay
A glorious angel. Then, if angels fight,
Weak men must fail, for Heaven still guards the right.

But Richard, with his extravagant claims, serves a further purpose. His half-inspired, half-insane religiosity sees in the holder of his office the immediate representative of God on earth, claims for the king a consequent divinity, and genuinely believes that the hosts of Bolingbroke will fall before the 'glorious angels' whom 'Heaven for his Richard hath in heavenly pay'. That there is something in what he says Shakespeare never, either at this time or before or after it, denies. In this particular play the very difficulty of dislodging Richard from the throne indicates it clearly, and in the earlier play we find that Henry VI is equally difficult to remove, while the courageous and astute Richard of Gloucester maintains his balance only with great difficulty and for a short time. There *is* something sacred in inheritance, and, though the evidence of the early plays has all pointed to the forming of this idea, it is in *Richard II* that, at a touch, it suddenly crystallizes out. Henry VI and Richard II, in their different ways inadequate men, have strong titles; and an unflawed title, if not half the king, is at least an important part of him. It is at least difficult to 'wash the balm from an anointed king' though it may not – and indeed does not – need 'all the water in the rough rude sea' to do it.

But if this hectic religiosity, this inflated claim of divine right, is fantastic in Richard's mouth, it is no longer fantastic when it haunts the broken dreams of the dying Henry IV. For the character and position of Henry IV introduce a set of problems the exact opposite of those of Richard II and new in Shakespeare's survey. Henry, fine statesman and excellent ruler as he is, is crippled and frustrated by his flawed title, and the sense of the sacredness of inheritance is as strong in him, who was perpetually reminded of his lack of it, as it ever was in Richard, and is accompanied by a far shrewder estimate of its significance.

The solution of the problems of the two parts of *Henry IV* and *Henry V* is the peculiar contribution of Shakespeare's Elizabethan phase to the summation of his idea of a king, of the man who should fit at every point the demands laid upon him by public office. Henry IV has all the qualities necessary to a king and avoids all the weaknesses of temperament in the portrayal of which the positive qualities have, so far, been implied. He has shrewdness, tenacity, and self-command that already approaches self-concealment; he has the true Tudor sense of the value of discreet popularity. He is as astute as a badger and has very much the same tough courage. He is not self-indulgent, he is not vain, he is not self-absorbed. He is not even a saint or a poet. He is an exceedingly able, hard-working statesman whose career reveals gradually but clearly the main qualification for kingship, the king's sense of responsibility to his people, that sense of service which, while making him no more than the state's greatest servant, makes all his privileges and exemptions, even a measure of autocracy itself, no more than necessary means for that service. Domineering he is, at times, like Shakespeare's prototype of Tudor monarchy, but he has, in the main, decent intentions, and he possesses, through thick and thin, an unfailing, humorous sense of proportion.

Having, then, such potentialities, why is he not the final figure in the group? The answer is obvious after the study of *Richard II*. The flaw in Henry's title, the fatal act of usurpation with which Richard had made such fine play, does indeed cripple his power and, through that, his mental stature, eating into his confidence and bringing down all loftiness of gesture or intention to the necessity of cunning and circumspection. Character no less than tenure suffers thus under the nemesis for an outrage done to the sacredness of inheritance. Henry IV is in nearly all things a potential Henry V and, trembling upon the verge of achievement, he looks into the promised land, and, as so often happens, speaks more explicitly of it than those who have dwelt in it familiarly. That is why it is, I think, impossible to understand Henry V as Shakespeare saw him, the Henry V who never speaks out, unless we can see his position and his intentions through the eyes of Bolingbroke's frustration:

> Heaven knows, my son,
> By what by-paths, and indirect, crook'd ways
> I met this crown: and I myself know well
> How troublesome it sat upon my head.
> To thee, it shall descend with better quiet,
> Better opinion, better confirmation:
> For all the soil of the achievement goes
> With me, into the earth.

It is left to Henry V to gather up in himself all that is fitting and necessary to a king and to remain as the epitome of the Elizabethan idea of the 'polliticke vertues'. Shakespeare has at last resolved his demands upon such a figure into certain clearly defined qualifications and summed them

all in Henry V, with his unflawed, hereditary title and his assured possession of all kingly attributes. With his broad-based popularity, his genuine
love of public service for its own sake, his strong sense of responsibility,
and his equally clear sense of its relation to privilege, his shrewd statesman's brain, successfully masked as that of a simple soldier, he stands
where, perhaps, no king in drama has stood before or after him. Church
and state, commoners and noblemen, soldiers and civilians, he knows
them all, with a knowledge rooted in the taverns of Eastcheap, and holds
them in his hand, too practised, popular, and secure to make a show of
mastery. He was a statesman fulfilling Burke's demand – he knew how
the whole world lived. He was a monarch, modelled upon the greatest of
the Tudors, Elizabeth herself. It probably happens to every man to believe,
at one time or another, for a time at least, that the greatest of the arts is
conduct. And it is some such experience as this, in Shakespeare's career,
that lies, I think, at the base of the great historical studies culminating in
the figure of Henry V.

But if this were all, the composite figure would be shorn of half its
subtlety and magnitude. We are aware already in this play that Shakespeare has gone beyond the experience he is primarily describing; that,
implicit in this carefully balanced study, this culmination of so long and
careful an exploration, is the germ of some later revulsion of thought
which refutes it, as the great destructive speeches of Timon refute
Ulysses' speech on the beauty of degree, of the ordered hierarchical state.
For a while, it may be, between the writing of *Henry IV* and *Henry V*,
Shakespeare believed the highest achievement of man to be the ordered
state he afterwards described in *Troilus and Cressida*, the image of the
ordered universe, of the cosmos with its regulated spheres.

> The Heavens themselves, the planets and this centre,
> Observe degree, priority and place,
> Insisture, course, proportion, season, form,
> Office, and custom, in all line of order: . . .
>   But when the planets
> In evil mixture to disorder wander,
> What plagues, and what portents, what mutiny?
> What raging of the sea? Shaking of earth?
> Commotion in the winds, frights, changes, horrors,
> Divert and crack, rend and deracinate
> The unity and married calm of states
> Quite from their fixture? O, when degree is shak'd,

(Which is the ladder to all high designs)
The enterprise is sick. How could communities,
Degrees in schools, and brotherhoods in cities,
Peaceful commerce from dividable shores,
The primogenitive and due of birth,
Prerogative of age, crowns, sceptres, laurels,
(But by degree) stand in authentic place?
Take but degree away, untune that string,
And hark what discord follows.

The keystone of this order was the figure of the perfect public man, of Henry V. All the implications of the foregoing plays point to this ultimate emergence of the complete figure. In all the anticipations that lead up to him, and particularly in the later scenes of the second part of *Henry IV*, Shakespeare has, he would seem to imply, 'in this rough work, shaped out a man'; the great art of conduct, and of public conduct at that, is at last truly understood.

But has he? Or has he, as it were unawares, and led already on to some perception beyond his immediate purpose, shaped out instead something that is at once more and less than a man. Henry V has indeed transformed himself into a public figure; the most forbidding thing about him is the completeness with which this has been done. He is solid and flawless. There is no attribute in him that is not part of this figure, no desire, no interest, no habit even that is not harmonized with it. He is never off the platform; even when, alone in a moment of weariness and of intense anxiety, he sees with absolute clearness the futility of privilege and the burden of responsibility, he still argues his case in general terms, a king's life weighed against a peasant's, peasant against king. No expression of personal desire escapes him; though he makes almost the same comparison as Henry VI, he is detached alike from king and shepherd, commenting upon them, but wasting no more strength on imagining what cannot be than on deluding himself, like Richard, with the empty glories of his state. He has inured himself so steadfastly to the life of a king, lived so long in councils and committees, weighing, sifting, deciding, commanding, that his brain automatically delivers a public speech where another man utters a cry of despair, of weariness or of prayer. It is in vain that we look for the personality of Henry behind the king; there is nothing else there. We know how his brain works upon any one of half a dozen problems; the treachery of Cambridge, Grey, and Scroop, the fomenting of wars abroad to preserve peace at home, the disaffection in the army, the difficulties of a formidable campaign, and the equally great dangers of a crushing victory. We see the diplomacy, the soldiership, the vigilant, astute eye upon the moods of people and barons, the excellent acting of a part in court and camp and council-room, and only when we try to look into the heart of the man do we find that it is hardly acting, after all, that the character has been converted whole to the uses of this function, the individual utterly eliminated, sublimated if you will. There is no Henry, only a king.

I think Shakespeare was profoundly interested in this particular study. Not, indeed, by the character, for there is no character, but by the singular circumstances of its disappearance. Neither we the readers nor Henry himself nor his God ever meets the individual that had once underlain the outer crust that covers a Tudor monarch, for there is nothing beneath the crust; all has been converted into it; all desires, all impulses, all selfhood, all spirit. He is never alone, even with his God – least of all when he prays, for then he is more than ever in the council chamber driving an astute bargain, a piece of shrewd diplomacy, between one king and another.

> O God of battles, steel my soldiers' hearts,
> Possess them not with fear. Take from them now
> The sense of reckoning, if th' opposed numbers
> Pluck their hearts from them. Not to-day, O Lord,
> O, not to-day, think not upon the fault
> My father made, in compassing the crown.
> I Richard's body have interred new,
> And on it have bestowed more contrite tears,
> Than from it issued forced drops of blood.
> Five hundred poor I have in yearly pay
> Who twice a day their wither'd hands hold up
> Toward Heaven, to pardon blood. And I have built
> Two chantries, where the sad and solemn priests
> Sing still for Richard's soul. More will I do,
> Though all that I can do is nothing worth;
> Since that my penitence comes after all,
> Imploring pardon.

This king, as Shakespeare portrays him, is indeed 'a wondrous necessary man', the keystone upon which the sixteenth-century state depends, and individuality has at last been subjugated wholly to the demands of office. But it is not for nothing that the generations of Shakespeare's readers have found little to love in this play. Unless we read it in the light of a certain bitter, underlying commentary, implicit in the orientation of the chief character, there is little there but that most grievous product of unremitting office, a dead man walking.

For the truth is that Shakespeare himself, now that he has built the figure with such care, out of the cumulative experience of eight plays, begins to recoil from it. It has been an experiment, an exploration, like, but for its larger scale, his brief but effective exploration of the system of Machiavelli, and, as he did with that system, so he does with this vast body of assembled evidence on public life: he rejects its findings as invalid before the deeper demands of the less explicit but immutable laws of man's spirit.

So much, then, for the Elizabethan phase of Shakespeare's portrait of the statesman-king, for the record of the period when he for a time believed that the wide canvas of public life was greater than the illimitable experience of the spirit. The contrast between the private and public virtues has been made clear, the qualifications of the great statesman have been slowly selected, tested, and built up into a single figure. Such characteristics as did not contribute to his public self have been eliminated (and they are seen, somewhat surprisingly, to be nearly co-terminous with character). More than this, certain of the loyalties, decencies, and ideals most prized in an individual are found to be incompatible with the public virtues. Henry, who rejected Falstaff in circumstances which cannot be forgiven, will also, in the moment of crisis, bargain with his God like a pedlar. His religion and his love for his people alike carry with them a tinge of expediency, a hint of the glib platform speaker.

It would seem, then, that in the very act of completing the figure, Shakespeare became aware of a certain insufficiency, and that dissatisfaction was already implicit in his treatment of Henry V, the culminating study of the series. What was there implicit is revealed by degrees in his treatment in the later plays of similar characters, or characters similarly placed. At the risk of straying a little from the immediate content of this discussion, may we consider Shakespeare's final comments? For the additional significance they lend to the subtlety, the implicit qualification that they bring to light in it.

Now, in the very play which concluded his Elizabethan picture, Shakespeare indicates already the tone and direction of his Jacobean commentary, which is at first merely dissatisfaction and disillusionment. In the course of the corollaries added in the Jacobean period it becomes clear that the disillusionment follows his perception of the true nature of Henry's supreme achievement, the whole and integral subordination of his individuality to the office of leadership. Shakespeare never again gives us a full picture of a successful ruler, with the exception of the figure of Claudius (the somewhat cynical implications of this selection constitute a study in themselves) and for the most part the men who fail, in the Jacobean plays, to meet the demands of public life are of interest not because they prove unfit for office, but because they are unfitted by office for something which Shakespeare increasingly perceives to be of deeper value.

Brutus is the first character in whom Shakespeare studied the wreckage that can be made of a man's conduct and career by the attempt to subject to the traffic of public life ideals deriving from values that cannot necessarily be carried into it. Brutus himself has an intuition of this when he pleads at the beginning with Cassius not to

> have me seek into myself
> For that which is not in me.

For what is in him, the clear sense of justice, the deep honourableness, the assumption that all other men's actions rest on the same spring of honour and clear vision, serve not to better the state, but only to wreck it and him. A coarser and shrewder mind, having the sense to 'hold the world but as the world', could have served the state more effectively. Cassius, from the first, acts openly 'in envy of great Caesar', but Brutus is blinded even to this by his preoccupation with 'the general good', unaccompanied as it is by the essential knowledge of how the world lives. The illumination of his nobler conception cannot be expressed directly in action – not, certainly, by the man whose function it is to transmit the illumination – and this inference, if we are justified in making it of Brutus, points on to the conclusion finally reached in *Antony and Cleopatra*.

But whatever may happen to the conduct and career of the man who mistakenly offers himself to public service, the personality, in this first study, survives the wreck unspoiled. Cassius is wrong, as usual, when he assumed that Brutus's

> honourable metal may be wrought
> From that it is disposed.

The most he does is to make Brutus deceive himself as to the nature of his function, not as to the nature or truth of his vision. Brutus does, indeed, a certain violence to himself in setting before him a picture of an ideal Roman citizen and insisting that he can and must become that man, a theme that Shakespeare explores again and more searchingly in Coriolanus. But Brutus escapes the last penalties even of this; 'I slew my best lover for the good of Rome', but he can in part redeem it, for he has, when it comes to the test, 'the same dagger for myself'. One other comment Shakespeare makes upon the relations of the private and public virtues, fast separating themselves in his mind, when he exposes, though in no way bitterly, the artificiality of this standard of public conduct. In Brutus's reception of the news of Portia's death – 'Portia is dead . . . Speak no more of her . . . Well to our work alive' – this becomes suddenly clear.[2] Ultimately Shakespeare was to overthrow the artificial and shallow conventions of conduct which public office, more than anything else, was likely to impose upon a man. In the meantime he is content to leave Brutus to reveal himself at death in the line 'I found no man but he was true to me' (the personal relations filling his thought at the last), and to conclude all upon the significant comment 'His life was gentle'.

After Brutus, the studies of the effect of public life upon the mind are, for a time, either cynical or tragic. All are studies of disaster in the soul, disaster which seems final in the Duke of Vienna, Angelo, Macbeth, and Coriolanus, and redeemed in Lear only by the miracle of suffering.

The companion studies in *Measure for Measure* stand together; the Duke, who has brought to cunning perfection Henry V's tactics in manipulating his people while adding to them a stronger spice of Machiavelli's, and Angelo, whom he chooses, with matchless irony, as an upright pillar of society. Public life has taken its part in the subversion of both these characters. They are not the only hypocrites in the play, but their particular blends of deception and self-deception are those that it peculiarly fosters. The deep and almost irreparable division in the mind of Angelo comes of the lifelong demeanour of a decent citizen unconsciously supported, like one of Ibsen's 'pillars of society', by the picture of himself that he finds in other men's eyes. The test of contact with Isabella discovers to him a self far other, that public life had hitherto allowed him to hide from. He would be, were it not for his conversion by exposure, as clear a case as could be found of the man

> Qui notus nimis omnibus
> Ignotus moritur sibi.

The two great tragic studies which contribute something to our knowledge of Shakespeare's Jacobean comment on the effects of office upon the individual fall into line rather with the latest plays than with the earlier. In Macbeth and in Lear the catastrophe goes deeper than with Brutus; nobility of nature is poisoned or driven askew by power rather than wrecked by the assumption of mistaken responsibilities. Personality itself is touched, but by the privilege of leadership, not by its demands. Though the theme of *Macbeth* is chiefly the Aeschylean one of crime begetting crime, yet the 'insolence of office' has its share in the growth of that megalomania which cries, 'For mine own good All causes shall give way'. The companion study in *Lear* is that of a man already formed, before the play opens, by the slower working of a more extended term of privilege. He, like an earlier king, was 'not born to sue but to command'; absorbed in the imperiousness that is the natural growth of unrestricted privilege, even in a magnanimous nature, he 'hath ever but slenderly known himself'. Had not catastrophe redeemed him, had it not been for the realization, 'I have ta'en too little care of this', he too might have suffered the fate of Seneca's king: Ignotus moritur sibi.'

Indeed, it is this hiding of the self from the man who escapes it in public life that Shakespeare examines in the last of the great negative studies of the Jacobean series. Coriolanus is the companion figure in the later period, to Henry V in the Elizabethan. The distinction between the figures of Henry V and Coriolanus reveals the distance that Shakespeare's mind has travelled in the interval and the finality of his verdict on his own earlier creation. For Coriolanus is a study of a man bred and reared to public life from infancy, regardless of the suitability of his temperament for the task. He has not, like Henry, subjugated himself to it deliberately; he has been dedicated by Volumnia to the code of his caste. From this springs a mind more deeply divided even than Angelo's, and from that in turn the catastrophe that overwhelms him and nearly subverts the state. Because the identification of man and office has not been spontaneous, the individual that was Coriolanus has been not transmuted, but suppressed. The natural character has never been allowed to grow, and so it has become stunted, thwarted, and ill-regulated, as unreliable and unpredictable as the Roman mob, which is its image in the outward action of the play. More even than Lear or Leontes, he 'hath ever but slenderly known himself', but unlike them he speaks a strange jargon of conventional Roman sentiment, appearing to think in terms of service and loyalties utterly alien to the ruthless, self-seeking underlying nature. For Coriolanus, throughout his career, is acting. But as he has not identified himself with his part and becoming lost in it like Henry V, his sedulous training in public life never quite serves to restrain the hysterical outbursts of rebellion from the inner self that he has never met. He is perfect in the words and gestures of a Roman noble; the generosity to his public foe, Aufidius, the little touches of would-be magnanimity to dependants, the blunt, honest soldier's refusal to take rewards or hear his 'nothings monstered', the deference to Cominius and the senior men of his own party, to his mother and to his wife (a deference which never, somehow, quite amounts to considerateness) – all these he has at his command, and so long as the situations are those he has been schooled to meet, he can present a tolerably coherent and unified front to life. He can say, almost in the words of Brutus, that

> brave death out-weighs bad life,
> And that his country's dearer than himself,

but the fine speeches, the schooled responses, the conditioned reactions, all collapse when the unknown, underlying self is touched by catastrophic failure. This life-long public self stripped away, the maimed personality does not (as indeed it cannot now) seek to discover itself, but only hurries, like a dislodged hermit crab, to find another shell. The ruthless training for office and public life has wrought its full and fatal effect.

As in the preliminary or minor histories Shakespeare gave a mainly negative conclusion on the nature of kingship and followed it up in the major histories by a positive study of what kingship was, so, in the Jacobean plays, he gives first a series of studies (though far less definitely orientated or closely correlated) of individuals sacrificed in one way or another to the exigencies of public life, and leads up to a final and positive study of the individual spirit triumphing over the less substantial claims, the more superficial values of the other. The last detailed comment is that of *Antony and Cleopatra*, which is like a symphonic rendering of the passionate theme of individual freedom, not the childish egotism of Henry VI or Richard II or that later modification in Lear and Macbeth, but the mature realization that upon the individual life of the spirit the world of affairs could have no final claim.

The whole course, then, of Shakespeare's survey of this problem, the choosing out by trial and error of the qualifications proper to a great statesman-king, the welding together of these findings into a single figure, the subsequent surveying of this figure and its implications from a distance and from a world of experience quite other, and the ultimate abandonment both of the figure and of the claims it represented, the whole course of this survey resolves itself ultimately into one conclusion, harmonious alike with the main body of Shakespeare's thought and with the conclusions reached simultaneously by the finest poetic thought of his contemporaries. It is a magnificent plea, first negative and then positive, for the supreme claims of the individual spirit. Shakespeare, from the first, sees, as clearly as Chapman, that there was little place for it in public life, that public life was not best served by it, but he sees equally clearly, and he sees it at the last, that neither is this spirit itself best served by public life. For

Shakespeare, the second conclusion, the final pronouncement of his experience upon this theme, is the valid one.

Of his view of conduct as itself a supreme art, Shakespeare surrenders nothing in this latest phase; but the quality of the conduct which interests him changes profoundly. He, no less than Ford or Webster, sees in it the possibility of sublimity, but, like them, and indeed like all the Jacobeans, he no longer finds its essential expression in the council chamber, the battlefield or the forum, but rather in the inner recesses of the spirit, revealed, if revealed at all, by chance or the accident of affinity. He must have recognized the echo of his own thought in Webster's words,

> For know, whether I am doomed to live or die
> I can do both like a prince,

the words in which his duchess declares her allegiance not to a pattern of conduct imposed by social demands, but to an inner aristocratic ideal, unrealized even by the character itself until that moment. For Shakespeare, too, had by then explored those minds whose purpose is not so much the presentation of a certain figure to the world as obedience to the guidance of certain perceptions, perceptions that not only cannot be directly expressed in public life, but may even be contaminated in the attempt at such direct expression. Henry V and Coriolanus are concerned to present a design for living whose main lines they themselves (with varying completeness) already know. But Hamlet, Lear, Timon, Cleopatra, Antony are concerned not at all with presenting a figure of such and such design, and hardly at all with that conscious uttering of principle in word and action that makes up public conduct. They proceed instead by a half-unconscious subordination of action, and even thought, to the guidance of some often undefined principle (itself perhaps at variance with the verdict of the world or unapprehended by it), which transmutes the character into something of which it itself would remain incompletely aware, unless released in a moment of tragic crisis.

That citadel of absolute truth, the inner self hardly known to the man himself, may be corrupted by the effort to stage himself to the public eye, and to surrender to the demand of public life may well be fatal to that core of the spirit wherein is stored its potential immortality.

Shakespeare's final position is an uncompromising declaration of individual freedom and responsibility, that supreme virtue of which the Jacobeans knew so well the value. 'I have in this rough work shaped out a man.' He has, indeed, throughout the Jacobean period: Brutus, Hamlet, Macbeth, Lear, Timon, Antony, Cleopatra, Prospero. And the shaping has involved the rejection not of Falstaff, but of Henry V.

It is the shaping out of this 'man', the creation of this figure which is no one man but an image to which many characters bring their parts, that makes the historical and political group organic.[3] To maintain that the political plays, even the four that make up the central group, are equivalent to an epic would be a piece of foolish extremism. A work of art cannot at the same time be two different works of art. But it is possible to consider that the sequence, through the continuous presence of this image of the statesman-king, is able to subdue to the dramatic form the vast and apparently undramatic matter of potential epic, without losing the peculiar virtue of epic material, coherent presentation of spaciousness, and of the multifariousness of life.

In Shakespeare's history plays we have, then, I believe, a second instance of hard-won reconciliation of seemingly alien content with dramatic form.

NOTES

[1] The group of plays with which we are mainly concerned here is the series *Richard II, Henry IV (I and II) and Henry V*, for in these four the simultaneous effect of epic space and dramatic concentration may be most clearly observed. But the gradually built-up figure of the king, which gives significance and unity to this central group, is supported by the exploration and commentary of the four earlier plays, and by various studies of kings and statesmen in the later. Accordingly, I have sometimes drawn upon these also for their contributions, whether as a preliminary group whose significant order is that of the writing, or as subsequent observations and conclusions revealing the implications of the main group. There is a certain apparent inconsistency in deriving the union of epic magnitude and dramatic concentration partly from the earlier group of plays for which (with the exception of *Richard III*) we cannot claim the highest dramatic quality, and partly again from several detached later plays for which we cannot claim continuity of subject. But it is more apparent than actual; the contributions of the three earlier plays are almost entirely in the form of negative conclusions and the substance of their findings recapitulated in the main group, while those of the later plays are a revaluation of the central image of that same group. The service of both to the present argument is that of revealing explicitly what is included by implication in the main, and central, group, and thus permitting it to be stated more briefly and with fewer qualifications.

[2] If further comment were needed, it is furnished by two still clearer episodes in the later play of *Macbeth*; one where Siward's stoical reception of his son's death is rebuked by Malcolm's natural humanity, another where Macduff makes his unanswerable appeal to genuine manhood against the artificial standard of conventional manliness:

> Dispute it like a man!
>   I shall do so.
> But I must also feel it as a man.

This, a far more assured and mature comment (not without interesting analogies in other contemporary dramatists), reflects back upon the conventional stoicism of the public man in Brutus and leaves us no doubt as to the conclusion Shakespeare had already drawn there.

[3]It may be urged that these plays are not a planned sequence, that there can therefore have been no continuous design (as in the *Oresteia*) and that the whole cannot have cohered in Shakespeare's mind as the living parts of a great work of art cohere to make an organic whole. In support of this it might be pointed out that the plays were written at fairly wide intervals. But the vast organism of a major work of art must always be held in the artist's mind through a considerable period of time, even if it finally takes the form of a single poem. Interruption of work upon it, the suspension of attention for a time, need not destroy the fundamental continuity of thought for the organic nature of the work of art that is finally produced. How long did Milton hold *Paradise Lost* in mind? And how long did Goethe hold *Faust*?

*the incompatibility of
men's endeavors and their
destinies ...*

VIII

*'Discord in the spheres': the
universe of* Troilus and Cressida

The great play of *Troilus and Cressida*, one of the most weighty in the
Jacobean period, has had a strange fate. Its readers have been variously
affected by it, and our reflections, when we have not taken refuge in
silence, have ranged from dismissing it as a piece of hasty work to
defending it as a failure on a grand scale. Commentators[1] describe, in the
one case, the ill-digested scenes mixed with graver, sometimes noble, matter, and in the other point out that, though Sakespeare had undoubtedly
something which he wished to say (and to say in specifically dramatic
terms), he for once mistook 'what may be digested in a play', and, by sheer
pressure of content, broke the mould he tried to use.

   By repeated readings of the play, helped greatly by seeing it upon the
stage, by trying to relate it to the criticism of life offered by some of
Shakespeare's Jacobean contemporaries (to say nothing of the criticism of
life implicit in some of our own contemporaries), I am driven to believe
that this is not enough; that the play of *Troilus and Cressida* is not a great
failure to record a phase of experience beyond the scope of dramatic form,
but a great achievement, perhaps one of the greatest, in the expression of
that phase, transcending those limitations to produce a living work of art.[2]
That the actual experience which is thus expressed is of deep significance
to our generation I no more doubt than that it is essential to our understanding of Shakespeare's later tragic and constructive plays; but for the
generations between Shakespeare's and our own it has been generally
avoidable, and therefore rare. It is no light matter to suggest that something in any way important to our understanding of the play should have

"disintegration + disruption" of current civilization places ideas of T+C much closer to our imagination

escaped a long succession of commentators. Nor would anyone venture upon doing so today, were it not that our actual experience of disintegration and disruption, so unlike that of any age between, has thrown fresh light upon the nature and foundations of what we call civilization; prospects once mercifully rare are now common and familiar, and much that has not, in the interval, been generally forced upon the imagination, now lies upon the common road for every man's necessary consideration.

The great plays that follow this one in psychological sequence,[3] *Timon of Athens* and *King Lear*, are expressions of a further phase of the same experience; disintegration is accomplished, 'Nature's germens tumble all together, Even till destruction sicken' and the judgement surrenders. In the moment of surrender the mind perceives another dimension of reality, and this perception leads in the end to the positive, spiritual revaluation in the last plays. But *Troilus and Cressida* stands at a lower point of negation in this sequence than *Lear* or even *Timon*. For, while its material is still that of the actual world, the mood is that of a man who has come to the end of that world's resources; emotional, intellectual, and moral values resolve alike into futility; even the imagination, the high constructive power, looking ahead into a dark night of the soul, sees no further ideal form, no 'unbodied figure of the thought' waiting upon creation. This last experience is an area of suffering peculiar to the artist's mind, but it can derive from an experience potentially common to all men, the vision of the disjunction and disintegration of civilization – the ideals it rests upon and the achievements it bequeaths – while these are still co-extensive for him with the universe of thought. It is, in fact, in this very image that Shakespeare chooses to embody his experience in this play. What is recorded in *Troilus and Cressida* is thus the acutest point of suffering in this sequence, before the understanding has surrendered its moral, intellectual, or imaginative synthesis and accepted disintegration; the fullest possible realization of imminent dissolution before its accomplishment brings anaesthesia.

Readers of drama often receive piecemeal the experience of which a play is the record, looking first at individual parts or aspects of it; indeed, it requires either the highest imaginative capacity or prolonged knowledge to receive so complex and so vast an artistic experience as is communicated by a great play. Let us concede to this habit for the moment, if only because it will take us by the shortest road to some essential truths about *Troilus and Cressida*, the consideration of various single aspects being a kind of preliminary exercise before we attempt to receive the communication of the artistic experience.

In *Troilus and Cressida* the aspect we are first aware of is, as in many plays, the material of which it is made. For the artist this has meant the choosing, from the infinite and unselected mass of life, of those groups of characters and events to which his mind turns for the purposes of its as yet undefined interpretation; it is the first step in the substitution of the form of art for the chaos of life. For the reader it means the subject-matter of the play and his general impression derived from it; the series of characters, the chronological sequence of events, the impinging of character and event upon each other. And in *Troilus and Cressida* this take the form of a succession of violently contrasted characters, events, and sentiments. Characters as discordant as Thersites and Troilus, Nestor and Pandarus, Hector and Cressida, Agamemnon and Achilles are forced into continual and jarring contrast, with no attempt to resolve the contradictions in an enveloping mood of humour or pity. Instead, the nucleus of the character-grouping, upon which our attention is continually focussed as in a well-composed picture, is that of Troilus and Cressida; a serious man, by nature heroic and an honest if confused idealist, and a light woman, equally by nature a

> sluttish spoil of opportunity
> And daughter of the game.

The same pitiless enforcing of contrasts is seen in the relation of character and event, the incompatibility of men's endeavours and their destinies; the ideal love of Troilus and the betrayal it meets at the height of its glory; the honourable, heroic code of Aeneas and Diomede, Hector and Agamemnon, and the collapse of that code in Achilles' murder of Hector; the clear, sustained thought of the debates upon principles and policy in the Greek and Trojan council chambers, and the relapse into petty feuds and ambushes, which serves to show how far that noble sanity can work upon event. And as we watch these passions, ideas, and achievements annihilate each other with no promise of compensation or solution, we fall more and more into agreement with Thersites, the showman who is ever at hand to point the futility, the progressive cancelling out to negation.

The materials of *Troilus and Cressida* are thus more obviously at war than those of any other play of Shakespeare's, and their discord has been a main factor in persuading its readers of the unevenness of the play, of the inconsistency in quality and treatment of the different parts, attributable, it might be, to indifference or weariness in the writer or to alternating and unreconciled moods of admiration on the one hand and expostulation, disgust, or disillusionment upon the other.

But what if this effect be itself art? What if disharmony be, not the result of a photographic reproduction of materials that the artist's mind has registered without full comprehension, but a deliberate commentary? For, significant and familiar as is the bitterness, the loathing of life which brought together the elements of *Troilus and Cressida*, the opposing of these is even more notable than the choosing. That aspect of a play which its readers think of as its form is itself a mode of interpretation of the material, having been for the artist the next step in the freeing of 'that unbodied figure of the thought, That gave it surmised shape'. The elements fall into such positions or relations within the scheme of his play as not only emphasize and disengage the nature and quality of each, but indicate the underlying values by which his interpretation of the material was determined.

This is revealed first and most obviously in the sequence of the scenes, and here the effect is best appreciated in a rapid production which preserves the Elizabethan tempo and forces us to see one scene running as it were into the next; by insisting upon their almost merging in presentation, it makes clear to us that they must be merged also in our interpretation; that they are, in fact, inseparable. Thersites or Pandarus (the explicit or the implicit statement of the mood of disillusionment) breaks in upon every scene in which nobility of conception, passion, or conduct is emphasized, following it up, almost before the echoes of the last words have died away. The induction and the conclusion are in the hands of Pandarus. Pandarus' talk precedes the great council-chamber scene in the Greek camp, where Ulysses builds his lofty image of the state; and Nestor and Ulysses (two of the wisest figures of the play) are hardly off the stage before the scurrilous venom of Thersites is poured upon them in the next scene. Straight upon this comes the corresponding council debate in Troy, with its penetrating analysis of one of the fundamentals of the play, the nature of value; and straight upon that again, Thersites calling up vengeance, 'or, rather, the Neapolitan bone-ache', upon both armies. Into this meeting of Thersites and Patroclus come again the Greek leaders, their lofty statesmanship tinged now perforce with politic cunning, and upon that again the scene (III. i) between Pandarus, Paris, and Helen; the feverish frivolity of the background of the war jars bitterly with the scenes of camp and battle and yet is inextricably interwoven with them. Straight upon their urbane and matter-of-fact jesting upon the habit of love, come Troilus's ideal, tremulous anticipations, and into this very scene again, Pandarus, that 'wondrous necessary man'. This handling continues all through the play, but the sifting together of the elements becomes closer and closer as it goes on; Pandarus is nearly always present with Troilus and

Cressida in Troy, and Thersites takes his place in the scene of Troilus's disillusionment in the Greek camp. The highest altitudes of chivalry are touched in the scene of Hector's visit to Agamemnon, where a noble code makes possible this courteous friendship between honourable enemies. The scene is set between that which sees Cressida 'wide unclasp the table of her thoughts To every ticklish reader' and that in which Thersites denounces Patroclus's relations with Achilles. This does not seem like accident.

There is something, then, in the form of this play which leads us to believe in its unity of intention. Moreover, the belief that it is not inconsequent and contradictory but intent and purposeful, is confirmed by our first experience of the imagery and the prosody. The tough resilience of the verbal music, the explosive illumination of the imagery are the marks of a causal, not a casual, direction. The speeches of Ulysses, Agamemnon, Hector, and Nestor are distinguished by close-woven, intricate, and virile imagery, and the ring of the verse throughout these scenes is superb. When Ulysses persuades the Greek councillors, he gives a noble smoothness and simplicity of line to his doctrine of hierarchical 'degree'. When Nestor is alone with Ulysses, a mind thewed like his own, he speaks with cryptic cogency a language of brief hints weighted with implications that he need not elucidate, so that, by the interlocking of imagery, the work of argument itself is done by the images. In neither of these quite different uses of imagery and musical units is there any suggestion of faltering power or purpose:

> Yet in the trial much opinion dwells.
> For here the Trojans taste our dear'st repute
> With their fin'st palate. And trust to me, Ulysses
> Our imputation shall be oddly pois'd
> In this wild action. For the success
> (Although particular) shall give a scantling
> Of good or bad unto the general.
> And in such indexes, although small pricks
> To their subsequent volumes, there is seen
> The baby figure of the giant mass
> Of things to come at large. It is suppos'd
> He that meets Hector issues from our choice;
> And choice, being mutual act of all our souls,
> Makes merit her election, and doth boil,
> As 'twere from forth us all, a man distill'd

Out of our virtues; who miscarrying,
What heart receives from hence the conquering part,
To steel a strong opinion to themselves?
Which entertain'd, limbs are his instruments,
In no less working than are swords and bows
Directive by the limbs.

It is this virility, the basis of the style, running beneath the froth and
fantasy of the Pandarus – Helen scenes, emerging suddenly in a different
tempo in Thersites' ecstasies of abuse, which binds the whole together,
showing one mind at work, and that an undivided mind, beneath the seeming variations. Moreover, the apposition (in such a speech as this of
Nestor) of images that, while leading in the reader's mind to a process
equivalent to arguing, do indeed fly off from each other 'with impetuous
recoile and jarring sound', plays its own part in furthering that impression
of disjunction which the art of the play, in major or in minor form, is
ceaselessly at work to enforce upon us. The persistence, in fact, of such
verse and imagery, right through to Troilus's last speech on the death of
Hector, indicates, in a very different way but no less surely than the ruthless choice and the sure handling of material, that this is no plaything for
Shakespeare. Here is a task upon which his whole mind was bent in
intense and terrific concentration. Metre and imagery alike wrestle with
their subject-matter. Every faculty works at its full height; the last
resources of intellect and imagination are in action.

The conclusion, then, from even this brief consideration of the subject
and form of the play, is that they collaborate, not fortuitously, but inten-
tionally, that the form illuminates and interprets the theme, is itself
ordered by it, each being in some degree an aspect of the other, precisely as
we expect in a play which is a major work of dramatic art. And so there is
confirmed the impression that here is no failure, nor even partial success.
For, given discord as the central theme, it is hard to imagine how else it
should be formally reflected but in a deliberately intended discord of form
also. Rare this may be – perhaps unique in dramatic art – but, as I have
suggested, the experience which the play exists to communicate is rare
also. As readers, we, in effect, testify, by the conviction that our impression has been conveyed by the whole, and nothing less than the whole
play, that the work of art we are contemplating is a living organism, a
single form of perceived reality, however vast, complex, or difficult of communication it may be.

With this conviction in mind, then, we can turn to the underlying ideas of the play, no longer expecting to find inconsistency in Shakespeare's treatment of the various parts.

It cannot escape our notice that, in *Troilus and Cressida*, the revelation of the writer's values[4] is not, as in most of Shakespeare's work, implicit only, and so dependent upon our ability to receive the artistic experience of the dramatist;[5] there is also much explicit discussion of the abstract question, 'What is value?' This is both easier to distinguish and a direct road to Shakespeare's implicit comment, and for both reasons it is well to consider it first.

Many of the characters – Troilus, Paris, Achilles, Hector, Ulysses, Thersites – are either involved in a bitter fight to harmonize the conflicting evidence of their universe, or are gradually relaxing their efforts and subsiding into a no less bitter equilibrium of disillusionment or loathing. As they make their different interpretations of the meaning or non-meaning of that universe, it begins to be clear that many of the main issues depend for them upon the question of whether value is absolute or relative; inherent in the object or superimposed upon it; objective or subjective to the valuer.

Troilus, at the beginning of the play, represents one extreme; he believes that the object of faith or worship (a woman, an ideal, a code, an institution) is invested with value precisely to the degree to which it is valued. 'What is aught', he exclaims, 'but as 'tis valued', and though it never occurs to him to consider the relation of this belief to his estimate of Cressida, there are signs of underlying misgiving in his constant questioning of her. The course of the play brings him out of his belief, through a process of disintegration in which the operation of reasoning is set against the faculty itself (V. ii. 139-43), to a state of equilibrium in which he repudiates the two great ideals of his life, love and soldiership, betrayed in the one by Cressida's perfidy, in the other by the murder of Hector. In their romantic defence of the war at the beginning, he and Paris behave like book collectors who pay £100 for a rare example containing certain typographical peculiarities, not because of its intrinsic beauty or interest, but because that market price has been fixed by other men's willingness to rise to it. For all its romantic dressing, this is at bottom the most purely commercial aspect of value presented in the play, equating merit with the price that can be got for a thing, Helen with so much warfare. When this is advanced in its turn as a reason for continuing to value her, it involves a bland *petitio principii* that neither of the hot-headed young men has time to observe:

Paris. There's not the meanest spirit in our party
   Without a heart to dare, or sword to draw,
   When Helen is defended... Then (I say)
   Well may we fight for her, whom we know well
   The world's large spaces cannot parallel.

If the fallacy of their arguments escapes their own notice, it does not escape that of Hector, the clearest exponent of the other view of value, value as something that must be primarily inherent in the object valued:

But value dwells not in particular will;
It holds his estimate and dignity
As well wherein 'tis precious of itself,
As in the prizer: 'Tis mad idolatry
To make the service greater than the God;
And the will dotes that is inclinable
To what infectiously itself affects,
Without some image of th' affected merit.

It is, as he implies later, for lack of this 'image of the affected merit' that the arguments of Paris and Troilus are 'glozed but superficially' and are indeed no reasons. He dismisses the strongest argument on their side, namely that its effect on its worshipper itself invests the idol with value (indeed, with all the value we need to seek), temperately making it clear that the sense of value depends for its stability upon something outside itself, objective and absolute, inherent in the object – in short, upon the 'image of the affected merit'.

But many other characters in the play are seeking, by different methods and with different incidental experience, for just such an 'image' – an absolute value by which to test the evidence of their experience. And they all either come to the same destructive conclusion or themselves furnish notable confirmation by their fates of the destructive philosophies of the rest.

Achilles, lazy in mind and body, is, when roused, no more defective in intelligence than he is in professional skill. The sting of Agamemnon's insults drives him to some effortless and quite lucid self-examination on the nature of reputation and, as he falls in with Ulysses at the peak of his exasperation, the discussion slides naturally into the major question of the play, 'Is there or is there not in anything an absolute value?' Achilles makes for himself the discovery that reputation (which he, being of the school of Troilus and Paris, equates with value) determines a man's own view of himself. Ulysses clinches it for him: a man 'feels not what he owes [= owns], but by reflection', but he carries the investigation a step further, and sees in reputation (the value other men put upon a man) the necessary completion of a process without which a quality does not fully exist. He equates it with the function of communication as we understand it in art or in love, without some form of which the process has not been consummated. Indeed, Shakespeare lets him use that very term:

> No man is the lord of any thing,
> (Though in and of him there is much consisting)
> Till he communicate his parts to others:
> Nor doth he of himself know them for ought,
> Till he behold them formed in th' applause,
> Where they are extended.

The essential relation between 'communication' and 'form' here is highly significant, as is the distinction between Ulysses' position and that of Troilus, Paris, and Achilles. Ulysses, who could speak later of the 'mystery, wherein relation Durst never meddle, in the soul of state', does not deny the possibility of the absolute value that Hector insists on. He merely points out the inseparable relationship between the two aspects, intrinsic value and assessed value, in man's experience, and declares that without the second the first is unfulfilled. 'Else a great prince in prison lies.'

When we remember how unusual are discussions of abstract themes in Shakespeare's plays as compared, for instance, with Chapman's, Tourneur's, and Beaumont and Fletcher's among his contemporaries, we may well pause to ask what it means in *Troilus and Cressida*. In all the plays in which something similar occurs (and never, not even in *Measure for Measure*, is it so full and so penetrating) it is also strictly integral to the main matter and so inwoven with the action as to be a natural commentary upon it. This is no less true of the discussions on the nature of kingship and government in the sequence of history plays, especially the two parts of *Henry IV* and *Henry V*, than of the reflections on the art of conduct in *Hamlet*. Arguing from this, we may wonder whether this continual talk of values, this debating to and fro not only of their nature, but of the question of their existence, is not equally essential in some way to the fundamental theme of *Troilus and Cressida*, whether, in short, Shakespeare ever suffered his characters to be deeply concerned with a question which was not the core of the play. Is Shakespeare, in *Troilus and Cressida*, himself revealing, through their conscious analyses as through their experience, a state in which such questions met just such answers in his own mind? I think he is, and I think this brings us to the root of the matter. The writer of this play is a man to whom values have become suspect.

Were the wisdom of Hector and Ulysses allowed to survive, in contrast with the rest of the play but without further comment, this might be less clearly implied. But actually it suffers defeat in both cases; in Hector's by the implications of his betrayal at the hands of a code in whose stability he had trusted; in Ulysses', first by the course of the action, which denies the truth of his idea by the contradiction of event, and, secondly and more specifically, by a later admission of his own, when, arguing that virtue must not seek 'remuneration for the thing it is', he goes on to dismiss the possibility of intrinsic value having, in practice and in the affairs of men, any effective alliance with assessed value:

> Love, friendship, charity, are subjects all
> To envious and caluminating time

so that the indispensable condition, without which intrinsic value cannot be liberated into reality, is never there. The reason for this is at once simple and irremediable, it lies in the nature of man's mind:

> One touch of nature makes the whole world kin:
> That all with one consent praise new born gauds,
> Though they are made and moulded of things past,
> And give to dust, that is a little gilt,
> More laud than gilt o'er-dusted.

That is, man's judgement (his capacity for valuing) is incapable of its task, and absolute value, whether or not it exists, is never discernible.

Even the acute intelligence of Ulysses then, having done its best upon the problem, has met with implicit and explicit defeat, and it is not surprising that the same fate befalls the other characters.

The last position, in descending order of negation, is that of Thersites. He has long taken for granted the conclusion that Ulysses has implied; mankind in his eyes is as incapable of worthy judgement as of worthy conduct; Ulysses, Nestor, Agamemnon, Hector and Troilus are reduced to their lowest terms, no less than Achilles, Ajax, Patroclus, Paris, Helen and Cressida. But he has travelled further. He does not waste time debating the existence of absolute value, or whether or not man can perceive and live by it; he assumes no criterion beyond that fallible human judgement of which he is so eloquent a satirist. Nor does the obscene casualty of fate and circumstance stagger him; for here the paradoxes of circumstances have long ago taken the wind of satire: 'To what form but that he is, should wit larded with malice, and malice forced with wit turn him to? To an ass were nothing; he is both ass and ox; to an ox, were nothing; he is both ox and ass.' In the world he offers us there is no stability in character, ideals, institutions, judgement, nor in imagination itself. The whole is a shifting, heaving morass where all is relative and nothing absolute, where pullulating worm and insect forms, seething upon the surface, are seen suddenly, as at the dissipating of some soft, concealing cloud, intent upon their task of disintegration and erosion, reducing all things to their own terms and substance.

And yet Thersites is an integral part of the play's form and matter, and that play is a living organism. It is upon the whole fabric that his mind is at work, driven by the passion of his disgust to break down the forms of things into lifeless elements that can never again be human flesh and blood nor even wholesome earth, but must remain barren and negative like deflowered soil. As we read his comment and relate it with the debates in these other minds, his is seen to be dominant of their scale. For he, to whom all the argument is a cuckold and a whore, who sees the common curse of mankind, folly and ignorance, as deserving only the dry serpigo and war and lechery to confound them, has arrived at his conclusion by the very road that they are travelling – Ulysses by his own reasoning, Troilus by the conversion wrought in him by event, and the rest by their betrayal of or at the hands of their codes. The starting-point of his interpretation is the conclusion to which they too are proceeding: there is no absolute value inherent in the universe imaged in the loves and wars of Greeks and Trojans. There *is* no 'image of the affected merit'.

Once we have isolated this central question (What is the nature of value and has it or has it not an absolute existence?), once we have traced the series of positions, from positive to negative, of Hector, Troilus, Ulysses, and Thersites and the relation of each of those positions to the general evidence of the play, matter and form alike are seen to derive from this conclusion, which makes of the whole a vast, complex but organic artistic experience. The conflict between conduct, ideals, and event which the choice of material lays so clearly before us and the idea of disjunction inescapably enforced by the structure of the play serve now to drive home the conclusion that in this play disjunction was a fundamental principle, if not the most fundamental, in Shakespeare's view of the universe of event.

But we are uneasily aware, at the same time, that this judgement is not limited to the universe of event. Were that so, we should probably find in this play a mood of partial negation only, as in the balanced conflicts of the tragedies, where the positive element contends on equal terms with the negative and the duality is essential in the artistic experience. But in *Troilus and Cressida* our sense of the artistic unity has derived, as we have realized, not from an impression of balance, but from an impression of evil enveloping apparent good; not from a picture of the accidental prevalence of mischance and injustice over wisdom and rectitude, but from the implication of a causal relation between disjunction in event and the absence of absolute criteria in the universe of thought. To make this clear we may look again at some of the noblest thought in the play and see how it is related to the enveloping and prevailing evil and how its destruction carries the principle of disjunction into the domain of the mind itself.

Let us take again Ulysses' defence of 'degree', the foundation upon which civilization and its achievement rests. The hierarchy of his state stands, in its nobility of conception, linked with the hierarchy of the heavens, a microcosm of the great universe:

> The Heavens themselves, the planets, and this centre,
> Observe degree, priority, and place,

and 'all in line of order'. The heavens maintain their courses and the world of man reflects their ordered process in 'The unity and married calm of states'. But if the planets 'in evil mixture to disorder wander', then 'Degree is shak'd', both in the cosmos and in society, the image of the cosmos created by man's mind. Then, in the two universes alike, in that of the material cosmos and that of man's creating 'each thing meets in mere oppugnancy', and chaos is come again. To this 'mere oppugnancy' the play leads us inescapably, by the matter and texture of the concluding acts. The towering thoughts and ideals topple down before a destiny as implacable as that foreseen by Ulysses for the doomed towers of Troy; and if we look immediately from these ideals to the last phases of the action, the ambush and murder of Hector, we have no choice but to measure the chaos and the discord by the gracious assurance, the magnanimity, and the seeming stability that they destroy. Just as we feel the value of the *Oedipus* or the *Oresteia* to be in one way commensurate with the depth and the power of evil which Sophocles and Aeschylus meet and transmute, so in *Troilus* the nobility of that order which in the end proved perishable gives us the measure of the destructive forces which triumph over it. The existence of the principle of cause and order (in the cosmos and in the affairs of men) is therein questioned; it vanishes, revealing destruction as the principle underlying all life.

The supreme reach, moreover, of Shakespeare's imagery and prosody in this play, with all that they imply of sustained imaginative thought, serve also by their association with the prevailing evil, to affirm the magnitude and universality of that evil when it does prevail:

> But the strong base and building of my love
> Is as the very centre of the earth,
> Drawing all things to it.

It is Cressida speaking; and when the base of the world, the centre of stability itself, is equated with Cressida's love, we have not much farther to seek for Shakespeare's comment upon that stability.

Moreover, the downfall of the principles of order and value in the world of man's creation, with the substitution of the negative principles of disjunction and chaos, is traced directly to that inability in man to imagine absolute value which we have already recognized; in Ulysses's words, to the 'touch of nature' that 'makes the whole world kin'. It *is*, indeed, man's 'nature'. Not only is the objective universe, then, the cosmos and society, found subject to this curse of disjunction; the universe of the imagination also is proved incapable of conceiving a stable value. Disjunction, chaos, discord in the spheres, this is the only irreducible and continuing thing. The denial of absolute value, of any real 'image of the affected merit', is, then, carried beyond the world of event within the play; casualty has replaced causality in the world of the imagination also.

It would seem, then, that this play is an attempt, upon a scale whose vastness is measured by the intensity with which every faculty of the poet's mind is engaged, to find that image (of absolute value) in the evidence of man's achievement, in the sum or parts of his experience or, if nowhere else, in the processes of creative imagination. Troilus' love, Agamemnon's chivalry, Ulysses's vision of the hierarchy of state are all, thus, experimental images, in which are tested the absolute value of man's passion, intellect, and imagination. In face of this test, this 'Quid hoc ad aeternitatem?', all fail. There is no absolute quality the evidence for which does not resolve itself into a mere subjective illusion of blood or fancy, a

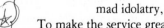

> mad idolatry,
> To make the service greater than the God.

The creations of man's spirit, hitherto exalted, are now seen to have survived only by chance, at the mercy all the time of a stronger, natural law of destruction; what in another mood might have appeared tragic accidents, the counterpoint in a fuller harmony, are now seen, instead, to reveal an underlying law to which all is recurrently and inescapably subject. This is the ultimate, indeed the only surviving absolute in *Troilus and Cressida*. The faculty that could perceive degree and the ordered form of a universe, the imagination itself, has been touched and the images of form no longer rise at its command. 'There is no more to say.' The dark night of the soul comes down upon the unilluminated wreckage of the universe of vision. The play of *Troilus and Cressida* remains as one of the few living and unified expressions of this experience.

The grand scale of this catastrophe blinds us. We do not willingly imagine this overthrow; some at least of us never to the end comprehend it, for it is like a note too deep for our hearing, or a landscape too vast for our experiencing. We probably come nearer to understanding the tragedies than this play which is no tragedy and is yet perhaps the record of the profoundest catastrophe in man's experience.

> Moving of th' earth brings harms and fears,
>   Men reckon what it did and meant,
> But trepidation of the spheres,
>   Though greater far, is innocent.

If we turn from this attempt to understand the nature of the underlying ideas in *Troilus and Cressida* and consider the form through which these ideas are revealed, we see that what has been achieved is in fact what we suggested at the outset. The idea of chaos, of disjunction, of ultimate form-lessness and negation, has by a supreme act of artistic mastery been given form. It has not been described in more or less abstract terms; it has been imaged. What seemed to be an absolute limitation of drama has been trans-cended and shown, in this rare achievement, to be but relative.

And in this case, even more than in either of those which we have just considered, the subduing of content to form is no mere act of virtuosity; it has a further significance as an instance of one of the ultimate functions of art.

That the experience on which this play rests is of profound significance at any time, and of peculiar significance to our own, needs no discussion. Whenever actual experience threatens to pass endurance, there is a measure of alleviation in discovering that it has already been met and recorded. The facts are not softened, but the sense of isolation which gives the facts a main part of their horror is mitigated; the desert is not less to be reckoned with, but something is gone if it is no longer 'terra incognita' nor utterly unmapped. When we find, as we certainly do in this play, not merely a record of actual experience, but a communication of an artistic experience, the alleviation becomes more positive; the actual experience, in that case, has not only been met, but resolved into form by the grandest of all human faculties, the artistic imagination. Once it has been encompassed by this imagination, at whatever cost, the bounds of human comprehension have been set forward in proportion as it had appeared incomprehensible. The value that we finally attach in this way, to Aeschylus, to Sophocles, and to Shakespeare rests upon the extent of their comprehension of evil, and upon the extent to which that vision of evil has been brought under the governance of those artistic laws which are themselves the image of the ultimate law of an ordered universe. Thus, in Shakespeare's *Troilus and Cressida* we meet a paradoxical dualism. The content of his thought is an implacable assertion of chaos as the ultimate fact of being; the presence of artistic form is a deeper, unconscious testimony to an order which is actually ultimate and against which the gates of hell shall not prevail.

This is made clearer still by the direction his thought takes in the plays that follow *Troilus and Cressida* and lead on in direct succession to the final group. This subduing of matter to form in the earlier play is then seen to be prophetic of a resolution not only of the technical problem of relating content to form, but of the dualism of thought implied in their conflict. The victory of form is no mere technical achievement; it has, as has form in all great art, a spiritual aspect and significance.

It is the development from *Troilus and Cressida* to the latest group of plays that gives to both their profoundest meaning. Our understanding of the latest plays bears strict equivalence with our understanding of this one; only so far as we imagine the abomination of desolation can we imagine beatitude. For the tragedies that follow represent a recovery of the balance between the perception of evil and a positive interpretation of it, whereas in *Troilus and Cressida* the writer looks upon the implacable fact of orderless evil in the mind and in the objective universe alike. In this play the judgement is unshaken, and there is no escape from the torment of the perception of evil, but in the later plays judgement is superseded. The conclusions from all its experiments meet in the tense yet motionless equilibrium of Troilus's last speech, but the revelations perceived by the mode of thought that supersedes it flash out in sudden phrases on the lips of Edgar, Gloucester, and Lear:

> Sit gods upon your thrones, and smile at Troy.
> I say at once, let your brief plagues be mercy,
> And linger not our sure destruction on...
> I do not speak of flight, of fear, of death,

But dare all imminence that gods and men,
Address their dangers in ... But march away:
Hector is dead: there is no more to say.

'Let your brief plagues be mercy'; Edgar in *Lear* learns at length that 'the worst is not, So long as we can say this is the worst', and his discovery rests upon the knowledge, carried over from *Troilus and Cressida*, that when we are at the worst 'there is no more to say'.

In the next phase of this experience, then, there is no longer this vigilant judgement presiding over implacable fact, for a break-up has set in and disintegration has overpowered judgement. In the picture offered by *Timon*, the play which appears to reveal the next phase in this progression, the universe of thought and imagination is riven almost beyond recognition and the matter and form of the play derive from the experience, not of imminent disjunction, but of chaos itself. This brings its own anaesthesia and, though the powers of the mind seem to have surrendered to disintegration, something that was invisible at the stage of *Troilus and Cressida* is beginning to appear. The 'strong base of the world', has indeed now broken up, but through the rift is revealed, at depths almost below man's vision, a new base not dreamed of, where the 'perpetual-sober gods' remain, untouched even by the 'trepidation of the spheres'. The emergence from destructive to constructive experience has begun again, though it may be revealed in *Timon* only in this one phrase. Our experience of each play is, I venture to think, incomplete without the other.

In *Lear* the indications of this are more frequent and the conversions that flow in rising and cumulative waves through the last two acts of the play all set towards a positive, though undefined, interpretation, resting upon this foundation. The tragic balance is readjusted. The perception of evil is as full as in the *Oedipus* or the *Oresteia*, but there is an undefined, but no less positive, perception of order emerging again from casualty.

Gloucester.   O you mighty Gods!
    This world I do renounce, and, in your sights,
    Shake patiently my great affliction off;
    If I could bear it longer, and not fall
    To quarrel with your great opposeless wills,
    My snuff and loathed part of nature should
    Burn itself out.

                                *

You ever gentle Gods, take my breath from me,

Let not my worser spirit tempt me again
To die before you please.
                . . . What are you?
Edgar. A most poor man, made tame to fortune's blows
    Who, by the art of known and feeling sorrows,
    Am pregnant to good pity.

There is, of course, no actual refutation of the conclusions of *Troilus*.
The commentary of *Lear* is rather a series of flashes out into a seemingly
limitless universe of positive ideas and the later plays extend and stabilize
these. But this kind of commentary does, by its very non-logical process,
indicate in part how the universe of *Troilus* was superseded. The brief
visions of circumambient reality, the 'perpetual-sober Gods', the 'great
opposeless wills', the 'ever-gentle Gods', suggest that the imagination
may in this way perceive what, in the earlier play, operating in a field of
actuality delimited by the judgement, it could not; Edgar could, if he
chose, refute Ulysses' argument, that the intrinsic value can never
become effective because man's judgement is preoccupied with assessed
value, by pointing out that it contains an undistributed middle on the
grand scale.

Simultaneously there comes into sight that earlier mood again in which,

There's not the smallest orb which thou beholdest
But in his motion like an angel sings,
Still quiring to the young-eyed cherubins;
Such harmony is in immortal souls.

and that, slightly later, in which Pericles, in face of the opening vision of a
universe of fundamental order and reconciliation, finds again the image in
which Shakespeare has clothed this idea, whether negative or positive,
throughout:

Pericles.   . . . But what music?
Helicanus. My Lord I hear none.
Pericles. None? The music of the spheres.

Already we are in sight of the harmony of the latest plays, and the
seeming finality of the vision of *Troilus and Cressida* is seen to be, after all,
not an end, but the birth of a new, infinitely extended and positive vision.
At the phase at which *Lear* completes and resolves the experience of
Troilus and Cressida, only the anticipation of this is indicated. *Plus ultra.*
'It is enough that there *is* a beyond.'

NOTES

[1]These, ranging from Coleridge in the early nineteenth century to Professor F.S. Boas in our own time, with the addition of the quite recent work of Professor Wilson Knight and W.W. Lawrence, however widely they differ otherwise, agree in remarking in some way upon the contradictions in mood and assessments of values to be found in the play.

[2]I was for many years satisfied to see in this play a momentary failure of Shakespeare's artistic power. The failure was, on the contrary, in my understanding. It would be well, no doubt, if every critic were to hang upon the wall of his workroom the timely admonition: ''Tis not Homer nods but we that sleep.'

[3]It is the psychological sequence rather than the chronological that mainly concerns us here. It is undoubtedly possible for a mature artist to produce works in an order which does not precisely represent the order of the phases through which his mind is progressing at that time. This is made clear in the cases of some later artists who have left, in letters and journals, a complementary record of their thought and experience. The letters of Ibsen, taken in conjunction with his plays, are, of course, one of the most familiar examples of this kind of record, showing this kind of variation, in modern dramatic art. With the Jacobean playwrights many factors, even including professional demands, would be at work, but more important than these would still be those revivals and recrudescences of earlier moods which often characterize the apparent irregularities of spiritual growth. It is for this reason that we may discover some of the relations between Shakespeare's plays more clearly by considering them in what we believe to be their psychological sequence rather than in what we conjecture to be their chronological.

[4]There is some difficulty in finding a term for this. Were the results of Shakespeare's implications positive, the term 'values' would be satisfactory. But the modern connotation is, rather, the categories under which a man apprehends the good (see, for example, Inge, *Philosophy of Plotinus*, Vol. II, pp. 74 seq.), and, since Shakespeare's conclusion is negative, there is an undesirable element of paradox in applying it here. The position is complicated by the fact that, while his absolutes become evil, he has reached his conclusion by the process of eliminating values. We should perhaps be technically accurate if we said that his metaphysical ultimate is evil manifested in the form of chaos – a negative form perhaps of Nietzsche's 'Umwertung aller Werte'.

[5]I think that it is still mainly so in *Troilus and Cressida*, and that it is our doubt or inability at this point that has led to the misinterpretation of some of the values indicated in the play.

IX

Coriolanus

In the plays of his maturity, Shakespeare reveals by secret impressions the underlying natures of his characters, so that, with the knowledge thus conveyed to us, we redress at unawares the balance of evidence given not only by those characters but by other parts of the play. Many of those in which this process can be clearly discerned are minor or subordinate figures, but a few are co-partners with the greatest[1] and it is found to some degree in all. Of none can we say with certainty that we know them until we have taken into account the hidden evidence thus disclosed, and it is probable that our unconscious awareness of every character is influenced by it. But in one play at least Shakespeare seems to determine by this mode our apprehension of the central figure itself; and this so modifies the total effect of the play, as to re-colour our interpretation of nearly every aspect. No detailed analysis of such a character can be attemped within the limits of this volume, but some indications may be given of the process by which unconscious knowledge finds its way into our imaginations.

The character I have in mind is Coriolanus, one that we have already glanced at; and the discrepancy between speech and fact, a certain conflict between the character's professions and his actions may prompt us to look further into the mind from which both, though seemingly incompatible, derive. And this in turn may lead to successive readings that reveal depth below depth in his nature, re-interpreting the surface for us and modifying our first inferences from it.[2]

With the character of Coriolanus we observe first the strife and turmoil created by his passions on the world around him, shaking the State of

Rome and bringing him to destruction, then the presence of bitter conflict in his own mind. From this point onward we are guided, I think, by deeper-lying and less evident indications of motive, until we reach a point where we depend wholly upon 'secret impressions' for the final interpretation. When we have reached this, we begin to travel backwards, in reascending order, as it were, to the surface which we first observed and to reconsider these earlier and it may be mistaken conclusions in the light of that final discovery.

Our first impression of Coriolanus in the first three acts of the play is familiar to all Shakespeare's readers and on this there may be little dis-agreement. He is a man still young[3] and of evident military genius, as brave and brilliant in battle as Hotspur, with powers of leadership in the field and a grasp of strategy akin to that of Henry V; a man whose valour and heroic wrath inspire men to follow him and carry them to victory (I. iv. 30 seq., I. vi. 66 seq.). As a statesman, he shows in an emergency the same grasp of the essential factors; he is a clear and pitiless judge of the plebeians and a shrewd and fearless prophet of the immediate future. His impatient scorn of the people's cowardice and treachery, of the contemptible custom of vote-begging (accepted even by his fellow patricians), though fierce and heedless, is also of a heroic mould. He is a man of equally strong attachments within his own class, to his fellow generals Cominius, Menenius, and Titus Lartius, to his wife and above all to his mother; a sincere man, hating flattery, with an irritable dislike of praise, even when he has fairly earned it. These are the elements of a noble character and he reveals them clearly in action and eloquently in speech. On immediate political issues he is as sound a judge as on the conduct of a campaign; great intelligence as well as firm definition of thought shine through the courage and vigour of his speech (III. i. 37-40, 92, 104-11, 124-38, 141-60). His military genius (and, within these limits, his statesmanship) exceed the others' as his imagination surpasses theirs. In these two domains he appears to achieve full and untrammelled expression; passion and thought are in triumphant union. And the fruits of this may be seen in the liberal frankness of his manner during the first three acts to his fellow-generals and to Menenius; this is a man in at least momentary harmony with his immediate world.[4] If we accept this reading, his fall results directly from behaviour of a piece with what he has already shown us, from his intolerant, unsympathetic and heroically undiplomatic treatment of the insolent Roman mob. But after his fall the balance of his nature seems to change, and though some change might follow naturally upon the shock of his banishment, it is not altogether easy to interpret this as a direct development from his earlier behaviour. Darker moods and purposes than we or his fellows had suspected in him take possession and lead to his unnatural alliance with the Volscians, his vengeful attack on Rome and so to his death.

Thus already, in the reading these brief indications suggest, we find ourselves troubled by a seeming hiatus[5] at this point in the play. The haughty, heroic, and magnanimous patrician of the earlier acts is transformed into a vengeful soldier of fortune. The man who could not stay to hear his nothing monstered now sees himself as a lonely dragon whom his fen makes feared and talked of, and he who could not speak mildly to save his consulship flatters Aufidius's fellow-officers to win control of a war of vengeance.

And so a second impression begins to modify our first, though still drawn from the evidence of character and conduct revealed by the outward action of the play. For in seeking, as we must, to reconcile these two contradictory phases of conduct, to trace them to a common root in character, we have in fact already assumed the second to be inherent in the first. And so we begin to look for indications, for flaws that may be no more than faint inconsistencies; but that points us back or forward to the presence of something hitherto unnoticed in his nature, secretly at work, it may be, upon his experience, transforming it to something whose effects are incalculable to him, to us, and to his Roman world. One of the most evident of these flaws is the hyper-sensitive modesty of the early acts, churlish and ungrateful sometimes in its repudiation of praise that was in part at least kindly and courteous (I. ix. 36-40, 40-53). It is, as we have already noticed, in flat contradiction to his growing preoccupation, towards the end of the play, with the effect he is producing on other people and so belongs, presumably, to a part of his nature later submerged by the crucial act of treachery. But, more important than this, it is also hard to reconcile with our first impression, that of a man in full and glorious exercise of his power as a soldier, a confident man who, though vehement and irascible, yet expresses his political vision with full and satisfying vigour, a man secure in his close, affectionate relations with his friends and the members of his household. Beneath the confidence and the security, then, we recognize disharmony. And we ask from what it derives.

This leads us to consider other passages in the play, where openly declared difference of principle and conviction breaks out in the scenes in which Volumnia and the patricians force Coriolanus to conciliate the Roman mob he has defied (III. ii, esp. 16-20). This might be no more than a clash between two positive natures, each equally confident and secure in its own convictions, but that, as we observe, the divergence proves wider than Volumnia had supposed and its disclosure takes her by surprise. And we recall, too, an earlier moment of insistence on her part and uneasy acquiescence on his, where we are momentarily aware of something in him that she has not recognized. 'My mother, Who has a charter to extol her blood, When she does praise me grieves me (I. ix. 13-15). This is not idle talk; it reveals a deep division of idea, even an unrecognized division of ideals. Comparing the two passages, we recall what we have learnt of Volumnia's influence over Coriolanus, of her heroic ambition which has moulded his character and career (I. iii). We have been seeking to recon- cile two contradictory phases of conduct in Coriolanus and have been led to assume the presence of division in his own mind. Now this assumption, at first suggested by that exaggerated sensitiveness, ungracious, ill- proportioned and at odds with his customary mood, is confirmed by the passages between him and Volumnia, which reveal not only the unexpected depth and inwardness of the division between them, but a like unformulated division in the mind of Coriolanus himself. For Coriolanus has been moulded in the ideals of his world (epitomized in his mother's) and though much in him has given them a willing response, we begin to question now whether they have been entirely of his own initiating, and whether they have in fact satisfied the whole of him. If his conduct, first in little, perplexing details of behaviour and finally in a great and catastrophic revolution, has pointed to a civil war within the mind of Coriolanus and if his mother's bearing and his relation to her has suggested a sufficient cause for this, can we go further and say that Shakespeare has revealed to us something of the nature of this war and of the conflicting elements in- volved, by further hints, in single phrases it may be, in momentary betrayals of something invisible and unknown to the speaker himself? For this would, if true, lead us to reconsider our earlier conclusions with the help of these impressions and so perhaps to come nearer to understanding what lies below the contradictions that first prompted our inquiry.

What picture does Shakespeare give us of this Roman civilization with which Coriolanus is in these passages at odds, which has yet shaped his habits, which has been his world and his devotion, to which his mother has dedicated him and to which he has offered his genius in eager and trium- phant service? We might set aside the part played by the mob (which, to his fellow-patricians as to him, is hardly Rome at all and certainly not Rome's civilization, but rather an enemy within the gates) were it not that the values revealed by its behaviour have a disquieting affinity with some that we find among the patricians and that it is precisely their submission to its demands that calls forth the opposition from Coriolanus that prompted our inquiry. For the truth is that Shakespeare has some- times drawn the patrician world in harsh, blunt lines. Bold, vigorous, and spirited, the Roman nobles are insensitive to nobility except for the specialized virtues of warfare and are redeemed largely by their generous respect for these qualities in each other and by the aristocratic imperturba- bility, the sarcastic detachment with which they face annihilation at the end.[6] Cominius is a good general, brave in war but no fire-eater, sensible and conciliatory in politics, knowing well the importance of Coriolanus's achievements and making a sane plea for public acknowledgement of it (I. vi, I. ix, esp. 53-5), a just man but no idealist; a man who lets himself be guided by custom and events instead of shaping them. He, Menenius and Volumnia alike believe in maintaining a balance between ideals and complaisance; convictions are one thing; to act upon them implacably, as would Coriolanus, is another. Volumnia betrays this as often as she speaks of the Volscian wars (I. iii, II. i), but she adds much also that the other patricians do not openly express. There is something crude and coarse- grained in her enumeration of Coriolanus's wounds; at least half her pleasure is in their market-value, they are something 'to show to the people' (II. i. 165-72). Her restless ambition is short-sighted and limited, carrying in it the seeds of bitterness and ultimate defeat; her son has 'outdone his former deeds doubly' (II. i. 151-2), but we question to what positive good this cumulative record-breaking is to lead. And so when she meets in him a resistance she cannot understand she assumes it to be a trivial folly (III. ii). But the reader, guided imperceptibly by signs invisible to her, begins to recognize that her limited and crude ambitions owe such dominion as they have over Coriolanus to childhood's training; his affec- tions have made them in some sort sacred to him, the only images in which he could clothe his innate aspirations and ideals.

The ideals of this Rome in fact are sometimes base, and precisely because of their limitations (II. i. 216-20); Volumnia gloats over Corio- lanus's wounds as a profitable investment, and crude butchery wins the respect even of Cominius, taking high place in his official speech to the Senate on Coriolanus's triumph (II. ii. 87-127). If these are indeed the roots of Rome's code and values we have much ground for disquiet; per- haps, at the end of the play, as we listen to Volumnia's noble prayer to Coriolanus for the Rome that has ruined him (V. iii), we hear also a discordant echo of her exultation over the slaughter in Corioli (II. i. 175-8). Perhaps, after all, the mob are but the crudest element in a state in which even the patricians sometimes accept low values and condone base customs. Cominius and Menenius admit fairly and frankly (IV. vi. 112-18, 137-9, V. iv. 35-8) that they deserve destruction for abandoning Coriolanus to the mob's decree and this is the belated recognition, by two of Rome's best men, that they have hitherto identified themselves with some of the very things he had denounced.

This, then, is the obverse of that image of Rome to whose service Coriolanus had once dedicated himself, and after the overturning of his world, it, or something very like it, takes the place of that earlier image in his mind. In Corioli he sees no other. As to those Roman friends with whom he had been in close and happy relationship – 'He could not stay to picke them in a pile Of noysome, musty Chaffe'. 'Rome and her rats' are no longer now 'at point of battle', but infamous allies.

But has this reversal come, after all, without all warning? Of the process by which Coriolanus finds his way from the first image of Rome to its opposite we can only guess, for it is hidden in silence – the silence of his disappearance into exile from a stage he had hardly quitted before, the silence of his strange new taciturnity and later the even deeper silence, though more significant, of smooth concealing speech.[7] But the new picture is so sharply defined that it seems to spring all but complete from some area of the mind where it has long been secretly forming. Can this be so? If this is Shakespeare's intention here, perhaps we shall find Coriolanus already, before the crisis of his fortunes, more nearly aware than he dare admit of the two Romes in his own mind; perhaps we, the readers, have had intimations offered us of that uneasy relationship.

Such intimations of the hidden depths of the mind we shall seek most naturally at the points of fissure, those moments when his behaviour is most nearly inexplicable to us, to his fellows, and to himself. We go back to the passages, that is, when his recoil from the customs of his world is most evident; in his abnormal hatred of its praises and in his deep-seated loathing of the election tactics of the patricians. In the second, he only hates more deeply (though from widely differing motives) a tradition that the patricians themselves dislike; he and they are at one so far. But in the first, in his discourteous rebuff to courtesy, his wanton repudiation of popularity, that draws down Cominius's merited rebuke (I. ix. 41-53), he finds unbearable something that the patricians approve, a ritual that for them has significance and value. This is a wide breach not to be explained away by modesty or even by vanity.' 'It does offend my heart' (II. i. 185). We have no reason now to take these words at anything but their face value; something contaminates the acclamations and praises poured upon him, so that they touch him at heart; there is nausea in the recoil. And thereupon, we observe, he turns to the figure that has stood mute in the midst of the clamour, to Virgilia. 'My gracious silence, hayle' (II. i. 192). Perhaps these words too mean precisely what they say; perhaps there is something lacking else in his world, a source of grace and wisdom, a silence the vehement cannot touch.

Light can be thrown back upon the question at this point by certain habits of speech that grow upon him towards the end of the play. The first clear signs of change appear when he parts from Cominius, Menenius, Volumnia, and Virgilia at the gates of Rome (IV. i), when both bearing and language begin to reflect the deep shock given to his spirit by his banishment. Already he is the 'lonely Dragon that his Fenne Makes fear'd, and talk'd of more than seene' (IV. i. 29-31). Moreover, it is he now who counsels calm and submission, quoting what were formerly Volumnia's own stoic *sententiae*. He sets up certain barriers between them and himself by this ominous steadiness of demeanour, this unnatural, even and measured phrasing. He behaves like a man who has summoned up a stoic dignity to compensate for loss, conceal a wound or deny humiliation; a man who has lost at once his world and his integrity. From this scene onward, the familiar outbursts of rage disappear.[8] Paradoxically, the shock appears to have integrated his character. (More probably, as we already divine, it has cut deeply into it and left him to rescue and integrate one part only.) From now, he practises a rigid and seemingly unbreakable control over his emotions, a cynical shrewdness in planning his treatment of men, an unscrupulous exercise of flattery in subduing them (V. vi. 21-6, 71-84). But, there are indications that this inflexible rigidity belongs only to the surface of his mind and that is now the surface only of a part. This demeanour is more ominous than the former, ungoverned outbursts of rage or irritation; the man is for the time hardly sane, though his madness does not touch, what nothing has ever troubled, his military genius. He appears rather as a man playing a part or a succession of parts and watching himself as he does so.[9] And in the end this declares itself in a habit of speech which throws light back over the whole play.

For again and again, especially in the crucial scene of the last act, Coriolanus speaks of himself as an actor or as a man determined to deny nature (V. iii. 24-5, 35-7, 40-2, 83-4, 184-5). The two recur in sinister conjunction and these related and iterative images begin to stir the reader's imagination.

The climax of this headlong career of perversity comes in the fifth act, when the man who revolted against a conventional untruth and hated even the semblance of exaggerated praise has now put his imagination at the service of deliberate fantasy and built between himself and the world a gigantic façade of megalomaniac shams. The familiar images of the actor recur here and the language and rhythms of his speech are a clear index of the severance of his conduct from his nature.[10] The complex syntax, the florid vocabulary, the imagery at once banal and theatrical, the slow and weighty rhythms that reverberate like a hollow structure are as far removed from those of the earlier acts, from the ringing athletic movement, the crisp hammer-blows of the syntax and the vivid, shining imagery, as this later Coriolanus is from the gallant and impetuous aristocrat of the beginning.

We ask ourselves whether this seemingly new habit is of purely recent growth, derived solely from his spirit's catastrophe and sequent experience, or whether this, like that major image, the new picture of the Roman state, has its roots also in some earlier phase, had already, in fact, been long preparing in secret recesses of his mind. And this question leads us back again to the middle of the play, to the triumphant return from the Volscian war and to the consular elections. For it is upon these scenes that we must turn such light as we can derive from the final phases of Coriolanus's behaviour.

'It is a part that I shall blush in acting' (II. ii. 149-50). The words are spoken in protest to his fellow patricians when they urge him to put on the 'vesture of humility' and beg the people's votes in the open forum. And in a later scene he recurs at intervals to this image (III. ii. 15-16, 105-6 (109-10, Volumnia), 112-15). To his fellow-patricians, this is something to be argued away by appeals to common sense and to custom, even if need be, by Volumnia's impatient scolding. But the disproportionate outburst of anger as he resists and the persistent returns to the image that accompany them point to something genuine in the words and deeper in the motive. Nor is the cause of it the pride of which Volumnia and the tribunes accuse him.[11] It is clear that he fears some consequences far graver than they, who think only of the practical effects, and that though his fear is instinctive and only half-articulate, he is aware of some deep inward harm that threatens if he consents. And as the pressure upon him increases, in the later scene (III. ii), and his resistance becomes more desperate, we realize that he is right, though he cannot communicate his reason to them. Their demand is dastardly and his ultimate consent disastrous, not because his failure brings ruin on him, but because the result is precisely what he foretells, and because in consenting to play a part he does indeed 'teach his Minde a most inherent Baseness' (II. ii. 120-3). To them the impersonation that they counsel is a sensible piece of complaisance and no man of the world would think twice of it. But to him the pretence, the attempt to be something other than himself, means the forfeit of his integrity. What follows, from the decision of III. iii to the end of the play is determined by this and if Coriolanus, after the shock of his banishment, appears to hide himself in a succession of parts, culminating in that of the inhuman world-conqueror which Volumnia herself is compelled to destroy, it is because he has lost the power to 'honor mine owne truth' (III. ii. 121), and has no other stay against the tide of hitherto unknown passions that sweep him onward.

If, moreover, we were right in thinking that this baser Rome, present alike in the easy-going patricians and in the violent and sentimental mob, acted unconsciously as an irritant in Coriolanus's mind, if we are persuaded that, by conceding to it the service of a lie, he has in his own eyes forfeited his honour and debased his mind, if we think that his loss of the integrity that had upheld him is the real cause of the histrionic and vindictive treachery of the last acts, can we go a step further and ask why this experience, which Volumnia would have carried so lightly, brings psychological disaster to her son? If we would do this, we must attempt to guess at what has all this while lain hidden, that part of Coriolanus's nature which was not expressed in the double career of heroic soldier and forthright but discerning statesman, that part which was outraged by the customs his closest friends took as matters of course, that part whose resistance was broken by his own consent to a lie. I think that here too Shakespeare has given us certain impressions that can guide us to a conclusion justified in the context of the play.

Some words of Volumnia's spoken at the height of her exasperation when Coriolanus, after winning their votes, has provoked the mob to fury, surprise us by their evident misunderstanding of the nature of his impulse. 'You might have beene enough the man you are With striuing lesse to be so' (III. ii. 19-20). Is there any truth in this or is it in fact valuable precisely as a mis-reading of his character serving to point us to an opposite truth? For, despite his confusion, Coriolanus appears to be striving rather to be the man he is, a man, it may be, that neither he nor she knows; the very fact of the strife is perhaps an index of his frustration. She accuses him of being 'too absolute' (III. ii. 39) and, again, this absoluteness may but indicate a man not yet on terms with himself and struggling to preserve what he cannot define. Her argument here (III. ii. 47-57, 58-61, 62-4) that the union of 'honour and policy' in war are a true parallel to the conduct she now urges upon him is specious and fallacious. For uprightness and deliberate deception in a statesman are incompatible, while valour and strategy in war are not. 'They do not go together' (A.C. IV. xv. 47), and this he certainly knows even if he cannot define or articulate his knowledge. The strife that is native to his mind is not this deep, inward conflict, but a forthright, eager strife for some glory, that cannot be measured or satisfied by success. It is a great part of his tragedy that this glory is undefined; nevertheless, his desire for it fires his valour as does Tamburlaine's aspiration or Hotspur's 'bright honour'. It has no commerce with Volumnia's well-defined aims of power and dominion (II. i. 188-94). The Coriolanus we see in the play, for lack of a clearer sight or worthier image, struggles to satisfy this passion for glory with things that breed in him disquiet and disgust. The state he serves, the class to which his love and loyalty are bound, are content with mundane aims baser than his, with ideals that offer him no scope.[12] The preoccupation with his rival Aufidius (I. i. 236-8), which appears early in the play, may be but another indication of this restless search for an ideal objective; Aufidius becomes in some sort a focus, though but a nebulous one, for this desire for splendour of life that the summit of achievement in Rome could never offer. Antium, 'this Enemie Towne' (IV. iv. 23-4), already in the third act calls forth a line ironic but also prophetic, 'I wish I had a cause to seeke him there' (III. i. 19). In this passionate desire to image an undefined aspiration (and, it may be, unrecognized ideals) Antium becomes the city of his dreams. 'A goodly City is this *Antium*' (IV. iv. 1, cf. III. iii. 133), and the violent recoil from Rome in the fourth act makes it certain that he will rush to embrace that world that his imagination has already sought in secret. For what has all along looked like pride in Coriolanus is but rebellion against standards and concessions that repel him; the reaction has been negative, disgust and repudiation, because he cannot focus his aspiration, but aspiration is there in him, as strong as ever it was in Hotspur or Tamburlaine, though stifled and perverted.

And so we return to the words whose significance we hoped to illuminate with the help of secret impressions made upon us by other passages in the play. 'My gracious silence, hayle!' The words are sometimes read as a kindly, half-teasing greeting; affectionate and gently bantering. If we have come near the truth in what we have suggested already, they will now mean more than this. They may well be the only overt expression in the play of two things deeply hidden in the mind of Coriolanus, of a longing for the balancing silences, graces, and wisdom banished from the outer world but vital to wholeness of life, and an acknowledgement, albeit inarticulate, that in Virgilia these values were preserved. The clamour around him is his everyday condition, the easily articulated code of his community, at once heroic and insidiously base, the only system of values he has seen defined. But the source of aspiration such as his, an instinctive longing for poetry of living,[13] contains within it an innate love for silence and grace and even for that Valley of Humiliation whose air Bunyan knew to be sweeter than all others. His need is for wholeness of life and he has harnessed the poetry of living to battle and bloodshed. What his aspiration sought of life was that it should be radiant, clear and significant. And for this bread of life his world has offered him success and dominion preserved at the price of complaisance.

> I thinke hee'l be to Rome
> As is the Aspray to the Fish, who takes it
> By Soueraignty of Nature. (IV. vii. 35)

This sovereignty, this greatness is probably our final impression, that and the simplicity inseparable from greatness that has been his undoing. It is not the military greatness that his fellow-soldiers Roman and Volscian acclaim throughout the play, though that is a partial image of it. It is something that they cannot define, in spite of their many attempts at definition,[14] yet it is something that each in turn perceives, gladly or grudgingly, and the reiteration of the word noble[15] reveals their momentary recognitions. But an unholy alliance between the debased and limited ideals of his world and the heart's affections that a meaner man would have put aside has impressed upon his imagination an image of that ideal as insufficient for him as it was too great for the thing it imaged. This magnitude of spirit and imagination was moulded from birth in the worship of the Roman state. But in time that imagination substituted for itself an ideal Rome, as, later, an ideal Antium, both nobler than the actual and indeed non-existent. This was the inevitable result of the attempt to bind such potentialities within such limitations and its outcome could only be the destruction of one or both. The movement towards destruction set in when, under pressure of the Roman state and its ideals, Coriolanus renounced his own undefined but hitherto unquenched aspiration. Then the surest principle of his being was contaminated and the sovereignty of his nature perverted.

I have attempted to show here, as in other parts of this book, that it is by secret impressions that Shakespeare conveys to our imaginations the nature of such a character as Coriolanus. So great is the contradiction between his outward seeming and his hidden self, so blinded and incomplete his self-knowledge, that nothing but some such disclosure could have led us to understanding (imperfect though it is) and nothing but the supreme tact of an evocative mode could have pointed us the way.

Coriolanus cannot himself reveal to us his nature and motives, for part of that nature is denied and part undeveloped. No other character in the play can direct us, for the presence of such a person, articulate and clear-sighted, would have provided him with an ally against his own confusion and the limitations of his world. Only Virgilia seems to preserve for him some source of peace, silence and wonder from which the thirst of his spirit can be assuaged and it is in his words to her that we find one of the most potent of those secret impressions that work powerfully upon the imagination.

*

It is sometimes worth while to make a running survey of the speeches of certain characters, pretending, for the moment, that the music is our only clue to character, for we may find that it does indeed sometimes offer clues of the kind we have just suggested. The changes of mood and bearing in the character, for instance, of Coriolanus receive some curious illuminations from this treatment.[16]

This first phase of Coriolanus's speech-music reveals certain aspects of his character that are simultaneously confirmed by a multitude of indications and a cloud of witness. In the rhythm of his first speeches (I. i. 173-94, 196-206, 234-57), all is alert and crisp; brief sections abruptly alternate with longer passages that are rapid but shapely; when his language becomes colloquial it remains rhythmical and when he is angry the rhythm takes on a swift, lilting movement like quick waves. His long speeches are thus complete and rounded, if simple, musical studies. The memory of this remains with us, so that when we meet him next in the battle-scenes (I. iv-viii) we observe that even anger, which breaks up his syntax but not his rhythms (I. iv. 30-42), leaves the impression of speed without hurry, of the leaping energy of a fiery spirit finding its natural music and secure in itself. This is, I think, of great importance, for, with the exception of his last great speech in the forum, I doubt whether Coriolanus is ever again in absolute harmony with his own deeds until the end. And I doubt, further, whether we should altogether realize how strong is that harmony here, were it not that the movement of the verse, which never stumbles, conveys to us at unawares this sense of the sure-footedness of his spirit in such surroundings.

Back in Rome, he still speaks the music of the opening scenes, but now with some modifications. An irritable movement sets in when he strives against Cominius's praises (I. ix. 13-19) and there is, as always, an interesting change of music when he speaks to Virgilia (II. i. 196-8), when the cadences become melodious if simple, the speed and force of movement

cease and the rhythms become clear and calm.[17] The Coriolanus of the
second act begs his votes in prose and so the characteristic music momentarily disappears. But, when he is alone for a few moments, he, like the
senators of *Othello*, chooses rhyme for his 'sentences' and converses with
himself in a slow, sardonic movement that should warn us against accept-
ing as final the earlier limitations whether of music or of character. In his
contest with the tribunes in the third act (III. i. 25 seq.) the familiar,
strong rhythms return; harder, but not so buoyant; graver, but no less
powerful. When rage quickens them, they have the pace of the earliest
speeches and the hardness of this new mood; there are long verse paragraphs (whose content is tough, hard thought, as well as passion), and
these are swift, but not now abrupt (III. i. 63-73, 90-111, 118-38, 139-
60). This is his finest and strongest music and the current of it is rapid and
deep. Finally the climax (III. iii. 118-33), the accents come like the
strokes of a hammer, driven home by alliteration and the sounds of hard,
splitting consonants. Yet there is measure and control in every prosodic
phrase and in its relation to others and to the verse paragraph which is now
the prosodic unit.

Although the last lines of this scene (III. iii) have thus a sound unlike
any we have met before,[18] it is with some shock that we realize in the
fourth act that part of their movement has become habitual to a character
which, in the final stages of that conflict and in the interval since, has
entered upon a new phase, suddenly and deliberately changing its outward
form. The music of the next three scenes is still measured, grave, and controlled; a solemn music and more nearly conventional although the cadences grow colourless and there is less of that individual syncopation that
came of the hurry and precipitation of syllables in the outbursts of wrath.[19]

The same measured, almost stately movement continues through the
rest of the act, commonplace in music as in the sentiment that the music
accompanies, sometimes with a high proportion of regular lines[20] in sharp
contrast to the rhythms of Act I, sometimes in sustained verse paragraphs
with long prosodic units from which the elasticity of the earlier leaping
movement has vanished. Yet the verse has taken on a firm and steady
tread, the image of a mood which seems compact of control and vigilance,
where only a phrase or two[21] remains to disturb our assurance. In his long
speech to Aufidius (IV. v.71-107), we meet this new Coriolanus, a man
seemingly controlled and wholly integrated, the music of whose speech
contrasts as clearly with the fiery, athletic movement of his earlier verse as
it does with the plain straightforward prose of North upon which it rests.[22]
By the end of this scene, after which we do not see Coriolanus again

until the final movement movement begins in Act V, the music of his speech has so grown in solidity and consistency that it almost drowns our doubts and bewilderments. This music is maintained, with certain modifications natural to the formality of the situation, through Act V, scene ii.

But early in the third scene of the fifth act a third phase is disclosed, a music which gradually overpowers the colourless, prosaic movement of the opening of the scene and, after some twenty lines, begins to break it up: a touch of a more vivid movement (ll. 24-6) picks up those scattered phrases which, with diminishing frequency, had recalled the rhythms prompted by the image of the dragon in his fen; for two lines (ll. 27-8) we hear again the music that from the beginning has been associated with Virgilia; after a brief assertion of control (ll. 29-33) a hurried, irregular, excited movement breaks in (ll. 33-6) recalling, though with certain differences, the rhythms of the early acts. This is a prosodically surprising passage. In less than twenty lines we have listened to four different and by now familiar kinds of music, three of which had been excluded with increasing rigour since towards the end of the third act. We have heard, that is, a significant piece of musical interpretation, perhaps the clearest intimation given us at this point[23] that buried passions are not dead, that they are battling for their rights against the metallic smoothness of demeanour imposed by Coriolanus's new impersonation and that their outbreak, like that of all suppressed and maltreated passion, may take unexpected courses and end in havoc. For much of the rest of the scene, these four movements will be found to contend with each other, but the rising excitement hinted at in the movement of ll. 35-6 begins (ll. 56-62) to dominate the rest. Its rhythms are blunt and commonplace, sometimes crude and theatrical, and sometimes deliberately repetitive in stress and cadence; suggesting the monotonous emphasis of an inexperienced speaker, italicising sound at regular intervals to carry conviction and to seem convinced. This is the perfect musical image of hysteria, of blind emotion fighting against blind control. After some lines of formal speech again and Volumnia's long speeches, the climax of this music of hysteria returns (ll. 183-93), its repetitions, the heavy, lurching movement of the lines, the loss of elasticity in the relations between stresses and vocalic quality, all revealing the false and theatrical emotion which finds its natural expression upon the imagistic plane in the recurrent picture of the actor. After this the formal movement returns, but now without the artificiality of the corresponding passages in Act IV and the beginning of Act V, and we never hear again any of the music peculiar to Coriolanus until a brief outbreak of the first phase (V. v. 129-31) closes the play.

The third scene of the fifth act, then, has made clear one of the dramatic functions of verbal music, it reveals faithfully the insecurity of the temporary integration of Coriolanus's character, the artificiality of his rigid self-command, the hysterical movement of false emotion in conflict with this false reserve and the return of his mind on to its balance again at the end, and this it does in terms of those musical movements that we have learnt to associate with certain of his emotions or states of mind throughout the play. The sound, that is to say, here images a hidden condition of mind which is indicated by no other means except the imagery. Moreover, that same agency has warned us in the early part of the play, by the peculiar music associated with Virgilia, that there may be such hidden depths and in these middle acts by the recurrence of the dragon's music that the problem of the injury done to those hidden depths of his nature is not to be solved by increasing the pressure of a blind control or by the deliberate impersonation of a man of iron.

But when we have once heard these indications we can no longer close our ears to them and the surface facts of Coriolanus's character and bearing now become of interest chiefly in terms of their contradiction to an unknown, hidden self. Once we have accepted the presence of that other self known to no other character except Virgilia – who is, as we remember, 'silence' – we read all other evidences with fresh eyes and may discover in Coriolanus, hidden, undeveloped, unexpressed and unrecognized, above all, to himself, a poet who delighted in the icicle 'that's curded by the frost from purest snow', a poet for whom the war's great business was his only image of glory, but whose mind at its most bewildered never forgot the nature of integrity nor, in its most seemingly triumphant impersonation, forgave to itself the crime of compromising with its own inward truth.

NOTES

[1]Such is the figure of Falstaff in which Maurice Morgann first discerned this method at work.

[2]The likelihood of an ultimate contradiction of his earlier judgement is sometimes suggested thus to the interpreter by the presence of conflict in and about the character, while sometimes it is conveyed rather by an uneasiness of mind recognized by the character himself but provoking no outward conflict. Sometimes, it may be, the contradiction offered to the surface and its evidence is so slight as to pass almost unobserved, as with the characters of Henry IV, Henry V, Volumnia and others.

³Coriolanus won his first campaign at the age of sixteen, like the historical Edward II, and had thus had time for much experience of war without becoming middle-aged by the time of the play. This makes Aufidius's taunt at the end – 'boy' – something that may justly infuriate and not a piece of mere gutter-snipe rudeness.

⁴Never is this modest magnanimity more clearly revealed than in the scene during the consular campaign where he puzzles in simple bewilderment over his mother's disapproval of his conduct (III. ii. 7-16).

⁵Menenius perceives this too (IV. vi. 72-4).

⁶Ironically, Coriolanus never sees the best of those aristocrats whom he hates for the sake of the city, the scenes in which, awaiting destruction in Rome, they mock the craven repentance of the 'clusters' (IV. vi and V. i.).

⁷See p. 147

⁸To reappear once more only, at the end of the play, after his reconversion.

⁹This is an almost complete reversal of his former behaviour. The modesty is gone and he courts publicity; resolved to 'exceed the common', he deliberately makes himself 'feared and talked of'. His 'love's upon this enemy town' and the measure of his reasoning delusion is to be found in his assumption that he will not find in Antium the human nature he had 'banished' in Rome. He is as short-sighted in his estimate of Volscian hero-worship as he was shrewd in his condemnation of the Roman.

¹⁰Especially in V. iii. 56-67, and 183-9.

¹¹The word 'pride' is used nearly a dozen times in the course of the play and some six or seven of the other characters agree in thus accusing him; the first citizen, Sicinius (twice), the first Senate Officer, Brutus (twice), Volumnia (III. ii. 126, 130 and V. iii. 170) and Aufidius, explicitly in IV. vii. 8 and by implication from that point onward. But it is to be noticed that all but one of these are prejudiced utterances; even Volumnia's are to clinch an argument or reinforce an appeal.

¹²Volumnia to the end never perceives this, but two other characters, Cominius and Menenius, come near to doing so when in the fourth and fifth acts they acknowledge that his fellow patricians have in some sort betrayed Coriolanus and identified themselves with what was base and contemptible in Rome.

¹³Certain of Coriolanus's images bear out this. It is at first glance surprising that he does not, like Antony, draw his images from the battle-field, but sometimes, both in the earlier and in the later part of the play, from a quite different world of fancy or imagination. There are sudden, momentary flights from the immediate and actual; in the midst of his abuse of the mob comes the picture of them throwing up their caps, not as though they would lodge them on the Capitol, but 'as they would hang them on the hornes o' th' Moone' (I. i. 217) and from the often hollow imagery of Act V, scene iii, there flashes out the description of Valeria 'Chaste as the Icicle That's curdied by the Frost from purest Snow, And hangs on Dians Temple' (V. iii. 65-6). Images from nature thus break through, 'pebbles' and stars, the 'mutinous windes' that 'Strike the proud Cedars 'gainst the fiery

Sun' (V. iii. 60) and are at once in sharp contrast with the hyperbole and self-consciousness of the actor and suggestive of something escaping from the depths of his mind under the final strain of this scene. My attention was first drawn to the presence of these images in Coriolanus's speech by Miss Jaqueline R. Dunn.

[14]I. iv. 52-61; III. i. 254-9; (IV. v. 66-8); IV. vii. 33-5, 48-53; (V. vi. 126-8).

[15]Some twenty-five in all are spoken of Coriolanus, but the word has echoes in the traditional application to the patricians as description of rank and the somewhat similar use among the Volscian gentry. The following are some of the references to Coriolanus: I. i. 169, 253; I. iv. 52; I. ix. 66; II. ii. 45, 134; II. iii. 9, 93, 141; III. i. 233, 254; III. ii. 40; IV. ii. 21; IV. v. 68, 112, 122 (all spoken by Aufidius); IV. vi. 109; IV. vii. 36; V. iii. 145, 154; V. vi. 126, 145, 155. (Aufidius's earlier images and 'devil', 'viper', etc.)

[16]It must be plainly admitted that there is an almost symbiotic relation between verbal music and imagery in the speech of Coriolanus. But the two are nevertheless individuals; their functions in the life partnership can be distinguished though they are hardly ever (or momentarily) at variance in their purposes.

[17]This special music evoked by Virgilia recurs in Coriolanus's speech whenever he meets her.

[18]Though they have in part been anticipated, as we later realize in movements in II. iii and III. i, notably at II. iii. 120-30.

[19]The pace quickens and some of the old movement returns momentarily to accompany the image of the lonely dragon (IV. i. 29-31). This too recurs in the final acts.

[20]In one short passage (IV. iv. 12-24), four lines are without variation and several others only slightly modified from the norm. This is quite unlike Coriolanus's earlier rhythms and its smoothness here is ominous.

[21]As in the lines (84-9) in the middle of the otherwise deliberate speech to Aufidius in IV. v.

[22]In this speech, in which the quantity and weight of the rhythm reveal the new Coriolanus, there are groups of lines (71-3, 77-9) in which the verbal music is the only substantial difference between North's prose and Shakespeare's verse; an unimportant word drops out, the position of another shifts, and the movement is completely changed, while leaving the content of the verse almost identical with that of the prose. In these, and a few passages which approach them in closeness to the source, we find the rhythm momentarily responsible for the differences in our impressions of North's and of Shakespeare's characters.

[23]Except, again, for that of the imagery.

X

The equilibrium of tragedy

Finally, we may consider one more aspect of the function of limitation in
drama.

There is, as we briefly suggested in the foregoing studies, a constant and
creative conflict between content and form, technique and medium. But of
no less significance is a conflict arising from limitation of mood. And the
equilibrium which here results is essential to the highest reach of dramatic
art. Indeed, in considering it we may perceive certain of the basic relations
between limitation and achievement in drama. It is seen most clearly in
tragedy, for tragedy depends most intimately upon the preservation of a
strict and limiting balance between two contrary readings of life and their
sequent emotions at work within the poet's mind. Such equilibrium is
thus the distinguishing mark of the highest achievement in this kind, individual works tending to approach supremacy in so far as they derive from
this conflict and reveal this resultant balance.

Other characteristics of fine tragedy must of course be present also if this
is to be achieved in any play. There must be strength of emotion revealed
through character and through significant related actions and underlying
thought which further relates passion and event. Again, as in all great
drama, directness, rapidity, and shapeliness of presentation must serve the
ends simultaneously of concentration and of probability, and the resulting
beauty of passion, form, and thought will constitute dramatic poetry,
whether the vehicle be prose or verse. Finally, this image of tragic circumstance which we call a tragedy must involve catastrophe, either material or
spiritual, arising naturally from the action and forming an integral part of it.

A rough description such as this allows us to reject, without further examination, certain types of play which bear a superficial or partial resemblance to great tragedy. Melodrama fails to integrate passion and event by thought, fails sometimes to relate the catastrophe to the action, and lacks in general that depth of imagination upon which the revelation of character and emotion depend; again, a mere chronicle of evil or of pathetic event, even though shapely, may fail to satisfy our sense of tragedy from lack of intensity in passion and in thought; and a play in which death or destruction comes by accident will fail again, however finely imagined, because the catastrophe is not integral to the play and to its underlying thought.[1]

But in great tragedy there is an element common to the individual plays, though differing in form and theme, an element which marks both the treatment of the material and the nature of the resulting interpretation: it is the presence of that conflict, to which we have just referred, between two impressions made by his experience upon the poet's mind.

The part of this experience which is most clearly revealed is the intense awareness of evil and pain. But in conflict with this specific response to fact and event is another of a wholly different kind; the intuitive and often undefined apprehension of another universe implying other values. Beyond the realization of evil and pain (and the work of art will be great in proportion as this is profound), beyond the apprehension of an alien destiny that appears to shape man's action, there is the perception, at once more comprehensive and less explicit, of a possible resolution, of some reconciliation with or interpretation in terms of good. The impressions in conflict may be of various kinds; of a malevolent and a beneficent world-order; of apparent lawlessness against underlying law, a casual against a causal, a chaotic against a patterned universe. And the unresolved conflict between them will at first give rise to a sense of mystery; to the assumption that evil can never be sounded, however thoroughly it be analysed, that its causes will never fully reveal themselves, even to the most passionate questioning.

It is here that, in the finest tragic writing, there is equilibrium. The reality of evil and pain is not denied; if it were, tragedy would not speak to man's condition as it has done from the time of Aeschylus to the present day. Nevertheless, something is revealed which makes possible the transvaluation of the values upon which this rests; the works of art which we call tragedies are distinguished from others, not only by technical characteristics of subject-matter or form, but also by the balance maintained between conflicting readings of the universe and of man's condition and destiny. The supreme works in this kind reveal that balance in the highest degree, thus satisfying most nearly man's need to find his complex and contradictory experience transmuted into the enduring form of art. Certain tragedies, it is true, fail to maintain complete balance, some lessening their hold on the imagination by presenting irremediable evil and a satanic universe, and some, with similar consequences, indicating remedies so immediate or so easily defined that men's judgement and innate sanity mistrust them. Both kinds may nevertheless remain within the category of tragedy, provided they do not destroy either of the elements in whose conflict the average man recognizes an essential part of his own dual experience.

The characteristic balance thus obtained results, as we have said, in a play of a certain quality. In content and in thought tragedy is, like all great art, an interpretation of some part of the universe of man's experience, but inasmuch as it is dramatic it is primarily an interpretation by implication, by the emphasis it lays on certain parts of that experience, the significance with which it invests them, rather than by explicit or direct commentary. The part of this experience which it selects involves suffering and some kind of catastrophe, and these significant of something more than the bare facts actually present. Balance is thus maintained in all great tragedy; suffering and catastrophe upon the one hand and upon the other a relation (often unspecified and undefined) with some fundamental or universal law whose operation justifies or compensates them. From this arises the conflict of impressions; evident evil against partially hidden yet immanent and overruling good. Thus far all tragedy is akin.

In what writers is this most fully and most clearly revealed? In none perhaps more than in some of the major works of Aeschylus, Sophocles, Shakespeare, and Ibsen. Here, though the evidence of pain and evil is never denied, the final position is not despair or rebellion, but a perception of that in man's destiny which resolves pain in exultation. (It may rise at times to a willing collaboration with the purposes of the unrevealed powers whose presence is felt though never fully understood.) Some such balance as this is to be found in the work of most of the world's greatest tragic writers and we may observe not only its nature but the various means by which that nature is maintained. In certain types of formally archaic tragedy the outer action or story my indicate the reading of life derived from the evidence of evil in fact and event, while that other universe and its differing values may, as in the Aeschylean chorus, be presented directly as comment. In another type, while the outer action may still present that first reading, the second may depend upon an inner action proceeding independently, though in close relation with the outer, and consisting of the experience of individual minds exploring the world of thought or of imagination. Shakespeare's major tragedies and such of his contemporaries' as achieve tragic balance seem generally to be of this kind. In a third kind again, where there is little or no comment and yet no clearly distinguished inner action, the implications of form alone maintain the balance. This appears to be the nature of the equilibrium in certain of the plays of Sophocles.

Some of the tragedies of Aeschylus present the two balancing perceptions – which by their balance make the tragic mood – in different and separate mediums.[2] To the action or story, which is the main part of the play, falls the presentation of evil and that measure of implicit comment, through emphasis and selection, which is inseparable from creative art. It is left to the choruses to make the explicit comment on the action which subordinates it to the surrounding universe of order and law whose significance would else be obscure. The balance is superbly achieved and maintained, but by a division of functions, the one reading of life being presented by strictly dramatic, the other by non-dramatic methods. The theme of the *Agamemnon* and the *Choephori* is the implacable evil of the responsibility for sin, but throughout the plays as through most of Shakespeare's, there are seemingly contradictory references to forms of good apparently outside the evil; Zeus is all-wise, all powerful, the 'Saviour', he who pities.[3] But, unlike Shakespeare or any but a few other dramatists, Aeschylus comments not only on the fact but on the relationship between the two balancing forces. Without reducing the significance of suffering or of evil, and while yet maintaining the equilibrium between it and the enveloping beneficence of Zeus, Aeschylus reveals the process by which the two are linked. Zeus does not merely pity, but leads man through pain to wisdom, so that the very suffering which arose from the presence of evil becomes the means of conversion and beatitude. Zeus himself became the all-comprehending by no other road.

In the two strict tragedies, the *Agamemnon* and the *Choephori*, there is little more than this indication of the relation between the two and the tragic balance is maintained. In the third play, when the Erinyes become the Eumenides, we pass from the drama of tragic equilibrium to the drama of beatitude, and the process is elucidated in Aeschylus's picture of the reconciliation of the two forces.

This method is not peculiar to the Greek drama of the fifth century B.C. Though it involves an interruption of the strict dramatic effect, it falls completely out of use only when naturalism has a fictitious value, as in the fourth-wall drama of the late nineteenth and early twentieth centuries in Europe. It will obviously be found in all imitations of or derivations from Greek drama at any period and in that breaking in of narrative method which appears to be natural to some drama, such as that of medieval Europe, in the early phases of its development. Modern variations may relate to either or both of these forerunners. Goethe, in the first part of *Faust*, assigned to his choric and prologue figures part at least of the function of redressing the tragic balance, and other kinds of extra-dramatic commentary are used for kindred purposes to the present day (as in Drink-water's *Abraham Lincoln*). Plays, again, which, with varying degrees of plausibility, temporarily invest certain of the characters from the main action with choric functions virtually use the same method. For so long as the choric commentary lasts (though it be only for a line or two) for so long the two balancing interpretations are presented in different and separate mediums. Many of the Elizabethans used this method, briefly and abstemiously, with fine effect: Webster had peculiar skill in this. And in much of the tragedy written in Europe during the last thirty years – to jump the intervening years with their many interesting uses, especially in Germany – the tendencies to expressionism on the one hand and to symbolism on the other have alike tempted playwrights to the same device, which they handle with confidence and fluency, but with some-what less than Webster's effectiveness.

The balance between manifest evil and immanent good is maintained by a widely different process in the work of Shakespeare and most of his con-temporaries. Except for a few extra-dramatic conventions irrelevant to the present issue, these plays are wholly dramatic in form, and such comment as there is is necessarily implicit. But here an outer and an inner action can be distinguished clearly; the outer, like the action of the *Oresteia*, presents by its story the reading of life which observes and admits the nature of evil and of suffering; again, as in Aeschylus's play, with that element of impli-cit comment which is inseparable from emphasis and selection. But behind this, coextensive with and yet frequently independent of it, is action on another plane of being which we may regard as an inner action, made up of the experiences of the minds, the thought-life of the characters. Though the distinction between the two does not become so marked in drama as to force itself upon the reader's observation until perhaps the middle of the nineteenth century,[4] it is already visible in that of Shakespeare, and it is upon this inner action that the function devolves of maintaining tragic equilibrium by counterpoising the presentation of evil in the outer action. The thought-world of Cordelia or of Kent has relatively little effect upon the course of those events in *Lear* that are shaped by and shape the other characters; but it is of immense effect in our final impression of the universe revealed by the play, reaching its triumph in certain passages that, looking through death, create the harmony of the play.

To some degree already in Shakespeare, as in all major dramatists, a third means of balance is disclosed, and in a few, of a rare quality, it appears to be the only means and to work alone. Perhaps the earliest instances of this kind are to be found in some of the plays of Sophocles,[5] where the interpretative function of the choric odes is less than in those of Aeschylus; here the balance is achieved within the strictly dramatic part of the play, yet without the help of any discernible separate inner action. The presence of a beneficent world-order, of immanent good, is implied in such plays as *Oedipus* or *Macbeth* by the presence of form[6] as an integral part of the work of art even when evil or suffering is the theme. The impression left upon the mind is of an equilibrium between the manifestation of evil and the embodiment of the principle of order. Beauty of form and expression then represent by implication the forces of righteousness and beneficence of which Aeschylus speaks directly in the choric odes. In plays of this group, harmony of form is achieved despite the inherent evil or hideousness of the theme, and so profound is the transmutation that it becomes an image of that reconciliation by which order and beauty convert all things into themselves, by which the Erinyes become the Eumenides and we pass from an *Inferno* to a *Paradiso*.

We have already noticed that on either side of this central group, in which the equilibrium of tragedy is thus maintained, there are to be found other types of great tragic drama in which the balance is threatened by a greater emphasis upon the positive or the negative interpretation, by the acceptance in the poet's mind primarily of the latent or potential good or of the manifest evil. Poets who differ as widely as Milton and Ibsen may be found in the first group and those as far apart as Euripides, Marlowe, and Strindberg in the second.

In Milton's *Samson Agonistes* we found a peculiarly clear instance of that overbalancing in the direction of positive interpretation which is inseparable from religious drama and renders its strict form incompatible with tragedy. What was there said of Milton may be said, with certain modifications in detail, of Calderon at one extreme and of certain modern plays at the other.[7] But not all the plays that overset the balance on the positive side are religious drama, nor is the dissolution of the tragic mood always effected by a progression into beatitude. The last hundred years have produced notable groups of plays which lay so strong an emphasis

upon the remediable nature of evil and indicate so strong a confidence in
the near or immediate removal of suffering by the modification of social
conditions that they cease to be tragedy as surely, though by a different
road, as does religious drama. Ibsen, whose social problem plays are
largely responsible for the growth of this kind, seldom wrote plays of even
technically tragic form while his belief in this social amelioration was at its
height.[8] But the heritage passes to his successors, Hauptmann and Toller
in Germany, Galsworthy in England, Odets in America, and a host of
others in both continents.

Characteristic of certain of their tragedies, though not of all in equal
degree, is the temporal nature of the suffering. Though not as a rule accidental or insufficiently related to action or to theme, it yet does not move
us as does suffering whose cause is in part at least inexplicable. For in each
of these plays a remedy is known or can be guessed at. In *The Weavers,
The Machine Wreckers*,[9] *The Silver Box, Justice*; in many of the plays of
Brieux; even in the work of Elizabeth Baker, Stanley Houghton, and
Granville Barker, social readjustments not utterly beyond human might
would resolve most of the evil that causes the suffering and so leads to catastrophe, material or spiritual.[10] In its extreme form such drama shades into
the propaganda play, which lies outside the scope of this study,[11] where the
remedy is specific and the case immediate; Clifford Odets' *Waiting for
Lefty* leaves no impression of pity or bewilderment, but focusses the mind
by indignation and wrath upon the remedy. This so lessens the significance of pain, through offering the assurance of a cure, that the play falls
out of harmony even with man's cruder impression of the fundamental
nature of evil. As Toller himself pointed out, there is a clear distinction to
be drawn between the drama which is primarily social propaganda and that
which is in reality tragic: 'For only unnecessary suffering can be van-
quished, the suffering which arises out of the unreason of humanity, out of
inadequate social system. There must always remain a residue of suffering,
the lonely suffering imposed upon mankind by life and death. And only
this residue is necessary and inevitable, is the tragic element of life and of
life's symbolizer, art.'[12]

The mood of this social drama, then, even when it assumes the technical
form of tragedy, is not in essence tragic, for the evil arises precisely out of
this 'inadequate social system', and more significant than the material
chosen is the emphasis and orientation given to it. Any given play of this
group, that is to say, might have been written in the tragic mood if the light
had been focused, not upon a defect in the machinery of justice (which is
adjustable), but upon that streak of innate injustice in man's nature

which is far less accessible, which would express itself no doubt in some other form if not in this. It is worth observing in this connection that the latter half of Ibsen's own career reveals a steady progression from the non-tragic to the tragic emphasis, from the examination of evil in its more readily remediable forms to the exploration of deeper and deeper-lying evil and, finally, to that which baffles prescription. As we pass from the *Pillars of Society* to *The Wild Duck*, we reach the borders of central, balanced tragedy and with Rosmer and Borkman we enter the world of Orestes and Hamlet. For all its earnestness, this social drama rests, in fact, upon a more superficial reading of life than tragedy 'of the centre', and in this it contrasts sharply with religious drama of which the finest kinds seek out and resolve the potent and seemingly ineradicable forms of evil. It is not without significance that few great dramatists have touched it or continued long to write it; most of them pass on to the profounder forms of meditative tragedy or to that drama which, as we have already suggested, passes beyond tragedy itself.

There are plays, on the other hand, that derive primarily from a negative or destructive reading of life, and these also serve to define the limitations of strict tragedy and to reveal the ease with which its balance can be destroyed by disregarding their boundaries. Here also deviations from the centre may be of two kinds, approximately equivalent to the two we have just traced. Just as the constructive thinker may destroy tragic balance by the assurance either of religious revaluation or of social readjustment, so the playwright of the opposite kind may destroy it by the assumption of a spiritually evil world-order or of an irremediable mechanism or chaos. The first approximates to Satanism, the second to pessimistic materialism; both destroy the balance in ways opposite and parallel to those we have just examined. The first, the Satanists, are necessarily among the rarest tragic writers, for their interpretation involves, not the mere observation of evil phenomena, but the assumption of a system. More common are the writers of the second group (to be set over against the social reformers), who view event and transcribe it with quiet or with savage despair and admit neither qualifying evidence nor hope.

A large part of the social-problem drama of our day, that part which is critical without being constructive, may be of this later kind: when, in addition, the form is that of tragedy, we find such plays as Strindberg's *Miss Julia* or *The Father*, Granville Barker's *Waste*, George Kaiser's *From Morn to Midnight*, the Capeks' *The Insect Play*, Elmer Rice's *The Adding Machine*, and Lenormand's *L'Homme et ses Fantômes*. Few of these plays are great tragedy and, as we suggested in speaking of the social-problem play of the preceding category, few can fairly be named with that tragedy of the centre which we took as our point of departure. And this follows naturally from the relaxing of that tension imposed by the inherent limitations of the tragic mood: except in the rare instances of the religious drama or of its anti-type, the Satanic drama, it is seldom that a play which for any reason evades this law of balance has greatness of passion and of thought. Many of them prove, however, of great interest in analysis, revealing clearly the destruction of balance by negation.

Such plays reveal a clear conception of misery, which they usually study (like their anti-type of the previous group) in terms of one, precisely-drawn social organization, though they too sometimes attempt to give this universality. Their theatre technique is often brilliant and nothing, in situation or emotion, seems forced or pretentious; such work may well be too savage and too honest for staginess. Even when a modern reader has allowed for the disturbance of his judgement by the immediacy of a contemporary theme, he may still see much that would grip the imagination of a generation that came to the play knowing nothing of those immediate conditions. In many of these plays the resources of episode, dialogue, setting, and theatre device are used with bare economy and striking effect, to show the imprisonment of the human soul in circumstance. We watch a vicious circle contract like the curves of a helical spring; the surroundings limit the experience, the experience limits the power of reason and imagination, and the maimed imagination then in turn avoids such experience as change of circumstance might allow. Nevertheless, we are conscious that what we have before us falls short in some way of tragedy. The presentation of evil and of suffering may be as implacable as the writer's strength can make it, but we are left with the disturbing conviction that what we have witnessed is an incomplete reading of life.

This theme and this treatment may be found in the characteristic play of the theatre at one extreme or in the reflective play of psychological analysis at the other, in plays as widely severed as Rice's *The Adding Machine*[13] and Lenormand's *Simoun*. The unquestioned assumption that suffering is the work of a malevolent machine does not satisfy our understanding, for it no more fits the whole of our experience than does Clifford Odets' opposite and parallel assumption that the evil of the world is remediable by a change of social organization. The interpretation in terms of a limited mechanistic scheme involves no equilibrium, for the play does not lead the mind outward towards a wider emotional and speculative affirmation; it imprisons it instead in a limited area of pain. Such plays place themselves outside the category of tragedy because, by laying the whole emphasis upon evil and suffering, they destroy all balance. And this is true of a large number of modern plays that haunt us by their simultaneous force and restraint, bringing home to our imaginations their themes of misery, grief, defeat, and injustice. Nevertheless we refuse to call them tragedy because they do not square with the whole of our experience.

Finally, there is the rare negative form which might be called Satanic tragedy, the drama which oversets tragic balance, not merely by denying immanent good, but by implying a Satanic universe, a world-order behind the manifestation of event as evil as the event itself. To this kind belong among others, some of the plays of Euripides, Marlowe's *Faustus*, some of Strindberg; among the more recent writers Lenormand sometimes approaches it.[14] This group of plays contrasts sharply with the two we have just considered, in that, at its height, magnitude of theme and power of passion again appear as distinguishing characteristics. This was true also of its direct opposite, religious drama,[15] for there also some attempt at interpretation of life formed a background of thought and found its way directly or indirectly into the total effect even of the outer action. But in the drama of Satanism not only is there a more or less clearly implied interpretation of the universe surrounding the events, but, by reason of its conflict with the systems of positive religion, this interpretation will generally be original to the writer. Thus, in the major Satanic drama there is presupposed a mind both comprehensive and original, strong and wide enough in scope to synthesize disparate material into an organic system and with an individualism tenacious enough to withstand the imaginative force of prevailing assumptions. Nevertheless, even the plays of this group disturb, in greater or less degree, that supreme balance which characterizes tragedy 'of the centre'. Though in less degree than the other negative plays, those of materialistic pessimism, they fall short by presenting a universe – even though patterned and not chaotic – which corresponds but imperfectly with the dual, if contradictory, experience of man.

The peculiar Satanic negation appears in different ways in the plays of Euripides and of Marlowe. Euripides uses the facilities of the Greek chorus to comment upon a universe controlled now by an evil world-order and now by mixture of casualty and cause, while Marlowe, in *Dr Faustus*, uses the more consistently dramatic Jacobean form to present a steadfast picture of an evil world-order on which there is no comment except by implication.

Euripides, through the familiar imagery of the old gods, reveals the irresponsible, meaningless or even malevolent forces that overbear man's valour. His gods, it is true, are more powerful than man, but certain of them are less noble, and from them comes the frustration which annuls creation, confuses valour, and cripples wisdom.[16]

Even in those plays where this interpretation is less clearly defined, the perception of pain and the poet's sympathy with it outweigh all else. And Euripides' nearest approach to a vindication of life's processes would appear to be Hecuba's in the *Troades*, where she justifies the sufferings of Troy as the raw material of art.[17]

Marlowe, whose tragedy appears at its height and in characteristic form in *Faustus*, takes up a unique position as a tragic thinker, because of the implacable paradox on which his reading of the universe rests; man's innate fallibility on the one hand, and, on the other, the infallibility demanded by inflexible law.[18] To this paradox there is only one conclusion: 'Why then belike we must sin and so consequently die.' The precision and finality of this deduction indicate a vision terrifying alike in its assumptions and in its omissions. For implicit in Marlowe's premiss is the predestination of man to destruction by some determinate power capable of purpose and intention, and, as such purpose can only be sadistic, the world order it implies must derive from a Satanism more nearly absolute than that of Euripides.[19]

But neither in this play nor elsewhere does Marlowe state this assumption in explicit terms and the implication itself rests on a few passages in *Faustus*.[20] Even there it is rather by silence and omission that he reveals his belief that evil is not only inherent in man's destiny but both irremediable and predetermined. Only a consistent vision of a Satanic universe could beget the initial paradox; never does Marlowe raise the question: Why, if the laws of the universe be such, should man, himself a part of that universe, be so irreconcileably opposed to them? To a convinced Satanist it is, in fact, no paradox. Given a sadistic and malevolent power directing the world-order there is no inducement to postulate a further transcendent power or intelligence, relating or reconciling the contradictions of man's capacity and God's demands. And so Marlowe achieves, not a balance between two interpretations of the universe, but immobility and rigidity of protest. In his drama the spirit of man is set against the universe, but there is no equilibrium between two worlds of thought. For Marlowe, at the time of *Faustus*, did not question the nature of the world-order. He saw it steadily and saw it evil.

So complete does Marlowe's Satanism seem in its indirect and outward expression that it is almost impossible to reconcile with its finality our persistent impression of tragic mystery in *Faustus*. How are we to reconcile the absence of tragic equilibrium in this, perhaps the most notable Satanic play in literature, with this recurrent and obstinate conviction that here, if anywhere, is tragedy? In part because the absence, even here, is more apparent than real. The framework of Marlowe's thought, the deductive process by which he arrives at his conclusion, is consistent and, within its limits, unassailable.[21] But there are indications that it did not take into account the whole of his experience. The Satanic reading of life may, it is true, permit Faustus (and Marlowe) to confound Hell in Elysium and see Helen's beauty fairer than the evening air; for if these are themselves destructible, by so much is the mockery of man's fate more hideous. But there is one thing that Marlowe cannot subjugate to that world-order that predestines universal damnation – his own inarticulate and hardly acknowledged conviction that it is evil. From what source springs this passionate judgement, he does not appear to consider; but 'Christ's blood streams in the firmament' and there escapes – coherently, it may be, only in this single line – the implication of a deeper division in his mind, that his else consistent, Satanic interpretation has left unresolved. In that division, imaginatively revealed, though excluded from the logical demonstration of his thought, lie the dualism and conflict essential to the tragic mood. It does not constitute a balancing of one interpretation against another, but the absolute Satanism is flawed and the reader left with the impression of a potential balancing force to challenge its absolutism. Thus, even in the extreme case of *Faustus*, the most nearly Satanic tragedy that can be found, it would appear that in so far as drama is Satanic it loses tragic balance and in so far as it is tragic it is not Satanic. Moreover, in Marlowe's play, though in less degree than in the tragedies of the centre, there is to be found the same balancing of content by form that we remarked in the work of Sophocles. A partial challenge to the suffering and evil in the outer action comes from that beauty of form and style which itself gives the lie to the implication that the fundamental order of things is evil. For this itself implies harmony; as in the work of Sophocles, though not so fully, the revelation of beauty in form is an unwitting testimony to that beneficence or immanent good of which beauty and form are manifestations.

Nevertheless, in the plays of this last group, absolute tragic balance is overset, although magnitude of passion and thought again become possible, since the action is related to a surrounding universe greater in scope and significance than the figures and events that make up that action. And even though the direct inference be to a universe of implacable evil, this does not detract from the grandeur, though it may from the wholeness and saneness of the final impression. Moreover, beyond this direct influence lies the indirect and seemingly unwitting testimony of the 'world of profit and delight' that, residing in beauty, in form and in the unacknowledged sources of the poet's vision, maintains a partial balance in the play, despite his logical and intentional Satanism.

Admittedly, the suggestions we have just considered might, if pressed to the point of forming an argument, involve a *petitio principii*, inasmuch as the tragedies upon which we draw for evidence are themselves selected (even if unconsciously) by a mind in which the conclusion we later reach is already dormant. But they are suggestions only on the nature of certain perceived relations and Pascal's law still holds, for criticism as for much else: 'Tu ne me chercherais pas si tu ne m'avais connu.' The disability, in fact (if it be one), attaches to and must be acknowledged by all subjective criticism, and criticism is always in the last resort subjective. The logician himself admits that the conclusion of every syllogism is implicit in its major premiss and all that interpretation can do is to elucidate what is indeed obvious once it has been suggested.

The balance between the evil that is observed and the good that is guessed at is so common a part of human experience as to be perhaps its highest common factor. It is because tragedy reveals directly this equilibrium of conflicting thought and emotion that it has its enduring power. And it has been the attempt of this essay to indicate, first, that when tragedy departs from this norm and loses this correspondence with a universal experience it forfeits a part of its potency and, second, that this characteristic balance is the differentia of fine tragic art. In other words, it is precisely in this correspondence, and not in any of the outward characteristics by which the form can be described, that the essence of tragedy consists. It is then a mere matter of elucidation to indicate how and in what ways this balance is in practice preserved and by what deviations it may be destroyed. It may be observed in passing that the last three groups we considered, whether they were positive or negative, differed from the first, the religious drama, in that they destroyed the balance essential to the tragic mood by failing to satisfy that impression of two conflicting worlds of experience which reflects, at a certain phase, the totality of man's experience. Religious drama, on the other hand, supersedes the tragic mood by calling in the evidence of a wider surrounding universe of being, and destroys the balance by resolving the conflict.

It is now clear that tragedy is doubly subject to the law of limitation in art and that its subjection may throw some light upon the function of limitation itself. For it would appear to be subject not only to that which arises from its distinctive quality as an art, but to its own specific limitation in thought. The first of these conditions has been indicated in the preceding pages. The nature of the second, though implicit in what has there been said, may perhaps be briefly considered in conclusion.

Drama – and consequently tragedy, which can never escape the conditions common to all drama, but only refine upon and specialize them – must use as its primary material the world of experience, those events and actions which constitute actuality. It is its distinctive task to bring the presentation of these, by the resources of its peculiar technique into the sharpest possible focus; to produce, that is, the impression of immediacy. The indications it can give of the interpenetrating world of spiritual reality must necessarily be reconciled to this (a task of rare difficulty) and are generally subordinated to it, though, as we have seen, the highest tragedy depends for its power and its authority on the presence of an element of this conflicting evidence in its total effect. When this underlying reality forces itself irresistibly upon the poet's mind, finding its way into positive expression, the balance of tragedy is likely to be overset. The play then, if it remain dramatic in any exact sense of the term, takes on a form which is in truth no longer that of tragedy; *Samson Agonistes* cannot strictly be called tragic, and Shakespeare passes through the phase of the great, balanced tragedies to a later form expressive of a change in the relative evaluation of the outer action and the inner experience to which that action serves as manifestation. At this phase, common to the experience of many of the greatest dramatists, deed and event are, it would appear, primarily significant as images which make visible and manifest the reality which was hidden but immanent.[22] What we in part discern in Shakespeare's thought, as we pass from *Lear* to the three concluding plays of his career, has its parallel in the passage of Euripides from the middle plays to the *Bacchae*, of Sophocles from the first to the second *Oedipus*, of Ibsen from the social dramas to the group which culminates in *John Gabriel Borkman* and *When We Dead Awaken*.[23]

There are, moreover, certain writers who appear never to touch the tragic mood. This mood is not, it need hardly be said, the prerogative of those who use the dramatic form called tragedy or denied to those whose age or race precludes it. Many writers in other forms, narrative verse or prose,[24] have revealed that perception of tragic balance which would in drama have produced tragedy; Virgil had, of all men, this note of the potential tragic poet; the world he saw was poised betweeen those two conflicting interpretations that I have attempted to define; the influence of pain and evil at war with that of nobility in the spirit of man. But on the other hand many of the world's greatest poets have never touched this mood, and it must sometimes occur to the serious student of drama, and of its quintessence, tragedy, that their names are among the noblest and their thought among the most profound in poetry. Whereas Sophocles, Euripides, Shakespeare, Ibsen, even Aeschylus in the *Eumenides*, pass through and out of the tragic interpretation, Dante and Wordsworth never enter it in the fullness of their powers, and their major work is conceived in terms which do not allow of that Manichaeistic balance from which tragedy springs. And it is hard to resist the conclusion that the relation between their interpretation and that of tragedy as we have described it in these essays is, in fact, that of the double vision of the mystic to the vision focussed upon the manifestation only.[25]

And in essence this is what we suggested at the outset, that the religious interpretation of phenomena which means in fact the perception that they are only 'appearances' is incompatible with tragedy, which forever doubts whether their significance is ultimate or relative. Religion, whether it be positive or Satanic, declares that the unseen world is real and the actual a varyingly transparent veil.[26] When, in its normal form, it is beatific, it transcends the tragic vision, even as Fox's ocean of light and love flowed over the ocean of darkness. The ends of tragedy can never be served by that interpretation which, while seeing with it that 'in the world ye shall have tribulation', sees also that which has 'overcome the world'. For tragedy's concern is with that 'tribulation' while it still fills man's consciousness to the exclusion of all but a doubtful and half-discerned promise of transvaluation. In the next position, that of religious drama, the 'world', which is the proper theatre of tragedy, has been 'overcome'; its seemingly solid structure has revealed itself as transparent in that irradiation which destroys the significance of outward event.

Tragedy then is an interim reading of life. And in so far as it does not rest its interpretation upon that ultimate conclusion, in so far as it maintains that balance which is the source of its strength and of its value, to that extent it is the result of relative limitation of thought. The paradox, again, is more apparent than real, for limitation, here also, has a specific function. Just as, in the sphere of technique, we discovered that the limitation of the art afforded strength to the orthodox dramatists and transcendent power to those who successfully challenged it (whether in the major questions of theme and scope or in minor problems of presentation), so now we observe that it is on the relative limitation of its thought that its universal and enduring value depends. Precisely because it is an interim reading of life, it speaks to the condition of all but a few at some period of their lives; for it reveals that balance, that uncertainty, which sees two worlds of being and cannot wholly accept either. It speaks more potently to those within its reach than any other literary kind, because it reveals this interim reading in terms of those very technical limitations which impose upon it the necessity for concentration of form and directness of method.

NOTES

[1] These are instances only of the types of play which fall short of the category of tragedy. Any reader of drama will readily think of many others.

[2] And with this method we may associate all subsequent imitations of the Greek choric method, the many plays in which a virtually choric function is forced upon certain characters and one or two modern variations which will be noticed later.

[3] *Choephori*, 639-45. Aeschylus uses the chorus for these references; certain of the Elizabethans assign a temporary choric function to characters within the action; Shakespeare always uses the pure dramatic method and his commentary or references come only from those characters whose nature is to speak them.

[4] But to this group belongs a great part of the tragic work of Shakespeare, Lessing, Schiller, Hebbel, Ibsen, and such widely differing moderns as, to choose a few names at random, Galsworthy, Synge, and Hauptmann.

[5] It is hard to find any other dramatist except Tcheckov in whom the tragic balance appears to depend entirely upon this, though it is a contributory factor to that balance in the work of nearly all great dramatists.

[6] The functions of imagery which have already been indicated (Chapter VI) and those of prosody contribute to this effect. But the significance of form is more than the effect of the specific formal details.

[7] We may instance among the moderns (taking as wide a range as possible) Yeats' *Countess Cathleen*, Lunacharski's *Faust and the City*, and Mr O'Neill's *Lazarus Laughed*. These have the technical form of tragedy, but it is clear that they are drawn away from true tragic balance by the overpowering strength of the positive interpretation, whether this last is explicit or implicit.

[8] Already in *Ghosts* and certainly in *The Wild Duck* there is the implication that no mere social adjustment will eliminate the causes of suffering, for these are too deeply rooted in man's nature to be reached from without.

[9] It is perhaps only in these two plays that Hauptmann and Toller imply clearly that a remediable maladjustment is the main cause of the suffering and sin. In general their tragedy is more nearly balanced and implies clearly that the continuance of evil has in it an element of mystery akin to man's nature itself.

[10] In certain of the later of these plays there is a tendency to combine spiritual catastrophe with material or to substitute it for it, while nevertheless implying that some at least of the causes are remediable. Such a combination is certainly 'enough to make it no tragedy'.

[11]Even when it has the superficial form of tragedy, the true propaganda play seldom maintains strict dramatic technique. It tends to revert to thinly disguised exposition. This may have many virtues but they are not those of drama.

[12]The quotation here is from the author's Introduction to the English Translation of *Seven Plays* (1934), but the same distinction is drawn in the *Letters* and is implied in *Masses and Man*.

[13]At the risk of becoming unnecessarily explicit we might examine this, a highly representative play of its kind. It is a study of the inarticulate and uncomprehending death-agonies of a human spirit imprisoned in the mean monotony and vulgar pretensions of present-day black-coat slavery. After the earlier scenes, of mingled naturalism and symbolism, have laid before us the process of this fate, there follows a group of scenes in a world beyond death whose analytic technique and freer tempo allow the author to generalize the experiences of the earlier acts in an implicit commentary upon the mis-using of the soul's capacity for life. There is no alleviation, poetic or comic; the only variations in the play are the skilful changes of tension. Life, through a succession of reincarnations, is controlled by a vast adding machine progressing rhythmically to a foreknown result. This mechanism, which cannot be called a world-order, for the inference is not clearly enough drawn in the play, tends only to evil and to destruction of spirit. There is no suggestion of surrounding law, but only of the self-contained laws by which the soul's downward and negative progression is determined – just as are the totals of the adding machine. There is no attempt to throw light upon this from any other direction; nothing conflicts with the impression of pain and evil because there are no other forces, except in the too easily stifled imagination of the central figure, the victim.

[14]The vision of an evil world-order in *Medea* and the *Troades* appears consistent enough to justify regarding them as Satanic drama. Strindberg at his most coherent and forcible makes a similar reading of life (in *Miss Julia* and *The Father*), while Lenormand, slender as is his contribution in general, approaches it in *A L'Ombre du Mal*.

[15]Provided always that we continue to restrict that term to the drama of religious experience and do not extend it to include all drama written in terms of given theological assumptions.

[16]Some at least of the repetitions of this passage must be presumed to be Euripides' intention. (*Medea*, 1415-19, *Alcestis*, 1159-63, *Helen*, 1688-92, *Bacchae*, 1388-92, *Andromache*, 1284-48.)

[17]*Troades*, 1240-45. Just so Deirdre, in the Cuchulainn cycle and in Synge's play, thinks of her sorrow as a song 'that shall be sung for ever'.

Both these passages put briefly and explicitly an estimate of the function of art in which is implicit the conclusion drawn a few pages earlier in discussing the relation of form to tragic balance in the Sophoclean tragedy.

[18]Like Fulke Greville after him, Marlowe, in the opening argument of the play, sees the

> Wearisome condition of humanity,
> Born under one law, to another bound.

[19]More nearly indeed, than that of any dramatist known to me.

[20]Principally I. i, I. iii, II. ii, V. i and ii. (The references are to Boas's edition.)

[21]It is remarkable, indeed, that so clear a piece of deduction should be conveyed (even though, of necessity, piecemeal) in strict dramatic form.

[22]In great poetry they always have this function in some measure; they most certainly do so in Shakespeare's tragedies. But in the later phase to which I am referring, it becomes increasingly difficult to put any other simultaneous interpretation upon them.

[23]Goethe, less innately dramatic than any of these, could express his final interpretations in nothing less than the later additions to the second part of *Faust*.

[24]We may instance, to go no further, Chaucer's *Troilus and Cresseide* and Tolstoy's *Anna Karenina*.

[25]As Mr T.S. Eliot puts it (*Family Reunion*, Part II, Scene iii):

> He sees the world as clearly as you or I see it,
> It is only that he has seen a great deal more than that.

[26]The materialistic interpretation, as we noticed earlier in this chapter, destroys the balance of tragedy equally effectively by seeing only the veil and declaring that 'there is no light behind the curtain'.